PAST
CRIMES

PAST CRIMES

*Archaeological and Historical Evidence
for Ancient Misdeeds*

Julie Wileman

ARCHAEOLOGY

PEN &
SWORD

First published in Great Britain by
PEN AND SWORD ARCHAEOLOGY
an imprint of
Pen and Sword Books Ltd
47 Church Street
Barnsley
South Yorkshire S70 2AS

ISBN 978 1 47382 319 8

Printed and bound in England by
CPI

Typeset in Liberation Serif by M. C. Bishop at The Armatura Press

Pen & Sword Books Ltd incorporates the imprints of
Pen & Sword Aviation, Pen & Sword Family History, Pen & Sword Maritime,
Pen & Sword Military, Pen & Sword Discovery, Wharncliffe Local History,
Wharncliffe True Crime, Wharncliffe Transport, Pen & Sword Select,
Pen & Sword Military Classics, Leo Cooper, Remember When,
The Praetorian Press, Seaforth Publishing and Frontline Publishing

For a complete list of Pen and Sword titles please contact
Pen and Sword Books Limited
47 Church Street, Barnsley, South Yorkshire, S70 2AS, England
E-mail: enquiries@pen-and-sword.co.uk
Website: www.pen-and-sword.co.uk

Contents

List of Figures

List of Plates

Chapter 1

Archaeology, History, Crime and Punishment

Introduction

Murder, assault, thievery, fraud – for as long as there have been groups of humans living together, these and many other forms of crime have been committed. In this book, we shall take a look at the record of crime and punishment in this and other countries, and at the contribution of archaeology, history and forensic science to the identification of crimes, victims and perpetrators, as well as forms of punishment. For earlier periods, archaeology must be our main source of information, while historical documents help to illuminate more recent events. Even when studying more recent times, however, archaeology is playing an increasing part in helping us to understand crimes and the ways in which societies have dealt with criminals.

In the 1970s and 1980s, police forces started to ask archaeologists to help find important evidence at scenes of certain types of crime. Subsequently, the methodology and skills of archaeologists were put into service for the investigation of other types of events, such as mass disasters, and the finding and identification of victims of war crimes. Today, the police and other agencies regularly employ forensic archaeologists to help them locate and evaluate material evidence at scenes of crime. Their job is to look for buried items – to give names to victims and to find items that may help to identify criminals, such as the weapons used in the commission of an offence. They are also asked to help find bodies and to establish how and when they died and were buried. Some of the most harrowing work in this area occurs during the investigations of massacres committed as war crimes. Not only is the forensic archaeologist responsible for helping to identify victims for their families, but also to recover the evidence needed to prosecute their killers. Forensic archaeologists work at disaster scenes such as air crashes and tsunamis to identify the dead. In addition they also investigate ancient crimes, using modern forensic science to shed light on murders that took place centuries

1

ago, and to try to determine whether a death found during excavation of an archaeological site was the result of unlawful killing, execution, accident, ritual or warfare.

The forensic sciences have a very long history, if not always firmly scientifically applied. In the medieval period, Chinese doctors learned how to distinguish causes of death, and fingerprints were used to validate documents, although they were not systematically recorded. One of the earliest stories about the use of a forensic approach to investigation suggests that, during the third century BC, Archimedes was asked to make sure that a golden votive wreath destined for a temple was actually pure gold, or whether a fraud had been committed. He could not damage the crown in any way. He realised that a wreath made of pure gold would be less buoyant than one to which a lighter metal had been added. He was able to prove that the wreath was fraudulent.

Physical evidence began to be used to identify criminals in the later eighteenth century, and analysis of the ink in a document is first recorded in Germany at the beginning of the nineteenth century, around the time when microscopes began to be used to identify bloodstains. Within a few decades, tests were establishing whether poison had been used, and providing ballistic evidence. The invention of photography added new dimensions to criminal investigations, both to identify convicted criminals and to record details of crime sites. Following earlier theorists, Sir Francis Galton published a book on fingerprints and their ability to help solve crimes in 1892. In the twentieth century forensic science began to be formally taught, the first university to offer courses being Lausanne, in Switzerland.

Medical, technical and photographic advances rapidly added to the tools available over the next hundred years, and new types of evidence were introduced – forensic botany which is used to identify plants, pollen and other vegetable material at a crime scene or on a suspect, forensic entomology to study insect behaviour at crime scenes, isotopic analyses and DNA studies for identification of victims and criminals. The very first police crime laboratory was set up in Lyons in 1910. Since then, the use of computers and the world-wide web have enabled investigators to collate, compare and share information internationally.

Many police investigations require the application of normal archaeological skills, such as stratigraphic recording, sampling of soils and microfossils, and meticulous removal of even the tiniest scrap of materials and artefacts from the ground. The techniques used to study the minute details of the past have proved to be very useful in providing evidence for court prosecutions in the present.

Archaeologists bring a number of particular skills to the table: the identification of ground disturbance from surface indications and from geophysics; meticulous excavation, detailed recording and the recovery of small objects; and the identification of decayed and fragmentary finds, particularly animal and human bone. Just as important is the archaeological awareness of context and sequence.[1]

Forensic archaeology

Forensic archaeology has been in the news lately in many countries, particularly Britain and the USA. Several cases have hit the headlines, such as the Jersey care home scandal and investigations into a possible serial killer in Margate. Following the discovery of two bodies at a house in the town, police believe that they may be on the trail of a serial killer who has been murdering women since the 1960s. Their suspect has moved around a great deal over the period and a number of addresses came under investigation. Forensic archaeologists examined the properties using the kind of equipment usually employed to identify archaeological sites, and have found a number of 'hot spots' within the houses and gardens that may prove to be the locations of other murdered victims. DNA evidence is also being studied and may link the Margate crimes to as many as fifteen other 'cold case' investigations.[2]

The meticulous approaches and skills of archaeologists were used in a case in the Midlands, following the murder of a prostitute. Her body could not be found, but her DNA was present in the flat belonging to a suspect. In the yard behind the flat, detectives noticed the remains of a recent bonfire. Archaeologists were called in to excavate the layers of ash in the bonfire and discovered cremated animal bones, but in the lowest layer they found tiny burned fragments of what they recognised as human bone, as well as a tooth and a set of door keys, which were identified as being those of the victim. In other cases, archaeologists have been able to find possible burial places of murder victims, and also to exclude certain areas from an investigation because they could demonstrate that these had lain undisturbed since before the crime.

Such successes are based on the first principle of archaeological excavation – an understanding of stratigraphy and context. Each event in the past is represented in the soil as a context; contexts occur in time and space, and the recording of these in relation to each other form the stratigraphy, or layers, of a site. If you were to dig a pit in your garden, you would be forming a series of contexts – there would be the topsoil and subsoils that you dig through, the marks your spade is making, and the remains of whatever you put into the hole, such as plant roots, fence posts or rubbish. Then the hole would be filled in – either straight away in one action, or over time by natural silting episodes, which might be visible in the section of the cut. By careful excavation, an archaeologist can recognise each of these episodes and actions, and reconstruct the whole sequence of events – the stratigraphy of your pit.

Stratigraphy helps us to understand the time sequences of a site. Soil forms over the landscape through a series of natural processes over long periods of time. But it can be affected by outside events – it can be eroded by wind or water, and soil can build up due to silts deposited by floods or by material washed down from hillsides. These episodes can often be recognised by identifying layers of different coloured soils, and by the degree of compaction of the layers. Generally, soil is uniformly compacted within a layer unless there has been some sort of disturbance. This could be animal burrows, agriculture, the digging of ditches or foundations, or the use of an area as a roadway. Archaeologists can recognise (often by the feel of the soil under the trowel) where these changes occur and spot marks left by tools or other agencies such as animals, which mark the borders of each different area, and can remove each layer very precisely, without disturbing older material below or around it.

Soil that has been disturbed is often less compacted than the surrounding layers, and (in Britain at least) frequently more damp, as there is more space between the grains of soil for water to collect. Much depends on the *type* of soil – sand, loam and clay are all very different – but in many instances, changes can still be visible below the surface after thousands of years.

Each layer or change represents a *context*. Each context is evidence of a change in the activity in and around the soil at some time in the past. To build up a picture of these activities, everything is carefully recorded in three dimensions, measured, described, drawn and photographed. The process is repeated for each layer that is exposed as the digging goes deeper into the site. Every context is given a unique number. Measurements, drawings and photographs are made of the vertical sides, or sections, of the excavation, which can illustrate the stratigraphic sequences of events in that place.

On an archaeological site, many stratigraphic sequences may be recorded, which can be combined and related to each other to give a picture of activities across a wider area and a longer time period. The contexts can be laid out in a table, called a Harris matrix, which can be used to establish the chronological sequences across a site to help date them. Clearly, under normal circumstances, the oldest events are also going to be the deepest, with more recent activity appearing closer to the surface. (This is not always the case, often due to various forms of disturbance such as animal burrows or later site use where older material has been brought to the surface, for example during the digging of foundations for a building, which can cause the order of contexts to be transposed). If the site is relatively undisturbed, there may be artefacts found in each context which can provide an approximate date for it – a coin, a potsherd – so that the different events represented in the stratigraphy can be assigned a chronological context as well as a spatial one.

The final result should be that enough information has been gathered for it to be theoretically possible to make a virtual reconstruction of the whole site, even after it has been completely excavated.

In cases of crime, the stratigraphic sequences can be used to establish a sequence of events, for example during the disposal of a body. Was a hole prepared in advance, or dug at the time of disposal? If an identifying object is found in the layers, was it dropped accidentally by the murderer, or could it have be deposited by someone quite innocent of the crime at another time?

Many new forms of analysis are available nowadays to aid archaeological, and by extension, forensic interpretation of a site. It is possible to recreate whole climates and environments, as well as activities, on a site by looking at the soils, insects, pollen and other natural materials it contains.

Types of analysis

Soil chemistry varies according to the underlying rock types, the way in which soils have been deposited (by wind, water, or human intervention), and the activities that have taken place on each soil surface. Soils may be eroded over time, but more often they build up, layer on layer, as plants die and rot back into the earth. Soils which have been cultivated with ploughs or spades have a different consistency from soils that have stayed undeveloped, or which have been covered by buildings or paving and may contain different chemical elements as a result. For example, soil that once formed the floor of a stable or a byre will have a higher level of phosphates than soils outside, as a result of urine from cattle or horses; sodium and potassium levels will be higher where there has been a hearth or a kiln where wood has been burned, or where an attempt has been made to destroy evidence of a crime by burning.

Traces of plant material can also be identified for similar purposes by archaeobotanists. A special form of study is palynology – the study of pollen grains. Pollen grains come in a vast array of shapes and sizes distinguishable under a microscope, making them identifiable at a species level in many cases (Figure 1). Pollen is remarkably durable, often lasting for many thousands of years, and each pollen type is subtly different, enabling very precise

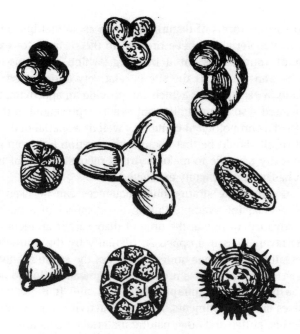

Figure 1. Some pollen grain varieties

identifications of exact species in a particular place at a particular time. Vast amounts of pollen are carried on the wind and settle on clothing and skin, and are even inhaled as we breathe. In some cases, the types of pollen found at a site can be very specific if they come from plants that are relatively rare, but each part of the environment has its own population of plants, and thus its own combination of pollens. The presence of some pollen grains can not only tell us what plants were present, but sometimes even the time of year when an event occurred, if the airborne pollen settled on the ground surface and was then quickly buried. Most pollens are released during the summer or autumn months, so finding a large amount of, say, wheat pollen in a grave would suggest that the burial took place in the mid- to late summer.

Pollen has been used in criminal investigations to determine the time of year during which a body was buried. This can help to identify the victim by comparison with the dates on which they were known to be still alive or when they disappeared, and can also be used to check the alibis of suspects. If the suspect was known to be a long way away at the season in which the pollen could have found its way into the burial, then he is unlikely to be guilty.

Other plant remains can be equally useful – seeds, nutshells, algae and diatoms can help to establish the environment at the time the context was buried, and can sometimes indicate the activities occurring around it. Changes in soil compaction due to digging will also help different plants to establish themselves on the site, and if there is a body buried in the soil, the decomposition will change the soil chemistry and encourage or discourage certain plant species. Clues like these may help to find bodies buried in wilderness areas, and can assist in identifying suspects, as in a case from New Zealand where a woman was assaulted and her house burgled by intruders who, when making their escape, brushed up against a flowering bush by her back door. Police were able to establish the presence of the bush pollen in large quantities on the suspects' clothing, helping them to proceed towards a conviction.

An early use of this type of evidence occurred in 1816. A young servant girl had been violently attacked and drowned in a shallow pond near Warwick. Police found trace evidence in wet mud by the pond – footprints and an impression of patched corduroy cloth, along with a scatter of grains of wheat and chaff. They were able to match the cloth impression to the breeches of a farmworker who had been threshing grain nearby.[3]

Identification of wood and other plant materials can also be used to establish where a piece of equipment or tool came from. If a handle, or other piece of equipment, is made from a particular type of wood or fibre that is not local, tracing its origin may lead to the place of manufacture, which in turn may lead to identification of possible suspects known to have come from, or visited, that area.

Fans of the *CSI* television dramas will no doubt be familiar with the study of insects and their behaviour in criminal investigations. In the case of burials, the presence of certain insects at particular stages of their life cycles can tell us whether the body was exposed before burial, at what time of year or day, and for how long. Temperature, climate, whether the body is inside or outside, large or small, covered or uncovered, all affect the rate of decomposition. During this process, various organisms are attracted to the body, including bacteria, fungi and insects. Flies prefer a body that is relatively fresh, while various forms of beetle move in as it dries out. Different species are likely to arrive at a corpse at different stages of its decomposition. Samples of the soil and materials in and around the grave must be carefully collected to preserve this type of evidence, and contamination must be strictly avoided. Under average conditions, flies will typically invade an exposed corpse within an hour of death. Within a day, their eggs will hatch into larvae, which go through further feeding and moulting stages until they are ready to pupate.

After a few more days, a new fly emerges, leaving the empty pupa case behind. Each stage takes a known amount of time, which varies according to the species, weather and so on and this enables experts to estimate the period in which the first flies laid their eggs, which will be close to the actual time of death. The speed of their development gives clues about whether the body was deposited at night or in the daytime, and whether the weather was warm or cold. Marks from scavenging animals such as rats or foxes can also provide further types of information.

Even in ancient burials, traces of pupa cases or the remains of beetles may survive. It is important to record where each fragment is found. Flies will normally lay their eggs in damp places such as the eyes or mouth, so concentrations of remains on other parts of the body may indicate that there was an open wound at that location.

As with all forms of forensic evidence, there are problems. A person killed in the winter may not have insect evidence on their body – few insects are very active in cold weather. If the body was sealed or wrapped after death, insects may not have been able to reach it. Nevertheless, the humble fly is a very useful witness.

Archaeological interest in the remains of insects and tiny snails reflects what these can tell us about both activity and climate in the past, and in some cases, about the kinds of plants that grew on that spot centuries ago. Archaeological entomologists can identify these creatures, many of which have very specific habitats and preferences. Some species like warm, wet places; others prefer dry environments. Some species are closely associated with certain types of food plants, suggesting the presence of those plant species was likely at, or close to, the site, even if today's environment is very different. Other species point to specific types of activity such as domestic housing. In Viking York, the remains of beetles, fly pupae, and even intestinal worms demonstrated that public hygiene was very poor in and around the houses of the inhabitants. Elsewhere, insects associated with cereal crops show where grain had been stored or processed. All these help us to build a picture of the life and activities of ancient communities.

A relatively new area of research uses isotope analysis from human and animal remains. Chemical elements such as nitrogen, oxygen and hydrogen have alternative forms which are basically the same but have a different number of neutrons from their parent elements. These are called isotopes. Some are stable and remain the same, and some are radioactive, decaying or decreasing over a known amount of time. The radioactive isotope Carbon 14 is widely used in archaeology as a tool for dating. Carbon is present in all

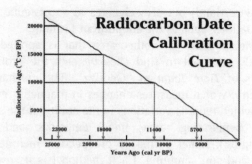

Figure 2. The carbon-14 curve (Source: HowardMorland/Wikimedia Commons)

living things, entering through food, water, and the air we breathe. It is constantly being replaced in our tissue. But when we die, that process stops, and the unstable radioactive isotopes begin to decay (Figure 2). In the case of Carbon 14, because we know how long it takes to decay and at what rate that happens, we can calculate how long it has been since the organism died – a tree, an animal, a person.

The combination of stable and radioactive isotopes can also tell us something about the diet of people in the past, where they were brought up as children, and where they lived in their later adult years. Carbon isotopes can indicate the climate in which a person grew up, because different plants take up varying amounts of carbon depending on whether they are growing in temperate or tropical environments; the amounts of carbon and nitrogen isotopes can also indicate whether a person's diet consisted of mostly vegetable foods, or meat. Isotopes of the metal strontium are present in food and water, and enter into our bones and teeth as we mature. The level of strontium in different places varies, so by measuring strontium isotopes we can establish where a person lived. Teeth are formed in the first decade of a human life, so the strontium levels in them will reflect the place where a person spent their childhood. Bones grow and change over time, so the levels of strontium in them are a reflection of where they lived in the last ten or so years of their life.

These analyses are useful in determining the identity of victims of disasters such as plane crashes – working out where each person came from can help put a name to their remains – and of course putting names to victims of crime. They are very useful to archaeologists, not only because we can track how people moved around in the ancient past (for example, finding out that a man buried near Stonehenge in the early Bronze Age came originally from Central

Europe, perhaps Switzerland) but also changes in subsistence strategies and diet in ancient populations, such as the adoption of farming.

Archaeological prospection is another area that is applied to forensics. Prospection methods are used to find sites beneath the ground. They are known to followers of *Time Team* as "Geofizz". The mechanical methods include magnetometry, which measures changes in magnetic responses in the ground; resistivity which records variations in the ability of the soil to conduct electricity; ground penetrating radar; metal detectors; and Lidar (Light Detection and Ranging). Other forms of prospection include land survey, aerial photography and soil sampling. Each method has its own strengths – magnetometry identifies areas where heat has affected the background level of the earth's magnetism, and so indicates the presence of hearths or structures made of fired brick among other things and it can identify areas of ground where there has been disturbance. Resistivity can be used to produce a map of walls and ditches hidden under the ground, based on the amount of electricity received back from a probe passed over the earth; loose damp structures like ditches will send back more of the current than hard dry ones such as walls and floors. It can also record the difference in electrical current in the ground where a body is present. Ground penetrating radar (GPR) machines send pulses of electromagnetic radiation into the subsoil and record the signals received back from structures beneath. GPR has been used to find bodies buried in concrete. Metal detectors, of course, find objects in the soil – marvellous finds like the golden objects from the Anglo-Saxon period found in Staffordshire, but also more mundane things like metal fittings from the remains of buildings or coffins, or buttons and zips on buried clothing.

Both aerial photography and Lidar use aircraft to view the ground surface from above. In the case of Lidar, a pulsed laser beam is scanned over the survey area and can measure between 20,000 and 100,000 points per second. A highly accurate plan of features that might be almost invisible at ground level can be created by this method and, unlike aerial photography, can even record traces of activity such as banks and enclosures in areas covered by trees. Aerial photography has been a useful archaeological tool since the First World War. From the air, changes in soil colour, cropmarks, the way water or snow is lying across a site, and shadows cast by low sun can all be seen in a way impossible at ground level. These marks can all indicate archaeological features – buried ditches and structures which, although virtually invisible, nevertheless reveal their presence when viewed from an aircraft.

Geophysical prospection has been used during many criminal investigations, such as the Margate case mentioned earlier, in 1994 with the notorious case of Frederick and Rosemary West, and in the search for the victims of Moors murderers Myra Hindley and Ian West.[4]

Human remains

In forensic investigations, the archaeologist may often have to deal with human remains. As well as identifying when and how the person was buried, a study of the body, even if only bones remain, can lead to identification of individuals, their age, gender, state of health before death, last meal, and cause of death. Osteoarchaeologists apply techniques drawn from medicine, anatomy, palaeopathology and many other disciplines. In the United States, and sometimes in Britain, these investigations are known as forensic anthropology.

In the past, police investigations into the grisly finds of murder victims could be pretty unscientific affairs. Half a dozen brawny policemen armed with shovels would simply dig up the remains, remove the body to the local morgue, and hope that a pathologist or medical examiner would provide them with sufficient evidence to pursue the killer. A vast amount of useful clues were lost until, by the end of the last century, it was realised that an archaeological approach would offer much more detail about events leading up to the death, the manner of the death, and the way the body was buried, aiding both identification of the deceased, and ways to identify and catch the criminal. Archaeologists in the past were also guilty of a lack of care in this respect – there are many instances where antiquarian diggers in the eighteenth and nineteenth centuries would dig randomly into prehistoric burial mounds searching for artefacts (particularly gold), simply discarding any bones they found in the process.

Thankfully, nowadays, strict protocols come into force when human remains are discovered, either during police or archaeological investigations. As a result, due care and respect are offered to the buried individual, and many details of their identity, life and cause of death can be recovered. Perhaps the first thing to establish is whether the corpse is male or female. Once the flesh has decayed to bones, only the skeleton can provide this information. In many cases, the larger the bones, and the more developed the places on them where muscles and ligaments were attached, the more likely it is that the deceased was a man – but there are also big, muscular women. Another problem occurs if the dead person was sub-adult – a child or teenager. Until we are fully mature, our skeletal shape is very similar despite our gender.

In adults, the pelvis is a useful place to start. The pelvis of a woman (or any other female mammal) has a wider sub-pubic angle than that of a man, to

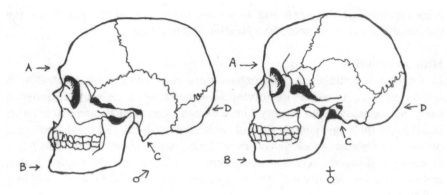

Figure 3. Male and female skull morphology – the arrows point to main gender differences

allow for the passage of a baby during birth. Men tend to have a larger socket for the hip bone than women. Another indicative area is the skull. Men often have squarer chins than women, and they have more sloping foreheads and protruding bone over the eyes (brow ridges), which women usually lack. There are also differences in the shape of the back of the skull and the point of articulation of the lower jaw (Figure 3). These indications are not foolproof, however. Gender is not an absolute. Indeed, some ancient societies recognised a range of gender statuses. There are women with masculine features, and men with feminine ones, and some people fall somewhere in between the two. This identification also depends on the presence of the symptomatic bones, and their condition. In some cases, the bones are too decayed to offer enough clues to be sure of their sex. Sometimes there are idiosyncracies in the skeleton which can identify people belonging to the same family, the small, outwardly invisible differences being inherited through generations. The age of an individual can be estimated in a number of ways – their teeth, whether the epiphyses (ends sections) of long bones and plates that make up skulls which at birth are separate to allow for growth have become fully fused together (meaning they had reached adulthood), and signs of age decay such as arthritis.

Osteoarchaeology can offer further information through the study of changes to the skeleton caused by disease, accident, trauma and even work. A number of diseases leave traces on the bones (though not rapidly acting infectious diseases). Leprosy is a good example – the disease eventually destroys bone material, which is reabsorbed into the body. It especially affects the bones of the central face and the small bones of fingers and toes.

Tuberculosis, syphilis, and some forms of cancer also leave traces. Study of the teeth can tell us a great deal about hygiene and diet, as well as age – how well developed are they, how worn, how many teeth have decayed because of poor diet? Dietary deficiency can also be seen – a lack of iron leads to anaemia, with porous holes developing, particularly in the eye sockets. A lack of Vitamin C leads to scurvy and tooth loss. A lack of Vitamin D can cause rickets as seen in the characteristically bent legs of children who have suffered the deficiency. Periods of malnutrition and disease also leave their marks, especially in growing children. Teeth and bones stop developing at a normal rate while the body is under stress, and these periods can be seen in X-rays as more opaque bands across the bone, or as ridges on teeth and fingernails.[5] These clues may be helpful in identifying individuals whose life history may be known.

More information can be gathered from a study of the stomach contents of the deceased. Even if only skeletal remains survive, there may be tiny clues about the diet of the person left in the soil – minute fish bones, seeds, traces of grains and so on. These can say something about the health and wealth of the individual. Where a body has been preserved in a bog, or in ice, more information can be gathered, as was the case with the body from the Lindow Moss in Cheshire, and the 'Ice Man' discovered in the Alps. Among other things, traces of poison might be present.

It is often possible to build up a picture of a person's life through the stresses their skeletons have suffered, and it is also sometimes possible to identify medical treatments.

Repetitive, heavy work leads to joint problems and changes in bone forms and the size and position of muscle attachment areas on the bones. Someone who has spent their life lifting heavy weights may have strong muscle formations in the arms and back, but also spinal deterioration. Archers, like those whose bodies were found in the wreck of the Tudor warship *Mary Rose*, had a shoulder condition known as *os acrimoniale*, caused by years of practice pulling back a heavy bow.

Trauma caused by accidents or injuries can also often be identified – places where bones have fractured or been crushed. Sometimes the person survived the injury for days, months, even years, and the degree of new bone formation can tell us for how long they lived after the injury. Some injuries to hands and forearms, known as parry fractures, can show whether or not the victim tried to defend themselves. However, an injury that is fatal does not necessarily have to affect the bones. It is probable that many injured people have died from soft tissue injury, through blood loss and infection, before modern medicine was available. Other injuries can indicate that the person was executed – by hanging or decapitation, for example.

People can die in a number of ways – naturally, as a result of age or illness, violently in war or as a result of murder, accidentally or by suicide – self-murder. Archaeopathologists will try to establish which of these is indicated by a close study of any visible wounds, identifying, if possible, the types of weapon or accident that could cause the particular damage visible. This may involve experimental use of tools or weapons on animal carcasses, to assess whether a suspected weapon could reproduce the exact wound found on the bones being studied. Was a sharp-edged instrument used, or a blunt one? From which direction and what height did the blow come? Was the victim standing up, kneeling or lying down? Determination of these factors can sometimes show whether a person was murdered, or judicially executed.

The bones recently attributed to Richard III, found in a car park in Leicester, have been studied and they have been shown to have belonged to a man in his late twenties or early thirties, matching the recorded age at death of Richard III, which was thirty-two. The bones belonged to a man of slender build, who had enjoyed a rich diet with plenty of protein. But he had suffered from scoliosis, probably in puberty, causing him to stoop and hold one shoulder higher than the other.[6]

Ten injuries were found on the bones, mostly to the skull, which happened at or around the moment of death. The cause of death was one or two blows to the back of the skull. It appears that his arms were tied together when he was buried.

Historical cases can also benefit from archaeological forensic work. A famous example from the United States is the Battle of the Little Big Horn, where General George Armstrong Custer's troops were massacred in 1876. Archaeological work at the site has established the range of types and capabilities of the weapons used by the Lakota and other Native American people against Custer and his men, the exact locations of some of the action, the manner of death of many of the soldiers and how their bodies were treated after death. We even now know the identity of the occupant of one of the graves, which proved to hold the remains of one of Custer's scouts.

The survival of bones in the soil is subject to a number of considerations – the soil chemistry, the depth of the burial, the presence of scavenging animals, insects, moulds or bacteria, the age of the individual and so on. If the soil is acidic, bone survival is very unlikely – sandy soils and granitic soils in particular rarely preserve bone. Many ancient burials, as well as those of more recent murder victims, tend to be shallow, which means that there is more

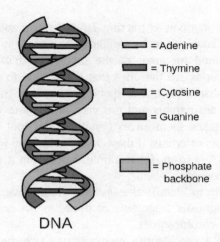

	= Adenine
	= Thymine
	= Cytosine
	= Guanine
	= Phosphate backbone

DNA

Figure 4. The DNA double helix (Source: Forluvoft)

oxygen and water in the soil around the bones, and that in turn means that living organisms that can destroy bone have easier access to the body. Disturbance by farming, building, or even by later burials, is more likely. The bones of children are less robust than those of adults and often decay more quickly. Only rarely are ancient bodies found to survive in good condition. These are usually in the form of preserved bodies such as Egyptian mummies, naturally mummified remains like the sacrificial child victims found high in the Andes of South America, bodies preserved by ice such as the Iron Age people in Siberia, and bodies preserved in anaerobic conditions, like the 'bog bodies' of Northern Europe.

Further evidence is now available to the archaeologist through the development of DNA analysis. DNA is found in most animal body cells including skin, hair roots, bones, teeth, saliva and other body fluids. DNA (deoxyribonucleic acid) analysis is based on the principle that every person has a different genetic fingerprint, except for identical twins. The DNA molecule contains the individual building blocks of this fingerprint for each living entity. Two strands of smaller molecules are linked into an entwined formation known as the double helix (Figure 4). It is made up of linked pairs of bases in specific sequences, different for every individual. There are two types of DNA – nuclear and mitochondrial; each cell in an organism has one copy of nuclear DNA (nDNA) inherited from both parents and up to 10,000 copies of mitochondrial DNA (mtDNA) which comes only from the maternal side of its ancestry.

Forensic analysis involves extracting DNA from a subject, then copying and increasing it to enable it to be studied. The sample is then separated out into parts, and scanned for areas of the sequences that repeat themselves. These repeating sections are the ones that are unique to each individual, as opposed to those shared within a species. They are made up of genetic markers inherited from parents and are very unlikely to be repeated in any other entity. This makes them an extremely useful tool for identifying the victims or perpetrators of crimes if they can be compared with known samples of that person's DNA – from, for example, hairs from a hairbrush, or blood samples already on record.

DNA can also help to identify the sex of a victim, even if the remains are no more than undiagnostic fragments of bone, as the sequences reflect the presence of X and Y chromosomes.

The use of mtDNA can identify members of the same family if they are related through their mothers, and because there is much more mtDNA than nDNA in a sample, it is particularly useful if there is little material to analyse, or if the sample is badly degraded. Like everything else, DNA starts to decay after death, but it is sometimes possible to recover usable DNA even after many centuries, from inside bone or tooth structures. However, great care has to be taken to avoid contamination – a speck of modern skin dust could invalidate the whole sample, so this is work that has to be undertaken in sterile laboratory conditions. Mitochondrial DNA was used to identify the bodies of the Russian imperial family found in 1991 and 2007. They had been killed along with some of their servants by the Bolsheviks in 1918. Using comparisons with known surviving relatives, including Prince Philip, it was possible to establish the identity of each member of the family, even though two of the bodies had been subjected to an attempt to destroy the evidence by burning.[7]

In modern forensic studies, DNA samples can identify victims and criminals, with just a one in 60 billion or so chance of being wrong. In more ancient cases, where DNA survives in bones or teeth, it can be used to identify the gender and ethnicity of an individual, their relationship to other bodies found nearby, and more rarely, their actual identity.

This has proved very useful for investigating 'cold cases' – providing new sources of evidence and allowing investigators to re-open old files to identify victims of crimes or disasters, and bring answers to their families. Archaeological crime scenes are, of course, the coldest of 'cold cases'! But even for very ancient cases, DNA is helping to provide clues.

In the case of the recent identification of the remains of King Richard III, it has been possible to compare DNA extracted from the bones with that of a living descendant of the king's sister, Anne of York, which seems to confirm that it is the body of the king that has been discovered. Further studies are continuing to see if it possible to check the Y-chromosome DNA from the body with those of modern descendants of John of Gaunt, son of Edward III, who was also an ancestor of Richard III.[8]

This is a developing area of science, and new exciting steps are being made all the time. It was recently reported that a skeleton found in northern Spain, some 7,000 years old, had surviving DNA which showed that this man had dark skin and hair, and blue eyes; he was also lactose intolerant and ate little starch in his diet. Surprisingly, his closest modern genetic matches were found in Sweden and Finland.[9]

Research into individual genomes may add much more detail to our study of both ancient and modern skeletal remains. It may eventually be possible not only to establish the gender and ethnicity of a subject and to identify their familial relationships, skin, eye and hair colour, but also to identify other mental and physical characteristics – a tendency to put on weight, for example, or whether they were extravert or neurotic personalities.[10]

DNA is also present in other organisms and material – animals, plants, and diseases have their own DNA fingerprints, and DNA can be found in animal and human faeces. This can help to identify possible causes of death like tuberculosis and malaria, even where there are no indications of illness on the bones. Genetic diseases can also be identified – conditions such as cystic fibrosis. Identification of the blood group of a body can also help to identify the relationships of the deceased with other individuals, and also to which ethnic group he or she may have belonged. Archaeologically, DNA can be used to identify animal families and movements, in tracing the ancestry of species such as the domestic dog, or the adoption of animal farming in the ancient world.

Facial reconstruction is a slightly controversial technique which uses the bones of the skull as a basis for attempting to recreate the appearance of a person when they were alive. The skull bones are scanned into a computer, and copied as a virtual or a physical 3D model. The anatomical structures of muscles, tendons and blood vessels are then superimposed on the model, along with the skin, eyes and hair, using average data. This can help to identify the victims of crime, and to give faces to individuals from the more ancient past. But there are many problems. The method cannot differentiate between a fat or a thin face, or recreate superficial marks such as moles, birthmarks or scars. Not all muscles attach directly to facial bones, and can vary a great deal between individuals. Nasal bones are often missing, and even when present, cannot accurately predict the shape and size of the whole nose. Age, ethnicity, and health status can all affect a person's appearance in ways which may not be visible from the bones alone. There are also problems about which sets of data are applied – various sets exist across the world and they do not all agree. And the person creating the reconstruction may also (not necessarily intentionally) affect the results through their own sense of aesthetics or even emotional response to the subject. As a result, different faces could easily emerge from the same skull if reconstructed by different people in different places.[11] Facial reconstruction is an art, rather than a science.

Despite the drawbacks, facial reconstructions can be useful for police and disaster investigators. For archaeologists, they can at least provide a possible image of the person under study, as has been done for Ötzi – the mummified body found in an Alpine glacier in 1991 – or the Iron Age man found in a bog at Lindow Moss.

Another area of work that has been carried out in the last decade or two is investigation into forms of judicial punishment, with excavations of execution sites and cemeteries, gaols and penal settlements. German and Dutch researchers have been studying execution sites and what they can tell us about the brutality of punishments during the medieval and early modern periods; American forensic anthropologists have studied Civil War prison camps, gaols associated with the black slave trade, and early prisons and lock-ups in colonial settlements; and Australian archaeological work has been carried out on the convict settlements and prisons set up in the nineteenth century to hold the criminals sentenced to transportation by British courts. All these studies are shedding extra light on history, sometimes confirming the historical accounts, and sometimes proving them to be inaccurate or incomplete.

Historical research
Historical accounts and documentary sources of evidence are used by both archaeologists and criminal investigators. Archaeologists study accounts of historical events, wills, estate plans, old maps, drawings and letters to gather clues about locations and the activities that have gone on in them, which may help to locate particular structures, or to interpret artefacts and earthworks. Crime investigators study evidence such as suicide notes, fraudulent documents, altered wills, receipts and other material to support or destroy alibis, and many more examples. Printers, typewriters and handwriting can be

studied to determine the source of a document and its author. Ransom notes received by the Lindbergh family in 1932 after the kidnapping of their baby son were identified as having been written by Bruno Hauptmann by comparisons of his handwriting, and although some controversy still remains about his guilt, Hauptmann was sent to the electric chair for the crime. The case of the Hitler Diaries in 1983, when the German magazine *Stern* published excerpts purporting to come from hitherto unknown volumes of the Fuhrer's personal record, employed analyses of the ink, paper, handwriting and content to establish that they were forgeries made by Konrad Kujau for a journalist, Gerd Heidemann, in order to embezzle money from well-known publishers. Kujau went to prison, but on his release he opened a studio from which he sold 'genuine' Kujau forgeries.[12]

Documentary sources provide many problems for archaeologists. The material may have been written years, even centuries, after the events described took place. The document itself may be a copy of a copy, with mistakes that have crept in over time, be in poor condition or have sections missing. Maps may represent what people intended to design, not what was actually there. The content may in fact be completely untrue – for a number of reasons. The original may have been simply a fictional story, or have been written as propaganda that coloured events to suit the aims of the writer and his audience, or be based on erroneous hearsay evidence. The police have similar problems with witness statements.

Much effort has been put into trying to confirm various events recorded in the Bible – Noah's Flood, the Exodus, and even the crucifixion. Another popular topic has been the Trojan War – did it take place or not? Julius Caesar wrote of his conquest of the Belgic tribes in the 50s BC – yet there is virtually no archaeological evidence to confirm his claims, nor has any evidence of his visits to Britain ever been found – so how much of his account is true?

On the other hand, historical accounts may be all we have – many events leave no archaeological trace behind them. History is most reliable when it is confirmed by multiple accounts, as well as by physical evidence, but it can be most enjoyable even when we know there may be a strong element of fiction in its records. Daniel Defoe enjoyed writing about criminals such as the famous highwayman Jack Sheppard and is believed by many to have been the author of a work entitled *A General History of the Robberies and Murders of the most notorious Pyrates,* which has become a rather romantic source of much modern imagination about the sea robbers of the eighteenth century. Whether by Defoe or not, and whether truthful or not, it became and remains popular reading!

PAST CRIMES

In this book, crimes and punishments will be described for many periods. Some very famous crimes have been left out, just because there are so many books already published about them. Some periods have more archaeological evidence than historical, while in later times, the opposite is true. In each case, however, an attempt has been made to place the crime or punishment in the context of its period in history and to give an overview of the development of the ways in which crimes were committed, detected, and punished from the stone ages to the beginning of the twentieth century.

Chapter 2

The Oldest Crimes

Prehistoric crime – problems

Even before people learned how to read and write, they were certainly committing crimes, and the evidence for some of these is still with us. Archaeology can only reveal a tiny fraction of such incidents. In most circumstances, little remains of the lives of prehistoric people apart from some stone tools, pottery sherds and bones. It is usually only the bones that can tell us about crime during the many thousands of years between the development of our species into modern humans, and the beginnings of literacy. We can presume that there must have been thefts and robberies, arson and rape, assault and fraud, but we simply do not have the proof, and never can have unless there are very exceptional circumstances of preservation.

Nevertheless, there is a tiny amount of evidence for possible assaults and murder in prehistoric and early societies. Only possible, because we are faced with an enormous set of problems in deciphering what happened from the shreds of fact that we can recover. There is evidence of armed attack on settlements in Neolithic Britain 5,000 years ago or so – burned houses, spreads of arrowheads showing attacks on gates in defensive ramparts of enclosures such as Carn Brae in Cornwall and Crickley Hill in Gloucestershire, and even sometimes the bodies of the slain. The problem comes in trying to decide whether these attacks were *criminal*. A mass grave, with a large number of victims, would suggest that we are looking at the evidence of a massacre or the aftermath of a battle (in which case the deaths could be categorised as the result of an act of war) or the resting place of victims of a sudden deadly epidemic. An alternative suggestion, which could apply also to single graves, is that we are looking at some sort of ritual sacrifice or slaughter. Study of the damage to the bones can help sometimes to distinguish which explanation is most likely. It is not normally the case that a criminal act would result in the deaths of a large number of people at once (although of course it can and does happen – in cases of arson, for example).

Single graves are even more of a problem. They are found more often than mass graves, and have even fewer clues. All the above explanations may apply as a cause of death – war, massacre, epidemic disease – but we have to add old age, normal forms of illness, accident, judicial execution and suicide to the list, along with murder. Even when a person has been deliberately killed, the evidence may not show up on the skeleton. Poison, suffocation, strangulation, drowning and soft tissue injuries leave little or no trace in many modern cases, let alone after hundreds or thousands of years. Even a relatively shallow wound can lead to a person bleeding to death, if it severs a major artery, but there would be no mark left on the skeleton for us to see if our only evidence is the bones. We also have problems to do with what happens to human remains in the ground (if the body was interred and not cremated). Bones decay slowly, but they do decay, and in some free-draining, granular and acid soils, they decay very rapidly indeed. Bones get disturbed in the ground, particularly if the burial is shallow – by burrowing animals, earthworms, flood episodes, erosion, ploughing and later building activities. The sheer weight of soil above a body can crush and distort it, leaving breaks and other damage on the bones. Bacteria and moulds feed on the remains, reducing them to scraps, and rainwater leaches out the chemicals within them. The archaeological osteologist has a hard task.

We also have to address social and religious problems. Over the millennia, there have been very different approaches to funeral rites. Ancient cremations rarely reduced whole bodies to ash, and often the remaining fragments were gathered together from the pyre and placed in bags, boxes or pots, which were then buried in the ground, perhaps with some offerings or possessions of the deceased. But many of the smaller bones, from hands and feet, for example, would be overlooked, and the fire itself would have distorted and mineralised the remains. We only have part of the information, and that itself has been distorted, although in some circumstances crucial evidence can be recognised by an expert.

Interments sometimes leave more clues. But the body may have been exposed before burial, even dismembered. Dogs or wolves may have gnawed the bones. In some societies, the practice of 'excarnation' has been observed – the body is placed in a sacred site until natural processes have removed the flesh, and only then are the bones gathered and placed in a grave. This probably happened in Britain, France and other parts of northern Europe in the Neolithic period, with the bones of at least some people gathered and placed in long barrows or chambered tombs. Various funerary treatments of the body may have been undertaken, such as mummification or coating the body in substances such as red ochre, a practice which has been noted on the remains of our extinct cousins, the Neanderthals, and in many societies around the world ever since. No-one knows why red ochre was used in this way – it is yet another archaeological mystery.

Bodies may simply have been placed in the ground, clothed or unclothed, or wrapped in a shroud. They may have been placed in coffins of wood or lead or stone. They may have been interred under a barrow mound, or in a simple grave, or within a specially built tomb, or in a cave or a bog. All these factors will affect how much evidence has survived.

There are also problems about the social context of ancient crimes. Before the adoption of literacy in the ancient civilisations of the Near East, we have no information about how communities maintained order without courts and police forces. How were suspects identified, apprehended, and treated? Which crimes were considered to be punishable and to what extent? Who decided guilt or innocence, and passed sentence? Without the arts of forensic science and the skills of lawyers working within a framework of published laws, it is probable that decisions were often made on the basis of public opinion or emotion, perhaps with guidance from chiefs, priests or shamans. It is possible to imagine that there were, at least in later prehistory, commonly accepted standards of criminality and punishment, which although not written down, were understood by most people. Indeed, there are some clues to this effect in later documents, recorded in succeeding literate periods, such as ancient Irish and Germanic laws.

The earliest law codes

The pre-existence of codes of behaviour is suggested by the form and nature of the very first recorded law codes. Evidence that ancient societies felt the need to establish law and order, and to deal with crime comes down to us from the earliest of the ancient civilisations to use writing. Clay tablets, inscribed with cuneiform script, recorded judicial cases and law codes, as did carved inscriptions on rock stelae or pillars. Cuneiform writing began around 5,000 years ago in the ancient Near East. It was used to make inventories, to record prayers, and to make a record of legal proceedings. For day to day purposes, a small block of fresh clay was prepared, and the symbols were impressed into it with the tip of a cut reed (Figure 5). It was a very flexible system, combining a form of alphabetical writing with types of shorthand that developed in complexity over time. The clay tablets could then be fired in a kiln, or sun-dried; once hardened in this way, they could, and do, last for millennia.

Figure 5. Cuneiform tablet (Source: Fæ/Wikimedia Commons)

The wedge-shaped symbols could also be readily carved into stone, and it is in this form that we find one of the oldest known law codes in the world – the Code of Hammurabi. It was carved in about 1772 BC on the orders of a Babylonian king. The stone pillar, 2.25m tall, was discovered in Iran in 1901 by a French archaeologist. Nearly 300 separate laws are recorded on its surface. Copies of parts of these laws have also been found on clay tablets excavated in Israel and other parts of the Middle East. The various sections cover a whole range of governmental concerns – military service, religious observance, trade and commercial practice, labour laws, as well as laws relating to criminal acts – and they also specify the appropriate punishments for transgressions. Earlier law codes are known – the code of Ur-nammu dates from 2112–2095 BC, in which in most cases, the punishments for crimes were set down in the form of fines. However, by the time of Hammurabi, things had changed and become more physical.

Acts of murder or assault were generally to be punished by reciprocal violence – if someone lost an eye, he was entitled to take out the eye of the one who had wounded him. If a son hit his father, he would lose the hand that struck the blow; if a surgeon caused a patient to lose an arm or a leg, the doctor would also lose a hand. Many of the punishments were simple and brutal in this way – a liar lost his tongue, or a duplicitous wet-nurse would have a breast cut off. The death penalty was enacted for a number of crimes, among which were rape, theft from the temple treasury or the palace, ordinary theft or receiving stolen goods (including slaves), kidnapping, keeping a tavern in which known criminals could be found without informing the authorities, selling bad ale, and for building contractors who caused death by putting up unsafe houses. Further capital crimes included abortion, and helping slaves to escape.

Other punishments included exile for incest, disinheritance for unfilial behaviour, drowning for adultery, whipping for attacking a superior, branding for slander against a married woman, and enslavement. However, the most common sentence was still in the form of a fine. Fines were detailed for damage, theft, breach of contract and many other transgressions, and were expressed in terms of double, treble or up to thirtyfold the value of the damage or theft.

The Code makes it clear that intention to commit a crime is important – penalties for accidental hurt or damage were either minimal or not imposed. Injury or damage caused by carelessness was another matter entirely. Stringent conditions accompanied orders for reparation and punishment, including warranties for workmanship and replacement of the full value of damaged items.

The Code also demands that in order to prosecute someone for a crime, they must be caught red-handed, and there had to be sufficient evidence presented to confirm his guilt. Oaths were administered to witnesses, and there were stiff penalties for perjury. Written evidence was greatly preferred to spoken testimony, and carried much more weight with the judges. This was a very bureaucratic society – all court judgements were written down, with the oaths of the judges, witnesses and officials, copied to all parties, and archived in the official department.[1]

By the time of the Middle Assyrian Empire, in the mid second millennium BC, harsh physical punishments were even more often applied. 'One Middle Assyrian law reads "... if a woman has crushed a gentleman's testicle in a brawl, they shall cut off one of her fingers and if the other testicle has become affected ... or she has crushed the other testicle in a brawl, they shall tear out both her eyes" – which casts some interesting light not only on Assyrian law but on social behaviour of the period!'[2]

The societies to which these law codes belonged were predominantly quite small Bronze Age city communities in the region of the Tigris and Euphrates rivers, ruled by a priest-king, or by a king supported by a temple hierarchy. They flourished from around 6,000 BC down to the final collapse of the

Assyrian empire around 1,000 BC, a time when there appears to have been a widespread disaster affecting most of Eurasia. Their settlements consisted of a maze of stone or mud-brick buildings in narrow alleys; some of the largest cities held up to 60,000 people, usually around a royal residence and temple complex, and a ziggarut. A ziggarut was a massive artificial mound made up of mud-bricks, sometimes glazed with bright colours, which rose in a series of terraces to a shrine on the top, which was believed to be the dwelling place of the city's patron god. The Great Ziggarut of Ur, dedicated to the moon god Nanna, was probably over 30m high.

Most houses were single-storey, but some of the wealthier residents had houses with an upper floor. There was some sort of sewage system beneath the streets, but there were no markets or workshops. These were confined to the temple precincts, under the control of the priests. Many cities were also enclosed by massive walls and gateways.

Surrounding the cities were the zones of irrigated fields and peasant communities who produced the food that supported the city. Compared to the kind of civilisations to be found in Northern Europe at the time, where small dispersed farmsteads made of timber were scattered across the countryside, without any major urban centres or central government, these Near Eastern cities were extremely advanced. At least to some extent, the development of cities was the result of a relatively harsh landscape – water sources were few, cropland had to be created through the use of irrigation techniques, and survival depended on co-operation and organisation. In the north, there was plenty of water and the land was richer – people did not need to band together to such a degree to survive. They had far more resources to hand, and could live more independently.

Life in the first cities revolved around the temples. They were not only religious centres, but also the places where scribes were taught writing and mathematics, where taxes and tribute were gathered, and where records were produced and kept. The society was highly stratified, with the king and his court, and the temple priests at the top and slaves at the bottom. This hierarchy was reflected in the way laws were administered, and in which criminals were punished. Legal disputes were debated before an arbitrator, and if a settlement could not be reached, the matter was referred to a panel of trained judges. If a crime was committed against someone from the upper classes, it was regarded as more severe, and carried a harsher punishment, than one committed against a lower class citizen. But if the criminal was himself from the upper classes, he could expect a harsher punishment than would a low class law breaker.

Ancient Egyptian law and crimes

Egyptian law also seems to have been recorded, but it lacked judges and courts in the early period of pharaonic government. In the early dynastic period, from about 3100 BC, at least through to the period of the New Kingdom, which ended around 1000 BC, state officials could act as judges when required. We do not have a law code for ancient Egypt although one seems to have existed in the later period, but there are records of legal precedents and royal decrees. In theory, everyone except slaves was regarded as equal under the law, unlike the hierarchical system of the earlier Mesopotamian cultures. However, punishments inflicted upon a criminal could also be inflicted on his whole family, including the children – they might all be exiled or imprisoned.

Deir el-Medina, the village of the builders of the tombs in the Valley of the Kings, excavated by Bruyère, produced numerous *ostraca* which recorded legal proceedings. *Ostraca* are pieces of fired clay, often broken pots, on which scribes wrote in lieu of papyrus. Deir el-Medina has also produced evidence of the use of oracles to decide legal affairs. It is not known exactly how this worked, but it appears that a document for each side of a case was prepared and placed either side of a street; an image of the founder god of the village was brought and placed between the documents, and whichever side the god turned towards was deemed to be the winner. Perhaps the statue of the god stood on a spinning turntable?

Other records from the village give details of punishments; in the case of stolen goods, a document sentences the thief to return the goods, and to pay a fine of twice their value. Further punishments included caning and branding.

In more serious cases, the matter could be referred to the pharaoh himself or the vizier, at a court called the *Great Kenbet*. Before trial, the accused could be held in a prison, although the exact nature of these is not really understood. They may just have been deep pits, or rooms in a temple. Prison as a punishment was not part of Egyptian justice. The worst crimes could be punished by exile, hard labour in desert mines and quarries, the loss of ears, nose, tongue or hands, or death. Executions were often in the form of impalement, but there are also records of beheading, drowning and burning.

In addition to the earthly punishment, ancient Egyptians also believed that the malefactor would face another trial in the afterlife, with further punishments there. The deceased would enter the Court of the Dead and be confronted by god-judges presided over by Anubis, jackal-headed god of the dead. His heart would be weighed against a feather from the wings of the goddess Maat, who represented justice, order and truth, and if it was too heavy with sin, he would be destroyed and denied eternal life (Figure 6).

Figure 6. The judgement of Anubis – the deceased's heart weighed against a feather (from an Egyptian tomb painting)

Citizens could petition local officials to investigate crimes on their behalf. One such petition tells of a crime 'perpetrated by the workmen of Nakhu-m-Maut. They went into my house, stole two large loaves and three cakes, spilt my oil, opened my bin containing the corn, stole Northern *dehu*-corn. They went to the house in the wharf, stole half the *killesteis* (a kind of acid bread) yesterday [baked], spilt the oil. In the third month of the Shemu-season, the 12th day, during the crown feast of king Amen-hotep, l.h.s., they went to the granary, stole three great loaves, eight *sabu*-cakes of Rohusu berries ... They drew a bottle of beer which was [cooling] in water, while I was staying in my father's room. My Lord, let whatsoever has been stolen be given back to me'.[3]

Towards the later period of the Egyptian civilisation, the post of judge became fixed and hereditary. Various texts show that judges were exhorted to be honest and unbiased, but other records show that bribery and corruption were not uncommon.

There were forms of police in ancient Egypt: at various times, men armed with staves and dogs or trained monkeys were employed to guard public places, and guards were recruited to prevent tomb robberies (Figure 7).

Tomb robbing was seen to be one of the worst crimes, because it not only took the possessions of the dead from the grave, but also stole those possessions from the deceased in the afterlife. The earliest recorded case

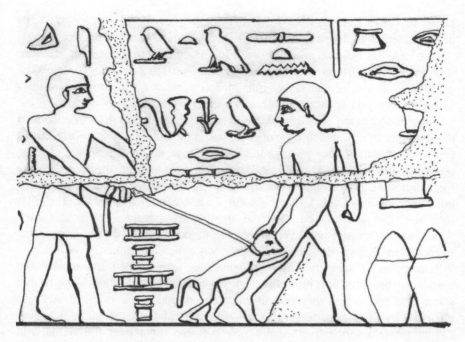

Figure 7. Trained monkey arresting a thief (from an Egyptian tomb painting)

comes from the time of Rameses IX (1129–1111 BC). Tombs were being looted, but the governor of the necropolis, Pew-re, was doing nothing to stop the robbers. Peser, the city ruler, reported the problem and a commission of enquiry had to be set up by the governor Pew-re himself. The commission reported that not all the tombs had been robbed, but that some had been despoiled, or attempts to break in were evident. The tombs of lesser people were much more badly damaged than the royal ones, often totally destroyed and broken. A few suspects were taken into custody as a result, but the main effect of the enquiry was that the commission had exposed the shortcomings of Pew-re and the commission members themselves. Not surprisingly, rather than make their findings public, the commission decided that it would be a good idea to dispose of Peser, the man who had blown the whistle. They set up a trap with a false confession, which Peser believed; gleefully, the commission proved that the confession was a lie, announced therefore that all of Peser's information was faulty, and charged Peser himself with fraud.

But the robberies continued, until the pharaoh himself set up a new commission. These officials obtained a confession from one of the thieves, a herdsman called Bukhef, who after being flogged, revealed a long list of names of his accomplices. It is a shame that we do not know the rest of the story!

One case has been recorded in detail in a document in the British Museum that dates to the reign of Rameses XI (1107–1078/7 BC). It contains the confession of a thief called Amenpenufer who robbed a pyramid. The thief was a builder, and with a gang of seven other workmen, they decided to cut into the underground passages of the pyramid. They found the sarcophagi of the king and queen, which they opened, and they stole the golden face masks from the mummies along with much jewellery and many precious objects, setting fire to what they could not carry. They divided up the loot between them, but soon Amenpenufer was arrested. He bribed a scribe with his stolen gold and was released. His gang went on to commit a number of similar robberies, but in the end three of them were caught. The others fled. Amenpenufer himself was eventually caught, although we do not know what happened to him. We do know his mother was exiled to Nubia.

Sometimes it was the priests themselves who robbed the tombs and temples. A group of four priests is recorded as stealing a gold necklace from a statue of a god, which they melted down and divided between them. Another gang led by priests made a habit of stealing gold from the gods, but were caught when a scribe overheard a row between them over the spoils, and began to blackmail them.

Virtually every Egyptian pyramid or tomb discovered by archaeologists had already been plundered in antiquity, and the problem was so well known and acute that the designers of the pyramids and tombs themselves went to great lengths to hide the entrances, to put in false corridors, dead ends and traps. The Great Pyramid of Khufu, built around 2,560 BC, included misleading passages that could be blocked by great slabs of granite, secret chambers and hidden entrances.

Even the most famous of all Egyptian tombs, that of Tutankhamun, had been robbed not long after the death of the pharaoh, probably within months, as some of the items stolen seem to have been perishable goods such as flasks of perfume. After this the tomb was resealed, the entrance corridor filled with rubble and the hole the robbers had made in the doorway was plastered over. In a nearby pit, known as KV54, materials associated with Tutankhamun were discovered, possibly the remnants of his embalming and a funerary feast. Similar items were found on the floor of the tomb's corridor, and it is believed that the items in the pit were removed there after the first robbery had taken place. However, a second robbery also occurred at a slightly later date, during which much of the rubble in the corridor was removed. One estimate suggests that about 60% of the jewellery that had been deposited in the chamber known as the 'Treasury' had been stolen. Tremendous curses were left in the tombs, aimed at deterring the robbers, but it is clear these had absolutely no effect.

The ancient robbers had no respect, either, for the bodies of the dead. The mummy bundles were ripped open to get at the jewels and amulets wrapped into the bandages, with limbs broken off and tossed aside.

Grave robbing was a profitable business, and whilst generally carried out in a clandestine manner, sometimes it was brazen – a stone tablet in the Cairo Museum records a rebellion which occurred around 2,000 BC, during which the peasants smashed open the royal tombs and stole the jewels and gold objects buried inside. A papyrus in the same museum, dating from the seventh century BC, records a case in Luxor. An official lay an accusation against a colleague, accusing him of raiding the tombs in the Valley of the Kings; the royal authorities set up an investigation, which at first found the accused not guilty, but new evidence caused them to change their minds, and the guilty man was sentenced to corporal punishment. This, and earlier contradictory evidence from judicial commissions, strongly suggests that there was a degree of collusion, graft and bribery among the officials responsible for the protection, and investigating the raiding, of the tombs.

It was not just in Egypt that tomb robbers were active. In 2012, Turkish archaeologists working at a mausoleum at Knidos found that graves had been robbed in the fourth century BC. This ancient site was an island connected to the mainland by a bridge and causeway, and was used for graves and for temples. The site's origins go back to around 750 BC, and it is currently undergoing restoration and further excavation. Proof of the robbery included a tiny gold ornament dropped by the thieves, and even a candle that they had dropped while escaping.[4]

Murder also occurred in ancient Egypt. In December 2012, it was reported in the press that CAT scans of the mummy of the pharaoh Rameses III had revealed a 7cm deep slash across his throat, that would have been fatal. The damage had been hidden by a linen scarf which was too delicate to move, and so had not been noticed until the scientific technique had become available (Figure 8). It was known that in 1155 BC there had been an attempted coup by Tiye, one of the pharaoh's wives, abetted by his son Pentaweret (or Pentawere), and that Pentaweret had been caught and committed suicide. The CAT scan now suggests that the coup had been successful in assassinating the king. Tests on an unidentified body of a

Figure 8. Mummy of Rameses III

young man found nearby, who was aged about 18, showed that he had the same DNA as the pharaoh, in a proportion typical of a father-son relationship, and thus was probably his son Pentaweret. This body had been covered with a goatskin, which would have been seen as a mark of disrespect. The neck of this second mummy showed over-inflation of the chest cavity and compressions in the skin that might indicate he had been strangled to death, rather than committed suicide.[5]

Modern techniques have revealed another even older Egyptian murder case. A group of six naturally mummified bodies was found around 1900 at Gebelein in the Upper Egyptian desert not far from Luxor. They date from the middle of the fourth millennium BC, and their bodies, including soft tissue, were preserved by the hot dry sand in which they were buried. One of these bodies, noted for his red hair (leading to his nickname 'Ginger'), that had been given to the British Museum, was subjected in 2012 to a CAT scan at the Cromwell Hospital. The results showed that this individual was a healthy young man (around 20 years old), who had been murdered. A copper or flint knife, estimated to have been at least 12cm long and 2cm wide, had been stabbed into his back, notching his left shoulder blade and breaking one of his ribs into fragments. It would have penetrated his lung. There was no evidence of defence wounds on his arms, so it seems he was attacked suddenly from behind by his murderer.[6]

Stone Age murders

Most cases of prehistoric murder involved only the skeletal remains. One of the earliest examples that has been suggested comes from northern Iraq, in the Zagros Mountains. Between 1953 and 1960, nine skeletons were found in a cave, called Shanidar. These people were not modern humans, but Neanderthals, the latest surviving hominid other than our own species, and have been dated to between 50,000 and 75,000 years old. The Neanderthal species existed for over 200,000 years, but seems to have died out just 20,000–30,000 years ago, so that they would have co-existed with modern humans for some time in parts of Europe and Western Asia. The species was first discovered in the Neander Valley near Düsseldorf in Germany. They probably diverged as a separate species from *Homo sapiens* nearly 400,000 years ago, perhaps even longer, and fossil bones have been found over a large stretch of Europe and Western Asia, where small bands roamed just south of the ice sheets that covered most of the north. Their tools and equipment have been found in southern England, in remains of hunting camps that demonstrate that they followed the game animals up into what was then tundra.

Neanderthals were stocky, strong people, whose anatomy seems to have been particularly well-adapted for life in colder regions. They made tools and weapons, and used fire. They created art, and probably music too. It is not known why they died out – it might have been that they could not compete with our own species, or they might have not been able to adapt to climate fluctuations, periods when the climate turned much warmer at a rapid pace.

Recent studies of one individual from the Iraq cave, known as Shanidar 3, who was a male in his later middle years, found evidence of a lethal wound which had sliced into one of his ribs. Many Neanderthal specimens show signs of wounds and accidental damage to the bones; theirs must have been a hard and dangerous life, hunting large game for food and seeking for shelter in caves and rock overhangs. Weapons damage has been noticed from time to time on Neanderthal bones, such as a scalp injury on a specimen from France.

Researchers from Duke University in North Carolina undertook some experiments to try to replicate the bone trauma found on Shanidar 3. They made some stone-tipped spears and fired them at pig carcasses. Pigs have very similar skin thickness and muscle mass to humans, so they make useful experimental subjects for comparison. The spears were of two types – light throwing spears, and heavier thrusting weapons. It was the lighter throwing spear that created similar damage in the pig carcass to that observed in the Neanderthal skeleton. The wound was not immediately fatal – it had started to heal before he died.

It is believed that Neanderthals had not developed throwing spears – theirs were the thrusting weapons, used at close quarters. The only people at the time with the more advanced throwing spears were modern humans – our own ancestors – leading to the conclusion that it was one of our own race who murdered Shanidar 3.

Recently, evidence has come to light which suggests that Neanderthals were not simply victims, but also that they killed others of their own species. In northern Spain there is a cave system called El Sidrón, which stretches for nearly three miles underground. In a cave about sixty feet deep, a number of bones were discovered, that seem to have been washed down along with soil and stone tools, from a rock shelter higher up. There were bones from six adults, three male and three female, three teenage boys and three younger children aged between two and nine years. The three men were possibly brothers, and two of the women were mothers of the smaller children. All the bones had been butchered, with skulls and bones split open to extract brains, tongues and marrow. The excavators believe that, one day 49,000 years ago, an entire family group was massacred and eaten raw (there were no signs of fire or burning) by a neighbouring Neanderthal party of hunters, using tools that were made just a few kilometres away. There were no modern human groups in the area at the time. Then there was a violent storm, which washed the remains down through a sinkhole into the cave below; one bonus of this is that the bones have not been contaminated by later contact with animals or people, and may provide one of the best sources yet for the extraction and study of Neanderthal DNA.[8]

Studies of prehistoric skeletons from South Africa, on the edge of the Kalahari Desert, have produced evidence for a very high amount of probable interpersonal violence in the Later Stone Age period in that region. It is not uncommon to find evidence of healed bone fractures in prehistoric specimens. There are three definitions of bone trauma that are used by scientists. Damage that occurred some time before death, and which had healed or started to heal, is known as 'antemortem' trauma; 'perimortem' damage is trauma which occurred close to or at the point of death, with no healing evident. Damage that occurred after death, as a result of breakages occurring in the burial environment, is called 'postmortem' trauma. In order to establish whether damage on a bone has been caused by interpersonal violence, it is necessary to determine when it happened, and to rule out other causes such as disease or accident. It is seldom possible to do this with most bones unless there is a

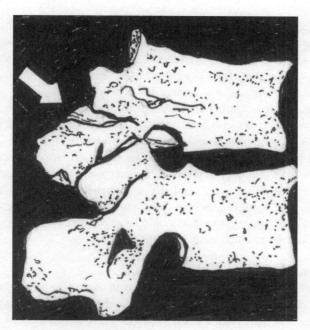

Figure 9. Bone point (arrowed) between the vertebrae of a stone age individual from South Africa

specific clue present. One of the skeletons studied in South Africa was that of a young female found near the southern Cape coast. Two arrow points were found embedded in her lower vertebrae, and the angle of these showed that she had been shot while lying face down on the ground (Figure 9).

Better evidence of violence can be seen in cranial wounds. A number of the skeletons studied had damage to their skulls apparently caused by a pointed object such as a hardened digging stick. The victims of this type of assault included three children in the Modder River area, as well as a number of other men, women and young adults from elsewhere.

The South African researchers have come to the conclusion that the rate of murder amongst these prehistoric communities was proportionally twice as high as the murder rate for New York City in 1990.[9]

Evidence for ancient violence has been found all over Europe – possible cannibalism in France, Denmark, Croatia, the Netherlands and Spain, and many examples of projectile or other bone or stone points embedded in bodies. There are also many examples of depressed skull fractures which may be the result of deliberate blows.

During the Mesolithic (beginning around 11500 BC) and the following Neolithic period from around 6500 BC, there were massacres of large numbers of people at several sites, frequently with more females and children represented among the dead than males. In these cases, we may have to designate these killings as 'war crimes' rather than murder.

In Britain, a large number of bodies from the Neolithic have been found with arrowheads in the grave, as well as skull fractures and other skeletal damage. It is often hard to know whether arrowheads in a grave were placed there as part of the deceased's equipment for the afterlife, or whether they had actually been shot into the body when the person was alive, and have fallen to the bottom of the grave when the body decomposed. There are a number of possibilities that could explain these finds – warfare between rival communities and hunting accidents could have resulted in deaths from arrows and spears. Murder is much more difficult to ascertain.

Ancient cannibals and sacrificial victims

Cannibalism may also be indicated in North America, in the case of the Anasazi people who lived in what is known as the Four Corners region (where Arizona, New Mexico, Utah and Colorado meet) between the first and twelfth centuries AD. These prehistoric people built a number of large settlements, often consisting of contiguous housing complexes on several levels, as well as 'cliff castles' – defensive communities placed on ledges high up in canyon walls. One of the most famous of these sites is Pueblo Bonito, with some 800 rooms or dwelling units, in Chaco Canyon. Here, and in some 40 sites across the area, nearly 300 possible victims of cannibalism have been found.

Evidence for cannibalism relies on several types of material: bones that have been broken open to extract the marrow, so-called 'anvil' abrasions on bones that indicate that a hammer stone has been used on them, signs of burning especially on the back of the skull which would occur if someone wished to extract the brain, an absence of spongy bone elements which would have completely disappeared had they been cooked and digested, and a shiny marking called 'pot polish' which appears on bones that have been cooked in ceramic pots. However, none of these clues alone prove that people ate other human beings.

Then in 1997, in a canyon called Cowboy Wash, the remains of 24 people were found, which represented about a third of the whole population of that area. The signs suggested that their bodies had been chopped and cooked. One other clue, however, was found at Cowboy Wash – a coprolite. A coprolite is a semi-fossilised piece of human excrement. When analysed, this coprolite was found to contain human myoglobin, a component of blood. Blood does not normally enter the digestive tract, unless it is consumed orally. The conclusion was plain – the person who had defecated did so after eating part of another human being.

This finding has been challenged by those who doubt the science, or are unwilling to accept that such practices took place among Native Americans. One theory has suggested that the cannibals who killed the Anasazi were originally from far to the south – perhaps a migrating group of people related to the Aztecs of the Valley of Mexico, where bloody sacrifices and terrible rites are known to have part of religion and government. However, more evidence would be needed to finally identify the killers.[10]

A particular category of prehistoric deaths in Northern Europe is that of the bog bodies. Most of these date from the Iron Age, which began in Britain around 700 BC. Bog bodies have been found in Britain and Ireland, the Netherlands, Denmark and Northern Germany, and they include men, women and children. The common factor is that after death, rather than being buried or cremated, the bodies were placed in marshes or bogs, where they have been rediscovered by peat cutters.

Bogs are good places for the preservation of bodies. They are typically low-lying, watery areas of land which have a build-up of moss and other organic material forming waterlogged acidic peat deposits. The acidic environment halts the action of bacteria that would normally break down a body, and the presence of tannins from the decaying mosses preserve skin as if it were leather. As a result, bog bodies can seem remarkably modern when found, and in the past, people have often thought they have unearthed modern corpses, either murder victims or unlucky travellers who have strayed into the mire. Hundreds of bodies have been discovered over the centuries, but only recently has the science existed to allow them to be preserved and studied. One of the earliest efforts to preserve a body came in 1950 when the remains of a man were found at Tollund in Denmark; two years later another man's remains were found at Grauballe, not far from Tollund. This person had a deep cut across his neck.

In 1984, a body was found at Lindow Moss near Manchester, after a foot was spotted on the conveyor belt of a peat-cutting machine. A little over two thousand years old, it was the body of a man in his twenties, with good teeth and carefully manicured nails. He had blood type O, the most common modern English type. He was generally in good health apart from some mild arthritis and a bad case of stomach parasites. Analysis revealed that he had received several blows to the head, been hit so severely from behind that one of his ribs was cracked, and a sinew cord was wrapped tightly round his neck. Clearly, his killers had wanted to do a thorough job.

A slightly later death occurred around AD 100. The head of a bog body from near Salford known as 'Worsley Man' has been put through a CT scanner. Found in 1958, the body was of a similar age to the man from the Lindow Moss, and like him had received a number of blows. The scan revealed the marks of a ligature round his neck that had strangled him. Finally, the Worsley Man was beheaded. This death occurred 150 years later, however, at a time when the Romans had invaded Britain and were rapidly bringing the country under their control.[11]

Why were these people killed and buried in the bogs? A favourite explanation is that they were ritual sacrifices. Some, though not all, seem to have been fairly carefully laid to rest. But there are exceptions. The body known as Huldremose woman, which was found in 1879, has been re-examined more recently. There was evidence of deep cuts to her legs and arms, and it seems her right arm had been chopped off before she died, although this is disputed. The damage may have been done by the peat cutters who found her. It can be very difficult to establish at what point such cuts were made because of the condition of the bodies when they finally reach the laboratory for study. In 1897 the body of a girl was found near Yde in the Netherlands. Just sixteen years old, she seems to have been strangled, and there was a knife wound near her left collar-bone. Two bodies found in 1904 at Bourtanger Moor, also in the Netherlands, were of men who had been buried together. One man had sustained a stab wound from which his intestines were protruding.

Strangulation is indicated in a number of bog body cases, as well as blows to the head and cuts to the body. Was this a widespread ritual practice, possibly as an offering to the gods in times of trouble? One explanation that has been given is that it was the advance of the Romans into Northern Europe that sparked a panic that demanded such sacrifices, but we now know that the practice of bog burials went on both before and after the coming of the Romans, as the dates of the Lindow and Worsley bodies clearly demonstrate.

Another possible explanation is that these were judicial executions of criminals. In his *Germania,* the Roman writer Tacitus recounts the legal practices of the Germanic tribes. He tells us that criminals were brought before a tribal assembly to answer for their misdeeds. If it was a small transgression such as theft, the penalty was usually the payment of some form of damages to the victim or his family, and to the tribal 'king'. For more severe crimes, however, the death penalty was demanded. Traitors and deserters were hanged. Cowards and those guilty of sexual crimes (including homosexuality) were accorded a more ignominious death – they were to be thrown into bogs where their moral pollution would be concealed from sight. Are we therefore looking at actual criminals, executed for their crimes?

Some Pictish carvings from Iron Age Scotland are thought to represent ritual murder or sacrifice. Another Iron Age victim has been discovered at Minehowe, on Orkney, but this man does not seem to have been a sacrificial victim. Archaeologists came upon the body of a man aged between twenty-five and thirty-five, buried in a shallow grave in a midden heap. The corpse had been unceremoniously crammed into a space too small for his whole body, around 2,000 years ago. His feet had been bent at odd angles to force them into the available space. Large stones had been laid across the body. Analyses at Bradford University determined that he had been around 5ft 5in tall, and had probably been right-handed, with strong upper arms and damage to his spine consistent with time spent lifting heavy weights. He had bad teeth. There was a diamond-shaped puncture wound on his left shoulder caused by a powerful blow, possibly made by an arrow or a spear. On the left side of his body there were a number of cut marks made by a sharp metal blade. They were deep and probably fatal, penetrating his chest, lung and kidney, as well as doing damage to his arm and hand.

That the damage was mostly on the left side of the body suggests that he might have been holding a weapon himself, in his right hand, but lacked a shield. His ability to defend himself had been severely comprised by the injury to his back, which seems to have been the first wound. It was not possible to be sure whether he had sustained any blows to the head, as the skull was too damaged for an assessment to be made.[12]

A famous murder victim

The most famous ancient murder victim found in recent years is certainly 'Ötzi', the frozen body found in the Alps on the border between Austria and Italy, in 1991. The body had been preserved in glacier ice for more than 5,000 years. More recent bodies have sometimes been discovered in glaciers, but the artefacts found with Ötzi quickly proved that he was far older. He comes from a period (the Neolithic) when only tools of bone, antler, wood or stone were used, and he carried a flint knife and a yew bow – but he also had a copper axe. This discovery meant that archaeologists had to reassess their dates for the end of the stone ages and the beginning of the Chalcolithic, or Copper Age. Clearly, knowledge of how to smelt and cast metal had begun several hundred years earlier than anyone had imagined.

At first, everyone believed that this 45 year old man had fallen victim to a storm or an accident in the mountains. He had evidence of a number of medical conditions – osteoarthritis and hardening of his arteries, and ridges on his fingernails (known as 'Beau's lines') showed that he had only recently recovered from another bout of illness, one of three in six months. Bouts of illness during childhood show up on X-rays of teeth and bones as lines of denser material, which occur when normal development is slowed or arrested by disease. These marks rest permanently in the body even when the person has grown up. However, fingernails keep growing throughout our lives, and can reveal much more recent events. Their growth is also affected by disease, but in this case, the illness may only have occurred a few weeks prior to death. Of course, it is extremely rare to find fingernails on ancient bodies, as they usually decay quite rapidly in the ground. The man in the ice had apparently resorted to a shaman or healer for help with the arthritis, having acquired a number of tattoos which in some societies were used as a form of acupuncture treatment.

Because of the problems involved in preserving Ötzi's body, which would have decayed very quickly if it had been allowed to thaw, further investigations into his health and cause of death were delayed while suitable low temperature accommodation was prepared. This took longer to establish permanently than it might have done as there was doubt about which side of the Austrian/Italian border his remains were actually found, which had to be sorted out at a high political level.

Finally, it was agreed that his body had rested on the Italian side of the border, and a special chamber was constructed for his preservation at the South Tyrol Museum of Archaeology in Bolzano. The finds were moved to their permanent home there in January 1998. Attention had originally focussed on the wealth of artefacts that had been found with the frozen body. His clothing had survived – a woven grass cape, a goat hide coat sewn with dark and light stripes of hair, a round bearskin cap that tied under the chin, and goat hide leggings, one for each leg, with ties to attach them to a belt and round his shoes. Below these he wore a goat leather loincloth. On his feet were shoes; the inner part was made of woven grass netting, fastened to a deerskin upper and a bearskin sole with leather ties. More grass stuffed into the shoes would have made them warm to wear, and quite comfortable as long as they stayed dry. There was also a calf's leather belt and a leather pouch in which he carried some of his equipment, including some flint tools and a bone awl. He also carried a fire-making kit in his pouch – tinder in the form of a dried fungus, and a piece of iron pyrite, which when struck against a flint, would have produced a spark.

Other tools and equipment were found around the body. These included a flint knife with a wooden handle attached by animal sinew, in a tree-bast net sheath, which he could attach to his belt. He had another net, possibly for catching rabbits or birds, and two small light birch-bark containers, one of which is thought to have contained the embers of his last fire, to be used to start the next one. There was also what has been called his 'first-aid kit', which consisted of strips of hide holding pieces of birch polypore fungus, an ancient antibiotic and styptic remedy, which also can help deal with intestinal parasites. Later medical analysis showed that Ötzi suffered from this problem too. He would have carried much of his equipment in his backpack, constructed of bent pieces of hazel wood supporting a leather sack.

He had a bow, 1.82m long, made of yew, which he had not yet finished making – tool marks were visible on the wood. It was covered in blood. He had possibly laid the bow against a rock before he died, and placed his quiver beside it. Made of a hazel frame and chamois-leather bag, the quiver had a decorated side pocket, but had been recently broken. Inside were antler tips, animal sinew and tree-bast string, and two complete arrows, with twelve unfinished arrow shafts. The arrow shafts were made of viburnum sapwood, and were around 85cm long. The finished arrows had flint arrowheads attached with birch tar and wound thread, and three fletchings attached the same way, with nettle thread. Interestingly, these two arrows had been made by different people – one right-handed, the other left-handed, demonstrated by the way the threads were wound.

The most astonishing item, however, was Ötzi's axe. Mounted on a 60cm long yew haft, the copper axe, 9.5cm long, is bound with birch tar and leather straps. The copper is almost pure, and the axe had been cast, and then cold-hammered to create the narrow blade. The blade showed clear signs of use. Traces of arsenic found in the hair of the ice mummy suggest that he might himself have been a metal worker. Arsenic commonly occurs with copper in local ore deposits, and a certain amount would have been taken up by the metalsmith's skin and hair as he worked. If Ötzi had worked the copper himself, he must have been one of the first pioneers of metal technology, one of the skilled few who brought the stone ages to an end and began the development of a whole new world of production and tools which has led, incrementally, to our own technological era.

Pollen analysis identified thirty different types of plant species in Ötzi's stomach. These, taken in with his food and drink, showed that he must have come recently from south of the Alps, possibly from the Schnal Valley, where one of the rarer types of tree species can be found, although he grew up in a region even further away. He had left the valleys just twelve hours before he died, a time period estimated from the degree of digestion of the pollens. The pollens also indicated that he died in the spring or early summer. He had recently eaten wheat, possibly in the form of bread or a porridge, dried sloes, and venison meat. Researchers also found that he had very bad teeth (and almost certainly bad breath), possibly caused by his diet, which would have been rich in starches. He seems to have had a very low sperm count. Recent DNA analysis revealed that he also suffered from Lyme disease, which is spread by ticks. He was a short man, just five feet two inches tall, had brown eyes, was lactose intolerant, had a predisposition to heart disease, and was related, very remotely, to a modern Corsican or Sardinian population!

He would have come from a small farming community, living in timber houses, and keeping sheep or goats. They were growing spelt wheat, and gathered fruit and wood from the surrounding forests, where they also hunted deer and chamois. It would have been typical of a large number of Neolithic settlements that had spread across Europe during the two or three thousand years since the introduction of farming and pottery-making to the region.

Further examination of the body itself had begun in 2001, ten years after the initial find. New X-rays were taken, which revealed an object in the left shoulder – a flint arrowhead. It had penetrated the shoulder blade and severed a major blood vessel. Ötzi would have bled to death from such a wound, although as the clotted blood in the wound had started to degrade, his death would have been slow. Further damage to his hand in the form of a deep cut, and a number of bruises, suggest that he had been in a fight before he died.

Detailed forensic study has established that someone pulled the arrowshaft out from Ötzi's back, but the arrowhead itself remained wedged in his body. Some of the injuries he had sustained, however, were beginning to heal, suggesting that the fight he was involved in had lasted for several days.

Some unconfirmed DNA analyses have claimed that traces of blood from four other people were present on his equipment and clothing – one person's blood on his knife, two others on the same arrowhead (which means he must have retrieved it after shooting two different people), and one on his coat. It is suggested that the amount of blood on the coat resulted from him carrying a wounded comrade on his back.

At some point shortly before death, he had fallen or been hit on the back of the head – there was a major bleed in the rear section of his brain, in which the condition of the blood proteins indicated a very recent injury. So it may have been this fall or blow which finally killed him.[13]

There is also speculation that someone actually buried him – it has been argued that the way the body and equipment were originally laid out suggests that they had been carefully placed under a cairn of stone. This was not immediately evident, as the body had been tumbled around by the moving glacier ice, but if this is the case, perhaps Ötzi did not die alone in the mountains.

The scientific researches have told us an amazing amount about this man, his life and death. They cannot tell us who killed him. However, we can imagine a number of possible scenarios based on the evidence. One theory suggests that he was killed by someone he knew – because they had taken the trouble to retrieve that arrowshaft from his back, which would have identified its owner, and because they did not take his valuable copper axe, again something that would have been recognisable. Was this a simple revenge killing? If so, what about the possible evidence of other people from the DNA analyses? Perhaps the bloodstains had been left on his equipment and clothing some time in the past rather than during his last journey in the mountains. Was he an outcast from his community who had to be hunted down and disposed of? Did his illnesses set him apart, or perhaps his metal skills made him someone to be suspicious about – such skills must have seemed very much like magic to people living a stone age life.

Was he in the mountains as a shepherd or herdsman, or crossing them to trade with other groups, or even, perhaps to hunt for more copper ore? Could he have been carrying something valuable apart from his own equipment, for which he was attacked and robbed by bandits? We will never know for sure. Perhaps more important than knowing how he died, however, is that the discovery of his body has allowed us to know that he lived at all. Ötzi has brought us face to face with a real person, with aches and pains, skills and a life history, who lived five and a half thousand years ago, at a crucial moment in the development of our world – the point where stone tools were being superseded by metal ones, and modern technology began.[14]

CHAPTER 3

Classical Crimes

Law and order in classical societies

The period of the classical civilisations of Greece and Rome is the era in which the evidence for laws and law-breakers starts to become more available. More sophisticated societies increasingly needed complex and formal judicial structures, and also started to think about how those structures needed to be organised in daily life. In the Mediterranean in particular, with its city-based societies, governments began to find it essential to find ways to maintain law and order, and they started to think about how to police their communities.

Athens produced a famous law-maker in the seventh century BC. He was called Draco, and his laws were very harsh. From his time on, very strict laws are called *draconian* after him. He was striving to put an end to the feuds that had become common in Athens as a result of a lack of written statutes, and he had his version of the laws carved on to wooden tablets and onto stone stelae, so that everyone would know what they were.

Punishments were very severe, and the death sentence was enacted for many offences – arson, murder, and even petty theft. A debtor of lower social status than his creditor could be forced into slavery. Eventually these laws proved too harsh for the Athenians, and most were repealed in the early years of the next century. Only the law of homicide survived; inscriptions that have been found suggest that it was the responsibility of the victim's relatives to bring a prosecution, and that whilst the penalty for premeditated or deliberate murder was death, if the killer could prove that he had not intended to kill the victim, he was just exiled.

The Greek god associated with law was Hermes. He was the messenger of the gods, and led the souls of the dead into the afterlife. He was the god of thieves, as well as of travellers, poets, sportsmen and inventors. He was a trickster god, who was known for his quickness, stealth and cunning. Zeus sent Hermes to serve mankind by teaching them the value of justice.

About 120 years ago on Crete, at a site called Gortyn, an inscription on stone blocks was discovered; originally, the blocks had been part of a circular building, which may have been the public law court, and have been dated to the early fifth century BC. The inscription is part of the law code of the ancient city, and is an example of the unique survival of Greek law in cities other than Athens. The parts of the code that have been found do not deal with all the laws, but included are provisions for family law, commercial issues, rights and freedoms, and 'moral crimes' such as adultery, seduction and rape. Cretan laws were, it was believed, given to mankind by Zeus, father of the gods, and this, of course, gave them added weight.

Law was maintained on the streets and in public meeting places by public slaves, controlled by the magistrates. They could arrest criminals and take charge of them, and were used to control crowds, but they did not undertake investigations – those had to be pursued by the citizens themselves if they wanted to bring a charge to a court. Athens had a body of 300 such slaves, from Scythia, who were provided with rods to defend themselves and to subdue wrongdoers. Using foreigners was supposed to ensure that local allegiances did not affect the pursuit of justice.

In Athens, the site of the highest court was at the *Aeropagus*, a hill northwest of the Acropolis. Legend said that when the god Ares murdered the son of Poseidon, god of the sea, it was here that he was tried. It was also here that the ruling council of elders met. When the laws were revised in 462 BC, this council lost most of its power, except as a court for hearing murder trials. That is why the playwright Aeschylus set the trial of Orestes for the murder of Clytemnestra at this scene. In the fourth century BC, the Areopagus also had responsibility for investigating cases of corruption.

The remains of an Athenian court were excavated on the southern side of the Acropolis. Among the artefacts discovered was a pedestal shaped like lions' legs, which was the support for a large marble table of the period 400-300 BC; there was also a piece of copper sheet, which the excavator believes to be the type of material upon which legal verdicts were recorded. The find seems to be part of a large complex and portico that has been tentatively identified as the Palladium. This was the building in which, according to the geographer Pausanius, writing in the second century AD, cases of manslaughter and the killing of people who were not citizens were heard. Killing people who were not citizens was generally regarded as a lesser crime than murder![1]

There have been plenty of examples of archaeological finds of people who died violently in Athens. Wells in the *agora*, or central plaza, of ancient Athens have yielded many skeletons, and while some may be victims of attacks on the city during war, some seem to have died as a result of other types of assault. Many of these may well have been victims of murder, their bodies thrown down the wells so that the killer could avoid detection.

Another type of crime for which there is much evidence from the Greek world is forgery. It was the Greeks who first invented coinage in the western world and this allowed the Greek cities to control trade, and to profit from the issuing of the currency. They took care to produce pure coins that would guarantee the flow of trade in their regions. But as soon as coinage began, counterfeiting started too. Despite the threat of dire punishments, forgers began to make large profits from the production of fake coins. A good fake coin must *look* like the real thing, but use far less precious metal in its construction. There are various ways to do this.

One of the first ways people tried to make false coins was to make a base metal 'flan' using lead or copper, and cover it with a thin sheet of silver, that appeared like the real thing. Making a die copied from a real coin, and using it to strike a fake made from a silvery-coloured metal such as tin was also tried. A base metal coin could be covered with silver foil, but that tended to wear off very quickly, and such coins were often spotted as it was hard to get the weight right. So more silver had to be added – thicker foil, or adding a layer of silver solder, or adding another type of solder which was then sprinkled with silver dust, that was then melted on under heat.

There are many literary references to counterfeit coins in Greek writings, proving that it was a common, well-known occurrence, so much so that an immoral person could be described as a 'fake coin', and everyone would know what that meant.

Counterfeit coins were produced for the local markets, as well as for foreign trade. The crowded markets of Athens and Corinth would have been good places to pass off these small value coins, while the faker could get away with passing larger denominations of coin abroad, where people were less familiar with the real thing. It is interesting to note that Diogenes, famous for searching the streets in a hopeless quest to find an honest man, was the son of a man who was an official coin-maker in the fourth century BC. Diogenes' father was convicted of adulterating the coins with base metals; the shame forced his son to leave home, and to conduct a lifelong campaign against the sins of luxury and avarice.[3]

Roman laws derived from the Law of the Twelve Tables which were based on Greek originals; early in the Republican period, a group of patrician Romans were sent to Greece to study the laws introduced by Solon, the Greek leader who had repealed the laws of Draco and created a new law code in the sixth century BC. In 450 BC the Romans recorded their findings on ten tablets, to which a further two may have been added later. These were inscribed onto bronze and set up in the Forum for all to read. Although the original tablets do not survive, much of their content was copied by later historians into other documents that have been preserved.

In some ways, the early Roman laws were similar to previous codes – the principle of 'an eye for an eye' continued, but the payment of fines was a frequent alternative. The death penalty was invoked for treason, 'nocturnal meetings', murder, arson, libel and slander, perjury, destruction of farms, and the use of magic. The stated aim of the laws was that they were applicable to all classes of society, but the provision that for many crimes, even the death penalty could be avoided on payment of a large enough fine, meant that the law was less severe on the rich than on the poor.

Over time, the laws were changed or added to, as society and the empire became more complex. There were originally no professional lawyers, but there were jurists – people who had studied the law and gave their opinions to private citizens. In the early period there were no judges either; the parties involved in a dispute would appoint a third party, on whom both sides agreed, to listen to the evidence and offer a decision. Later, this system was replaced by the appointment of magistrates whose responsibility was to define the matter under dispute, state the relevant law in the case, and refer it to an appointed judge.

Professional lawyers appeared as Roman life became more controlled and bureaucratic. They would make speeches for or against the parties involved, and commanded very large fees. Many became extremely rich, and were notable for their large staffs and rich attire. The writer Juvenal said 'Legal eloquence does not often appear in rags'. There was also a lower class of lawyer to represent poorer clients – they did not enjoy the luxury or status of their upper class colleagues. Various Roman writers noted how corrupt lawyers could be!

Information on criminals could be gained by the use of slaves. A system of slave-informers was used, to identify wrongdoers and amass evidence against them. Initially, these informers were asked to 'grass' on fellow-slaves, but over time their role expanded to include the gathering of evidence against citizens. There was a massive slave population in Rome – possibly even larger than the Romans themselves were normally aware. Owners were forbidden in most cases to make slaves dress differently from other citizens or in particular liveries, in case once so identified, the slaves would realise how many of them there were in the city, that they outnumbered the citizens, and could rise up in rebellion. Successful slave-informers were promised their freedom but there was a drawback. In order to prevent slaves bringing false accusations against free citizens, Roman law dictated that evidence from slaves was only acceptable if it had been obtained through torture. It was common for all the slaves in the household of a suspected criminal to be rounded up and tortured to gain the necessary evidence for a conviction. Nevertheless, the system was successful enough that citizens coined a saying – 'Every slave, an enemy'.[4]

In most provinces of the Empire, the task of maintaining law and order fell to the Roman Army, with perhaps some local watchmen. When crimes were committed, the victims or their families were obliged, as in earlier times, to inform a magistrate, and set up their own investigation. In Rome itself, by the beginning of the first millennium AD, the population had risen to nearly a million, and a more formal system was clearly needed. Two functions were combined – that of fire-fighting, and that of apprehension of criminals and escaped slaves. The city was divided into fourteen districts, to which were posted seven cohorts of *vigiles,* each cohort having responsibility for two of the districts. A prefect was appointed to oversee this force, with a sub-prefect and a tribune for each cohort. Each cohort was divided into seven centuries, each with its own commander, who oversaw the activities of around 70 men.

They were given equipment to fight fires – buckets, pumps, axes and hooks to pull down burning walls. Straw mats soaked in water and vinegar were used to smother fires. The *vigiles* had medical orderlies and priests attached to their units, reflecting the dangerous nature of the job. In addition to fighting fires and catching criminals, the *vigiles* acted as night watchmen, and with the support of the soldiers of the Urban Cohort, helped to maintain order. Some of the cohorts were stationed at Rome's ports, rotating these duties with those in the city. It was not a popular job at first, and incitements had to be offered to recruit enough men – such as full citizenship and a cash bonus after a number of years' service.

Their policing duties were mostly concerned with small crimes, safeguarding properties, and breaking up disturbances, while major crimes fell into the province of the Urban Cohort, a much more military band.

At first, the *vigiles* stations were just buildings compulsorily seized for the purpose by the state, but by the middle of the second century, purpose-built stations were built, and later sub-stations were added. The sites of four of the seven second-century stations have been identified. The sub-stations, or watchhouses, were called *Excubitoria.* One of these, a watchhouse of the Seventh Cohort, has been identified from a graffito found on one of the walls (Figure 10). This site, in the Trastevere district, which was found in the 1850s, fell into disrepair until restoration began in 1966. It consisted of a hall with a

Figure 10. Vigiles graffito found in Rome

central basin and a small chapel, a possible bath suite, a storeroom and two further rooms.

Roman law courts were divided into civil and state-controlled groups. The state courts were only concerned with criminal activity that threatened the security of the government and the political system – sedition, forgery, assassination and so on. The civil and private courts dealt with the more ordinary crimes. Most cases including theft and robbery, criminal damage and injury were settled with fines and reparations. The amount of the fines for theft varied according to whether the thief was caught in the act, and whether the stolen property was recovered during a formal search or by chance. Ordinarily, a citizen was not allowed to kill a thief unless the incident happened at night, although even then he was not allowed to use a weapon and had to call for witnesses. After the second century, no form of killing was allowed. The victim of the crime had to prove that the thief had acted with malicious intent, and that the items had actually gone missing, or had been misappropriated without consent.

In assault and rape cases, much depended on the status of the victim – penalties for attacking a slave were far less than those for assaults on citizens. Rape was a capital crime, punishable by execution or exile. However, it was up to the woman to prove that the act had not been consensual – if the rapist claimed that she had consented, she could herself be accused of perjury or adultery. Not surprisingly, many women were forced to keep silent.

Roman punishments

There were prisons in Rome, and part of one survives under the church of San Guiseppe dei Falegnami on the Capitoline Hill. It is known as the Mamertine Prison, and may date from the seventh century BC. Two damp underground cells, one above the other, can be found here, and it remained in use until at least the late fourth century AD. Imprisonment was not in itself a punishment – prisons were used to hold people before their trials, or executions, some of which took place within the prison. Not until later in the Empire did long-term imprisonment become more common, and then conditions seem to have been very bad, as sometimes imperial intervention was required to stop the worst abuses of torture, poor accommodation and treatment within these institutions. Tradition has it that Saint Peter and Saint Paul were held in the Mamertine Prison, as was the great Gallic hero Vercingetorix. Not far from the Mamertine were the Lautumiae – quarries for tufa stone – which were used to incarcerate slaves and low-class criminals.

Punishment for slaves was usually harsher than that for citizens, but unless a major crime was involved, there was an incentive not to inflict permanent harm – slaves were property, and in killing or maiming a slave, the authorities would also be punishing the owner, who might otherwise be an innocent party. Slaves could be whipped, or have a heavy weight suspended from their necks that they were forced to carry at all times. Public slaves (belonging to the state) could be sentenced to hard labour in mines, quarries or in mills.

Punishments for citizens ranged from simple fines to whippings, enslavement or exile. The death sentence was generally reserved for cases of treason and patricide but non-citizens could be executed for other crimes. Various methods of execution were used, including being whipped to death, beheaded, strangled, crucified or thrown into the sea, river or from the Tarpeian rock (Plate 1). The latter method was particularly popular for patricides, and involved bringing the criminal to a public place, blindfolding him, whipping him in all parts of his body until the blood ran, then sewing him into a leather sack along with a snake, a dog, a cock with a sharpened beak and claws, and/or an ape, before pushing him from the rock or into the water. The dog and the cock represented the watchers of the household who should have raised the alarm, the snake because it was believed to kill at the same time as it gave life, and the ape to symbolise the lowest form of human life to which the criminal belonged. This reflects the patriarchal nature of Roman society, stemming from its tribal origins. The *paterfamilias*, or head of the household, held absolute power over the other members of the family; therefore killing one's father was seen as equating to treason against the state, because it demonstrated a spirit of rebellion and refusal to accept proper social order.

The Roman army had its own laws and codes, and its own punishments, much as modern armies have today. Polybius, in his *Histories,* gives us many details about these.[5] Roman generals had the power to order punishments and executions independent of other state laws for 'military' crimes and for 'unmanly acts'. Major military crimes such as desertion, treason or theft would be subject to a court martial, followed by fines, flogging, or execution. Soldiers guilty of deserting or betraying their comrades would be stoned or beaten to death by their own units in front of the assembled troops. The category of 'unmanly acts' included mutiny or cowardice; punishments ranged from having rations cut, being given extra and unpopular duties, suffering a beating, being reduced in rank, or execution. When a cohort of soldiers was accused of such a crime, they were divided into groups of ten men who would select by lot one of their number to be killed by the other nine; the remaining nine soldiers of each group were further punished with being given inferior rations and denied the protection of the fort at night, having to camp outside it.

There is some archaeological evidence for judicial executions in the Roman period. Excavations in Cambridge unearthed three decapitated bodies, one of which displayed evidence of sword cuts in the neck area delivered from behind, and at Dunstable, eleven decapitated bodies were interpreted as having been killed by sword blows from behind while the victims were in a kneeling position. We must assume these were judicial executions.

Some headless bodies found in late Roman graves may have been mutilated after execution, as part of the public degradation of their remains. Dr Katie Tucker has undertaken a study of Roman decapitation burials; she has said that 'the most convincing examples of decapitation as a mechanism of death are in those individuals where there is evidence for slitting of the throat in association with decapitation (presumably to release the blood, and why carry this out on a corpse, where the blood would not be released by such an action?); and individuals with evidence for other peri-mortem trauma such as stabs to the lower abdomen or lower back, chopping blows to the knee, fractures of the distal upper limb, or blunt-force trauma to the cranial vault. These all seem to be related to attempts to incapacitate or immobilise the individual prior to decapitation, and again, this is not something that is likely to have taken place on an individual who was already dead'. An individual from a Winchester site shows evidence of a chopping blow to the neck that could only have been delivered to someone still alive, who was in a kneeling position.

There are, however, other explanations for removal of the head, which seem to have been the case with seven late Roman burials at another site in Winchester, Lankhills. All these individuals had been decapitated with a knife after death, and the heads placed near the legs. Two bodies had other possible signs of violence on their bones. A further headless burial discovered at the site was of a very small child. Clearly, the child is not likely to have been a criminal, so was the beheading a ritual act, possibly to deter its ghost from haunting the living? The Romans were very superstitious about ghosts, and firmly believed in the power of the dead to rise from the grave to wreak harm on the living. Iron Age societies in Europe are said to have believed that the soul resided in the head, and practised decapitation after death to allow the soul to become free. It is likely that this practice continued throughout the period of Roman occupation among many of the local people, and the practice even seems to have been revived in the later centuries of the Roman period.

There are other examples of what are called 'deviant' burials from Roman Britain. There are people who were buried without due reverence, or buried face down, or show signs of violence. In some cases, the prone (face-down) burials may simply represent a burial rite of a minority religious sect, but in other cases, something else seems to have been going on. Some bodies have large blocks of stone weighing them down in the grave, and others have been buried tied up. In Colchester, two prone male burials were found just outside the formal limits of the cemetery – each had their wrists tied together. At Bratton in Wiltshire in 1955, excavators found a prone burial with arms bent back behind the torso, probably indicating that they had been tied. A man buried face down in Dorchester had been mutilated at the time of death, his right forearm and hand having been cut off. A woman buried in the prone position in the Eastern Cemetery in London had her arms tied behind her back, and two others had blocks of stone weighing them down. Three per cent of the burials found at this site were prone burials, which might suggest that there was a place of execution nearby.[6]

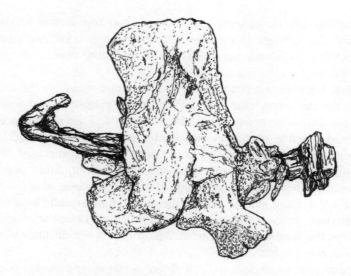

Figure 11. Crucifixion bone and nail from a site in Israel

Crucifixion was generally reserved for common criminals, and in the same way as the public gibbets of early modern England stood as a ghastly reminder of the wages of crime, the crucified victims of Roman justice served as a warning to others tempted to sin. It was generally a very slow, painful way to die, and to the agony was added the public humiliation of hanging in public view, naked and vulnerable.[7]

Israeli archaeologists have found the remains of a first century AD crucifixion victim in Giv'at ha-Mivtar in northeast Jerusalem. One of the nails used to fix him to the cross remained embedded in his heel bone (Figure 11). Its position suggested that each foot was nailed to the side of the upright beam. We know the name of this man, because after his death his bones were placed in an ossuary on which was scratched 'Jehohanan, the son of Hagakol'. Splinters attached to the nail were of olive wood which suggest that the cross was not very high, as olive trees do not grow very tall. The nail was stopped by another piece of wood, this time acacia, so that the condemned man could not have dragged his foot free. His legs had been broken, which seems to have been a common practice intended to hasten death, but such mutilation also formed part of other punishments that did not involve crucifixion. No other nails were present, possibly because iron was expensive, and thrifty officials recovered the nails when the body was removed. The nail found in the heel had bent at the tip, and could not be readily pulled out, so it was left behind. A scratch on the right radius bone appears to indicate that another nail had been driven into the arm just above the wrist, as the wrist bones were unbroken. However, this evidence has been challenged and cannot be taken as completely secure.

Another form of execution was condemnation to death in the arena, reserved for the worst criminals and traitors. Typically, executions would occur around midday, between wild beast shows and the afternoon gladiator bouts. People who wished to avoid the execution spectacles would leave the arena to go and eat their lunches. Such executions often included the use of wild animals to kill and devour the defenceless victim; lions, bears, bulls, elephants and other beasts were imported for the purpose, to such an extent that certain species of animal, such as the Asiatic lion, actually became extinct in the Roman period (Plate 2). It is said that the emperor Caligula fed prisoners to the beasts, no matter what their crimes, when the price of meat for the animals rose too high.

Sometimes the executions took the form of staged re-enactments of Greek dramas and myths – Orpheus eaten by a bear, and Hercules burned to death, for example. Famously, Christians were thrown to the lions; their crimes were officially that they followed an unauthorised religion, using magic, offering sacrilege to the official gods and the divinity of the emperor, and holding unlawful assemblies. Others who might suffer the same fate included deserters, poisoners, counterfeiters and political prisoners. The practice was not ended until AD 681. A large cemetery of the third to fourth centuries AD has been excavated near the Roman amphitheatre in Trier in Northern Germany. At least forty-six graves were found, with very few grave goods, and the position of some of the bodies, or indications of missing skeletal parts, suggest that these burials are not normal. Some of the dead may have been gladiators, others executed criminals.[8]

One of a number of skeletons discovered at York had evidence of a bite on his hip which must have been made by a large animal such as a bear, so perhaps he had died in just such a spectacle. The bodies at York were mostly of robust young men with developed musculature, suggesting they had taken part in weapons training. Captured prisoners, criminals and runaway slaves could be sentenced to gladiatorial schools, where they had to fight for their lives time and again, although there was a remote possibility of survival. If they won enough bouts, and managed to save sufficient money, they might be able to buy their freedom.[9]

The punishments inflicted by the Romans seem to us to be horrifying; but we must remember that their perspective was different.

'The Romans saw harsh public discipline, at least for the lower orders, as an appropriate form of retribution and an effective deterrent to wrongdoing. The arena was only one place of public punishment; criminals were also crucified along roads and at crossroads. Both the widespread belief in the inferiority of those lower down the social scale, and also the longstanding idea that criminals deserved to feel pain, facilitated the crowd's ability to distance itself from those in the ring and watch their deaths with excitement and pleasure. The art depicting combats and executions takes for granted an emotional distance between viewer and viewed.'[10]

Piracy in the Roman period

Evidence for crimes in the Roman period includes examples of murder, arson, forgery and theft, and there are accounts of many others including the famous incident when Julius Caesar was captured by pirates. This occurred in 75 BC and is described by Plutarch. Aged about twenty-five, Julius Caesar was aboard a ship off the coast of Turkey on his way to Rhodes to study the art of oratory when he was captured by Cilician pirates. The pirates demanded a ransom, but Caesar said the amount was too low – he was worth much more. He apparently acted as if the pirates were ignorant savages and began to order them about. Caesar was clearly never a shrinking violet, even as a young man!

The (higher) ransom arrived after about five or six weeks, and the pirates released their captive at Miletus, a port along the coast. Caesar immediately set about his revenge, putting together a fleet which he directed to the pirate stronghold. Most of the pirates were captured and their loot was seized. Then all the captives were crucified – although in a spirit of mercy, Caesar had their throats cut first!

Piracy along the eastern Mediterranean coasts was a continuing problem for the Romans, necessitating a naval base and a programme of building of fast galleys. Pompey the Great was given vast resources to combat piracy in 67 BC, after the pirates, with increasing boldness, started to raid Italy itself. There was also a political aim – to reduce the power of Mithridates, king of Pontus, who controlled much of Anatolia, sometimes financing his state from the rewards of piracy. Pompey is credited with removing the pirate menace in forty-nine days, but this seems to have been mere propaganda, as later accounts include details of further actions against them.

Outside the Mediterranean, piracy became a problem in the English Channel and North Sea in later centuries. The *Classis Britannica*, or British fleet, was charged with maintaining safe links with the Roman provinces of Gaul and the Low Countries. By the third century, Saxon and Frankish pirates were active in the Channel, raiding the coasts of Gallia Belgica and Brittany. The commander of the Roman fleet was a man called Carausius, who soon became a suspect in the eyes of the emperor, Maximian. It seems that Carausius may have been stealing the pirates' loot, and even failing to pursue the pirates until he knew they had loot he could steal! His execution was ordered, but Carausius got wind of the order, and in an extraordinary move, declared that he was now the emperor of Britain and Gaul. His ships defeated a combined Roman, German and French fleet, and he moved his operations to Britain. His breakaway empire did not last, and by 300 the Romans were back in charge, but the fleet continued to combat piracy.

The *Classis Britannica* was based in a number of forts along what came to be known as the Saxon Shore of Eastern and Southern Britain, and Northern Gaul, the main fort possibly being at Dover or Boulogne. Several forts survive, including Lympne, Portchester, Pevensey and Boulogne, and other evidence for the fleets is found in a number of altars and inscriptions, and in tiles marked 'CL-BR' discovered at iron-working sites in the Kent and Sussex Weald, dating from the late third and early fourth century. The Painted House at Dover seems to have been a *mansio* attached to the fort there. (A *mansio* was an official hotel for the accommodation of travelling functionaries and imperial messengers). It is not clear whether all the forts were built by imperial order to keep Saxon pirates and invaders out, or whether some of the earlier ones were built by Carausius to keep the Romans out! Either way, the expenditure on building and manning these stone forts demonstrate the extent of the pirate problem.

Cursing the thief

Theft of property might seem a very difficult crime to prove by archaeological excavations or finds, but in fact there are cases where such evidence is at least indirectly visible. For the Roman period, evidence of theft occurs in the form of curse tablets (Figure 12). These were messages to the gods inscribed on sheets of lead, which were then rolled or folded up and placed in a shrine or sacred place, such as a spring. There may have been professional curse writers, who would inscribe the lead sheets in suitable terms for their customers. One curse which had not been rolled up was found in Leicester, and was dated to the third or fourth century AD. The inscription read: 'To the god Maglus, I give the wrongdoer who stole the cloak of Servandus Silvester Riomandus ... that he destroy him before the ninth day, the person who stole the cloak of Servandus ...' followed by a long list of possible suspects. It is interesting to note that among these names, some are Roman, such as

Figure 12. A Roman lead curse tablet (Source: Marie-Lan Nguyen Creative Commons)

Germanus, and some are British including the name Cunovendus. The name 'Maglus' for this god could translate as 'Great One' or 'Prince'.

Other curse tablets have been found in the waters of Aquae Sulis (Bath) at the Temple of Sulis Minerva. Lavernisca had her cape stolen, and Cantissena's bathing tunic went missing. More seriously, someone has had a slave, Vilbia, stolen. This curse tablet asks the goddess to ensure that the thief should 'become as liquid as water', and also includes a list of names, both male and female. Cloaks were certainly a much-stolen item, presumably as they were left in the outer cloakroom of the baths or shrines, and other stolen items include a rug, and silver coins.

We have the text of a curse written by one aggrieved cloakless person, who possibly found himself having to walk home in the chilly British weather without his warm coat:

'Docilianus…to the most holy goddess Sulis. I curse him who has stolen my hooded cloak, whether man or woman, whether slave or free, that…the goddess Sulis inflict death upon…and not allow him to sleep or children now and in the future, until he has brought my hooded cloak to the temple of her divinity.'

Such hooded cloaks could be expensive items. The *birrus britannicus* was a long semi-circular hooded garment, made of oiled wool, that kept the rain off.

By the late third century, this form of cloak had become so sought after that it actually received a mention in an Edict of Prices issued by the emperor Diocletian in AD 301. Representations of this form of cloak can be seen in the figure of 'Winter' in a floor mosaic in the Roman villa at Chedworth, and in carvings of three enigmatic figures standing together, known as the Genii Cucullati, such as the example found at Housesteads fort on Hadrian's Wall. The cloaks were popular across the Empire, and were a major British export item.

In all, some 1500 curse tablets have been found; about 1000 were written in Greek, and 500 in Latin, and about 250 of these Latin curses have been found in Britain, most at Bath or the temple of Mercury at Uley, Glos.

Robbers and counterfeiters

More extreme forms of theft are also recorded. Roman soldiers were not above doing some tomb robbing – as they marched through Italy and Greece they found ancient and richly appointed tombs, which they broke open for the bronze statues and antique pots inside. These were sold to antique collectors back in Rome.[11] Eventually grave robbing was established as a crime in Roman law, with the death penalty attached to it, as Cicero recorded.[12]

Forgers were very active during the Roman period, and counterfeit coins have been found throughout the region covered by the Roman Empire. Many of the fake coins are in small denominations; they were designed to fulfil a need, especially in the provinces. It was often the case that insufficient amounts of small denomination coinage reached the provinces, and so *unofficial* coins were struck or cast, often quite crude in their execution, and clearly recognisable in comparison with the official issues. They made ordinary commerce possible, allowing small change to be given so that people could purchase smaller items, which cost below the value of gold or silver coins.

This explanation probably accounts for the large groups of copper *asses* (one of the smallest denominations) found in Roman Southwark dating from the period of the emperor Claudius. In the years following the conquest of Britain in AD 43, it is probable that insufficient small change reached this far-flung province, so that the soldiers stationed here would have needed to be supplied with some sort of small change in order to make everyday purchases.

As early as 81 BC, forgery of silver coins had been made illegal, with penalties including banishment or death. However, there was no mention of copper or bronze coins in the law; in fact it is not until AD 438 that such a law is recorded. Silver and gold coins were officially issued on behalf of the emperor; the lower denominations were made in local centres more or less officially. Sometimes this became quite a vast industry. One site in Egypt has produced some 15,000 clay coin moulds for issues of the later third and early fourth centuries AD. This site was close to a Roman military camp, but it is unclear whether the military authorities approved of this forging activity or not. Other sites in Egypt and the Near East have also produced large quantities of moulds dating to the early-to-mid-fourth century. Most of these moulds would have produced copies of small denomination coins for local circulation, and indeed many such cast coins have been found in excavations in the port city of Alexandria. It is obvious which coins are real when viewed under a scanning electron microscope, which clearly shows the different microstructure of (official) struck coins compared to (unofficial) cast ones.

The production of the fake coins was of itself very professional in some cases; a real coin was pressed into wet clay moulds, which were then stacked together. The molten metal was then poured through the connected moulds, producing many coins in a single operation. Although the quality of the casting is often poor, the sheer quantity of the forgeries and the moulds suggests that these coins were probably more often found in use than the real versions, and that the forgers were not often apprehended by the authorities. It seems probable that the governors were prepared to turn a blind eye to these activities, simply to keep trade flowing.[13.]

Clay moulds for producing fake coins have been found across Britain too, and many of the lower denomination coins that have been found here have been of the 'unofficial' types.

Counterfeiting of precious metal coins was another matter. An unusual group of forgeries came to light when found by a metal detectorist in Somerset in 2002. Among a hoard of 670 coins, seventy-two were found to be forgeries. Dating from the fourth century, they were among coins from many different official mints; oddly, some of the forgeries had an identical or higher silver content than real coins. Stephen Minnitt of the Somerset County Museum, said: 'They were probably an unofficial attempt to keep coinage supplies up to required levels. A few did have a copper base and were then plated with silver and those are the more genuine forgeries.' If that is not a contradiction in terms!

Plating base metal with gold or silver was the usual way to forge higher denomination coins, as it had been in the Greek period. Unless the plating was particularly thin, the deception could have gone unrecognized for some time while the coins remained in use. Only if the coin was scratched or broken would the base metal core become evident. One example of a forgery, however, might have been easier to spot. A 'silver' denarius was found by a path near Brighton in Sussex in 2010. A coin of this denomination would have been worth a day's pay for an ordinary worker in the Roman period. The coin seems to show a commemoration of the Battle of Actium in 31 BC, when Octavian (the future emperor Augustus) defeated the forces of Mark Antony and Cleopatra. The fake coin was made a little later – by a very poor faker. It has the wrong emperor on one side, and on the reverse, the crocodile is facing the wrong way. The forger has even spelled 'Egypt' incorrectly. It was struck from pure silver, so the forger would not even have made a profit. His motives for making the piece have baffled even the experts at the British Museum![14]

Another British find demonstrates a further monetary crime – coin clipping, the cutting off of slivers of metal from round the edges. In 1992 at Hoxne in Suffolk, a massive hoard of late fourth and early fifth century AD Roman gold, silver and other objects was discovered. Originally buried in an oak chest, there were nearly 15,000 coins and some 200 pieces of jewellery and tableware, including some magnificent silver salt cellars or spice pots, which can now be seen in the British Museum. The coins date the hoard to after AD 407, right at the very end of the Roman occupation of Britain.

A study of the silver coins in the hoard found that nearly every one had been clipped, something that has been noted in Britain, but seems to have been rare at the time elsewhere. The clipping was fairly carefully done to avoid damaging the face of the emperor on the front of the coins. The spare silver taken from each coin could have been melted down for profit illegally, or even perhaps could have been done deliberately by the authorities to acquire more bullion. By the start of the fifth century, the British province was rather isolated from the official money supply from Rome. Barbarians had poured across the Rhine into Northern France and the Low Countries, barring the way for the traditional transport routes from the Mediterranean, and from the mint in Lyon, a major source of Roman coinage for use in Britain. The late Roman officials may have become desperate to find a way to maintain the money supply for the province, not only for trade but to pay the wages of soldiers and administrators trying to keep the local government together.

Clay moulds for coin production have also been found in Scotland – but they date from *after* the Roman withdrawal back to the line of Hadrian's Wall. The moulds were used to make counterfeit *denarii*; at the time of these moulds, the Roman currency had become severely debased, and even the official 'silver' coins could contain less than fifty per cent pure metal, and have a thin silver wash over high-tin bronze. This would have been the counterfeiters' job easier, as the silver wash wore off quite quickly in use. X-ray fluorescence analysis (XRF) of the moulds found no silver at all – there were traces of base copper alloys, lead and zinc. It is possible that these coins were being made to use in trade with pedlars and merchants bringing goods north from the 'civilised' province into the wild tribal lands of the Picts. However, as they had a high value, it is thought unlikely that they would have been accepted without suspicion. Another explanation that has been offered is that these coins were to be used as replicas for religious offerings, much cheaper than using the real thing![15]

The burning of Rome

One of the most famous alleged crimes in ancient Rome was arson – specifically, Nero's burning of the city. Did he do it or not? The fire destroyed Nero's own palace, and there are accounts of him hurrying back to Rome to help with the fire fighting personally. Accidental fires were very common, and the poorly built high-rise slum tenements were particularly susceptible to fire, lit as they were by oil lamps, and with only crude brick stoves and open braziers for cooking and heating. On the other hand, the fire also destroyed the houses of members of Rome's aristocracy, who were not wholehearted in their support of the emperor. Our account of the fire comes from the writings of Tacitus, who was convinced Nero was to blame. He maintained that only arson would explain how the fire spread to burn down the stone houses of the aristocrats as well as the hovels of the poor in different districts.

Modern fire research tends to disagree with him, and experiments have shown that the rich houses could have burned as readily as the poor ones. Tacitus also says that the south easterly wind could not explain how the fire seemed to move in contrary directions, but we now know that a large fire produces its own winds that can fan flames over a wide area despite the prevailing breeze. Recent excavations in the area of the Forum have found melted nails from the roofs of burned buildings, a charred gate and collapsed masonry, along with many coins possibly dropped by victims who were unable to escape the fast-moving firestorm.

Another archaeologist however, remains convinced of Nero's guilt for a slightly different reason. The senate had opposed Nero's desire to build a grand new palace – so to get round their block, he burned down that area of the Forum where they had their houses and offices. It effectively curtailed the power of the aristocracy, leaving them homeless and allowing Nero to seize power more directly. The only area to survive was the open centre, which later became a sort of shopping mall, taking the place of what had been the aristocratic centre of Rome.

A third explanation is that it *was* arson but committed by the Christians, who had been subjected to tyrannical persecution by Nero. A German scholar has discovered that just before the fire, Christians had been publishing leaflets and messages predicting a devastating inferno that would destroy the city. There was also an ancient Egyptian prophecy that foretold the fall of Rome on the day the star Sirius rose in the sky – 19 July in AD 64 – the day the fire started. Did the Christians use this prophecy in an attempt to bring down their persecutors? The case remains open.

Assassination and murder

Roman history is replete with tales of assassination and murder including, of course, the killing of Julius Caesar, a story which has come down through history and literature in all its gory detail. Some Roman murders, however, occurred in much more secret ways. In Modena, Italy, archaeologists have come across three partial skeletons while digging in advance of a new development project. The site was a cremation cemetery which ran alongside the ancient Via Emilia, and a Roman irrigation ditch. It was in the ditch that they came across the skeletons, and they came to the conclusion that these individuals had been thrown hurriedly into the ditch, and weighed down with bricks so that their bodies would not float to the surface.

This happened around the end of the first century BC or the start of the first century AD, a date suggested by amphorae fragments and other rubbish also found in the ditch. All three victims were male. It is assumed that the missing body parts had been washed away in periodic flooding events since the time in which the bodies were dumped. The skull and arms of a youth around sixteen to twenty years old lay between his pelvis and legs; small deep cut marks were visible on his legs. A thirty-year-old man lay with his wrists behind his back, probably where they had been tied, but the lower half of his body was missing entirely. The third man was aged between eighteen and twenty-five. Only part of an arm, his shoulder and head remained.

Roman law and practice about burials was quite specific; these bodies would not have found their way into the ditch through any legal process. Were they murdered runaway slaves? Not likely – slaves were valuable and would have been returned to their owners. Victims of a feud? Unlucky travellers set upon by brigands? We shall probably never know.[16]

A number of murders carried out in Britain during the Roman occupation have come to light in recent years. Along the A2 road near Faversham, in Kent, archaeologists have found the body of a girl who seems to have been stabbed in the back of the head by a Roman sword. The site dates from just a handful of years after the Claudian invasion in AD 43, and the shallow trench which contained the body may have been dug to hold rubbish from a Roman marching camp that was being cleared before the soldiers moved onwards in their campaign. There were also fragments of military equipment and pottery in the ditch. The indications are that the girl, aged between sixteen and twenty, was British. She was otherwise healthy, but was struck down while kneeling by the wielder of the sword. The implication is that this girl, willingly or unwillingly, was used by the soldiers while they were in the camp, and then disposed of along with the trash when they were ready to move on, perhaps one of many similar tragedies that occurred during the invasion.

A much younger child, whose gender could not be certainly identified, died further north. She or he was perhaps ten years old, and was found buried in a shallow pit in the corner of a barracks at Vindolanda, one of the Roman forts along Hadrian's Wall. Like the Modena burials, this would not have been a legal way to dispose of the dead in the period, which was the mid-fourth century AD.

Analysis of the tooth enamel showed that, until the age of seven or eight, this child grew up in the Mediterranean – either Southern Europe or North Africa. Was he or she a slave, or part of the family of one of the soldiers? In theory, soldiers of earlier armies were not allowed to marry or bring their families with them, although many local liaisons did occur, but by the middle of the third century, these rules had been relaxed. If there were families, they probably lived outside the fort, in the *vicus*, the civilian settlement outside the gates, which provided services and entertainment for the troops and a local market for the natives. The child's hands appear to have been tied and the head had been crushed, although it is not clear whether this happened at the time of death, or was later damage caused by the weight of earth over the burial. However, as all the other bones had survived quite well, it is possible that the cause of death was a heavy blow that fractured the skull. The nature of the burial suggests that the killer wanted to hide the evidence of the crime from the authorities. Presumably it would have been hard to smuggle the dead body out of the fort without being seen by sentries, so this clandestine burial was undertaken. But each barrack room would have been home to eight soldiers, who could hardly have failed to notice the smell as the child's body started to decompose, which suggests that there must have been a conspiracy of silence. This certainly does suggest murder.

This is not the first evidence of murder to be found along Hadrian's Wall, as two bodies were found under a floor at Housesteads fort in the 1930s, one of which had a knife blade still stuck between the ribs.[17]

Another cemetery in York has produced some thirty skeletons from the Roman period, showing evidence of violent death. Some had been decapitated, their skulls placed between their knees or at their feet. One was wearing heavy iron shackles on the ankles. All the bodies were of men, and microscopic examination showed marks of axes or swords on their bones. One burial had a large hole in the skull, and was buried face down. It is now believed that these men were murdered as a result of the would-be emperor Caracalla's vicious endeavours to seize the throne for himself. He ordered purges across the empire, to rid himself of all possible opposition, one of which took place in AD 211, which would agree with the dates for these skeletons. A number of prominent men in York were publicly executed – we even know the names of two of them. One was a tutor called Euodus, and another was Severus' own chamberlain, a man called Castor, and it seems these unfortunate men paid the price of Caracalla's ambition – but after just five years, Caracalla was killed by one of his own generals.[18]

Black magic

Black magic was a crime that carried the death penalty. Even the imperial family were at risk from attack by witches. According to the historian Tacitus, when Augustus' grandson and Tiberius' heir, Germanicus, died in AD 19, his house was searched for evidence of witchcraft that might have caused his death. The searchers found 'the remains of human bodies, spells, curses, leaden tablets engraved with the name Germanicus, charred and blood-smeared ashes, and others of the implements by which it is believed the living soul can be devoted to the powers of the grave.'

Ahead of the construction of an underground car park in the Piazza Euclid in Rome, archaeologists found parts of a fountain dedicated to a minor Roman goddess, Anna Perenna. Amongst the mud and rubble they found a cache of 'voodoo' dolls and lead curse tablets that had apparently been hidden there in the fourth century AD. Many of the dolls had been placed in lead canisters; on one these was a thumbprint, that according to the Italian police fingerprint laboratory, was probably that of a woman.

A curse found in a grave at Messina was rather specific – it named 'the evil-doer' Valeria Arsinöe, and wished that 'sickness and decay attack the nymphomaniac!'

The popular impression was that witchcraft was women's work, like the use of poisons, although it was also common to implicate some men, particularly if they came from Egypt or the east, where knowledge of medical and sorcerous practices was believed to be both common and advanced. These experimenters were in fact the forerunners of the much later famous

Arab scholars and scientists, but for the Romans, they were a source of superstitious horror.

When the Romans conquered a province, they tended to leave local laws and customs more or less intact. Roman law applied to soldiers and Roman citizens in that province, but not necessarily to the natives. However, over time, and with the extension of citizen rights to more and more people, Roman law became the *de facto* norm, especially after AD 212 when most free people in the empire were given citizenship status. The laws changed again late in the Roman period when Christianity became the official religion, but the collapse of the Western Empire left much of Europe to go its own way, create its own forms of government, and its own laws and codes of punishment. Roman law survived in the Eastern Empire, and in AD 534 the emperor Justinian published a final Roman law code, which offered a clarification and modernisation of the many laws passed since the original Twelve Tables. Justinian's Code held good for most of the next millennium, until the Eastern Empire finally fell to the Ottoman Turks in 1453, and formed the basis for the canon law of the Roman Catholic and Eastern Orthodox churches. Renaissance scholars rediscovered the Roman law codes, and they were used in the formation of later law codes such as the Napoleonic Code and the laws of the emerging state of Germany, and influenced the codes of a number of other countries even later, including Japan and the United States.

CHAPTER 4

Dark Age Crimes

Difficult times

After the fall of the Roman Empire in the west, centralised order broke down. From the early 400s, few areas were left with effective means to maintain law and order in any formal sense. There is some evidence that those Roman towns that survived in the northern provinces, including England, hired their own mercenary protection, and these forces may also have had a function in policing the community. It is possible that in many places, people returned to pre-Roman practices, which may well have survived in the background during Roman rule. There is a vague hint of this in a document recording the state of affairs in Brittany at the end of Roman rule. It seems to say that the Bretons ousted the Roman administration and began to hold their own assemblies to decide law issues 'after the example of the British'.

The fifth and sixth centuries were difficult times. Without the structure of the Roman governmental system, struggles for land and power characterise the histories of many countries during this period. Local leaders turned themselves into warlords, some holding on to Roman forts such as Pevensey, and surrounding themselves with bands of loyal warriors. In England, France and the Low Countries, new settlers arrived – Franks, Jutes, Angles and Saxons, bringing with them their own customs. Many of these newcomers came from lands that had never been part of the Roman Empire, and their ideas were based on tribal customs and pagan religious beliefs. It is probable that population levels fell – a result of the combined effects of strife, plague and a deteriorating climate. In some places, particularly in Southern Europe, the emerging kingdoms tried to adopt old Roman laws, but there was little organised effort to control ordinary crime or to protect ordinary citizens.

John Chrystosom, archbishop of Constantinople at the beginning of the fifth century, wrote of the common crimes in his period, including house-breaking and robbery. Brigands and pirates attacked travellers, and kidnappers stole people to sell as slaves. Paedophiles seduced children and even priests and monks stole from their churches and monasteries. People lived in fear of burglars – they left lights burning in windows so that it would seem that someone was home, they bought dogs, installed locks and bars, and drew magic eyes on their walls for protection. Masked gangs of housebreakers would nevertheless often break in. Chrystosom's advice was that the best way to avoid being robbed was not to gather too much wealth! Even tombs were robbed for the precious goods buried with the dead. One practice to avoid desecration of the dead was to wrap the body in cloths soaked in myrrh, which glued themselves to the corpse, making life difficult for a would-be robber. Prisons in Chrystosom's diocese were extremely harsh places – no food was provided unless by relatives or friends, torture was used, and punishments included flaying and the cutting off of limbs, as well as hanging.[1]

Little by little, the situation stabilised. Small kingdoms developed in Britain, and other parts of Europe, often matching their boundaries to pre-Roman, tribal areas. Kings began to rule more or less effectively from new royal centres. In England, a number of early law codes were created. The earliest is thought to be that of King Æthelberht of Kent in the early seventh century. Others were established in Essex and Wessex. The laws of King Ine of Wessex, dating to around 694, survive because Alfred the Great incorporated many of them into his own laws in the ninth century, and they are recorded in a manuscript which still survives at Corpus Christi College, Cambridge. Ine's laws encompassed fighting, theft and belonging to a band of thieves, prevention of damage caused by neglecting to maintain fences, and looting. The existence of organised bands of robbers is implied by the definition of the numbers of people involved in criminal activity – up to seven men were simple thieves, seven to thirty-five were a 'band' and over thirty-five men constituted an army of looters and brigands. Many of the laws concerned the 'wergeld' (worth) of individuals, and the amount of compensation payable to victims and the king for a variety of crimes. Alfred attempted to bring together an assemblage of laws from the other kingdoms, and combine them with Christian principles and older folk customs.

Administration of the law was in the hands of free citizens at an assembly called a 'moot', although there may have been some legal advice from 'doomsmen' (Figure 13). These individuals are recorded, but we do not know much about how they operated or what power they had to influence the moot. Moot sites can sometimes be traced through place-name evidence, a form of documentary archaeology. The title of a borough in Surrey records a moot site associated with a tree – the name Spelthorne derives from 'the speaking thorn

Figure 13. Anglo-Saxon moot

(tree)'. Moots were usually marked, both in France and in Britain, with some sort of recognisable symbol – a stone pillar, a tree, a wooden post. At the seventh century Anglo-Saxon royal centre of Yeavering in Northumbria, a wooden 'theatre' structure has been excavated, which included an upright wooden post, and may thus mark the site of a royal moot. A number of moot sites are found close to prehistoric burial mounds, shrines, temples or other monuments, something that is also seen in Scandinavia and in Ireland. It is thought that placing the moots in these sites added to their legitimacy through a connection with ancestral power. The sites chosen were also often at the edge of territories, away from normal habitations, to underline their impartiality.

Justice and punishment
Crimes were dealt with on a personal basis – communities were expected to police themselves and to stand surety for good behaviour in their neighbourhoods. In this way, it was in everybody's interest to make sure that

the guilty were caught and punished, and it was presumed that the identity of a miscreant would not be a mystery for long among his friends and neighbours. Everybody knew each other, many were related to each other, and in Anglo-Saxon society, the concept of a 'Neighbourhood Watch' was fundamental. There were, of course, problems. Personal animosities or friendships could easily affect the judgement of the moot, and they could be at the mercy of gangs applying intimidation tactics. But on the whole, the system seems to have worked.

Evidence was asked for, however, in cases of wounding, especially in Irish laws. In Ireland, a physician was called to testify as to the severity of the wounds and whether or not the victim was likely to die or be permanently maimed.

Judgements were often on the basis of local knowledge of the character of the accused and the witnesses, but where innocence or guilt was unclear, the matter could sometimes be solved by the application of a trial by ordeal, in which God would make his judgement clear to all. Trial by ordeal is often misrepresented. It was only used in particular circumstances, where a defendant insisted on oath that he was innocent. The priest would impose a fast for three days on the defendant, and say a mass that included an invitation to confess the crime. If he still maintained he was not guilty, the defendant could then choose whether to undertake a trial by water or by iron. The water ordeal was of two kinds – cold and hot. The cold water ordeal consisted of drinking holy water and then being thrown into a river or pond. The guilty floated, the innocent sank. (And were pulled out before they drowned!)

In the hot water ordeal, first mentioned in the sixth century, a stone was placed in a container of boiling water, which the defendant had to take out with his bare hand. In the ordeal of iron, he had to carry a glowing bar of iron for nine feet (Plate 3). In both cases, his hand would then be wrapped in bandages. Three days later, it was unwrapped, and if it was healing cleanly, his innocence was proved. These ordeals took place in a church before witnesses.

A less physical but more psychological ordeal was recorded in Franconia. The defendant had to give a solemn oath that he was innocent, and then take the Eucharist, swallowing down the blessed wafer or bread. He would know that if he lied, he would either choke to death or be dead within a year by God's hand. It was the force of suggestion that would decide the matter. It has been described as a sort of early lie-detector – the guilty would betray themselves with their reaction, while the innocent would know they were safe.

Law and judgement in the later Anglo-Saxon period was increasingly codified. Each shire, hundred (a part of a shire nominally supporting a hundred ploughs) or borough had a court. Catching criminals and bringing them to trial was the responsibility of the residents of each borough or hundred, and the court was presided over by an official appointed by the crown. More serious cases went to the shire court or the king himself. The shire courts usually met twice a year and also dealt with matters where there was a dispute between different hundreds.

All free men aged twelve or over had to take an oath to act within the law, and to denounce criminals. The oath was to the crown – to break it amounted to treason. There was a hierarchy of responsibilities, duties owed from the local 'tithingman' responsible for a small group of citizens, to the 'hundredman' who oversaw a hundred division of a shire, to the shire-reeve and ultimately to the king. It was the hundredman who had the authority to raise a posse to pursue criminals.

Every four weeks, the hundred court would meet at a central neighbourhood site to hear local matters about landholding, local government and criminal matters. They could then set a date to hear criminal cases. The first stage was for the victim of a crime to make a statement on oath, name the perpetrator and demand that he be brought before the court. The court would then decide if the matter was legitimate and proper. If they thought it was, they would name a date on which the accused had to appear before them. The defendant then made an oath as to his innocence, which had to be supported by oath-helpers. If he did this, he walked free, but in a small intimate society, his problem would be to make sure he had enough oath-helpers who believed him and were willing to back him up. If he had a record, or had been caught red-handed, however, this option was not open to him. Instead, witnesses to the crime swore on oath that he was guilty. The only option then for the accused was to accept trial by ordeal and hope that God was on his side!

A probable court site has been found under a car park at Dingwall, in the Scottish highlands, which dates from the Viking period. The name 'Dingwall' is thought to derive from Norse words meaning 'the place of the assembly'. The car park covered an earth mound, levelled in the 1940s; it was used in the eighteenth century as a burial mound for the Earl of Cromarty, marked by a stone obelisk. Ground-penetrating radar has identified a large ditch round part of the site, perhaps originally defining the enclosure. Further excavation is planned to discover more information about this site.

Sentencing by the courts did not involve imprisonment – there were no prisons in Anglo-Saxon England. Where people were locked up, it was just to make sure they would appear before the court, or so they could be held while awaiting execution. The usual penalty was a fine, the amount of which depended on the victim's social status and the severity of the crime. The 'wergeld' system was complex, and amounts payable for damage or death varied according to the rank of the victim. High-ranking church officials were valued at twice the rate of ordinary priests, and nobles were worth many times the value of an ordinary free man. Even murder was punished by the imposition of payment of the wergild of the victim to his family until, in the ninth century, murder was made subject to the death penalty. The system was intended to reduce the likelihood of cycles of revenge occurring. Schedules of amounts were agreed upon – fifty shillings for the loss of a foot, ten shillings for a big toe, fifty shillings for the loss of an eye, and so on. By accepting this compensation, the victim avoided any loss of personal honour, an important aspect of Anglo-Saxon society, and the community as a whole could regard the matter as settled and done with. Wergeld also applied to property – a value was set on stock, buildings and land, which had to be repaid in cases of theft, slaughter or damage.

Welsh laws of the period also had a system of wergeld. As well as crimes against people, the Welsh laws included cats and dogs – a cat was worth fourpence once it had proved its worth by catching mice, twopence before that, and just a penny while still a kitten that had yet to open its eyes. The killing of mice was an important function, because mice infesting stored food and grain could destroy the provisions that a community relied on for its own survival. Likewise, guard dogs were valued – at twenty-four pence – unless the dog was killed more than nine paces from the door, when no fine was levied. The moral was that you should keep your dogs on a lead!

The reeve collected the fine on behalf of the king, and arranged for compensation to be paid to the victim or his family. Non-payment of fines resulted in being outlawed or being enslaved for a set period of time. As royal authority became more developed, death became the penalty for the worst crimes – murder, treachery, arson and robbery – by hanging, beheading or drowning. Arson was a particularly heinous crime – in a period when everybody lived in wooden and thatched houses. Fire destroyed their shelter, belongings, means of work and sometimes their lives. A death in a deliberate fire was regarded as murder. Usually, there was no distinction made between murder and manslaughter in this period.

Anglo-Saxon execution cemeteries have been excavated in a number of counties across the country. Excavations at Walkington Wold in Yorkshire have shown this execution site to date from the mid- to late Anglo-Saxon periods. The place had begun life as a Bronze Age barrow grave, and had seen occupation and activity in the Roman period. It was not unusual for such prehistoric or ancient sites to be selected for execution places, due to the perception of their ancient power in the landscape. It is also close to an Anglo-Saxon boundary between two hundreds; execution sites were often 'liminal' – on the edges of normal life. Samples of bones from the site were sent for radiocarbon dating, and a range of dates between 640 and 1040 were extracted, suggesting that the site was used sporadically for several hundred years.

Twelve skeletons were analysed; two retained their heads, ten did not. Some bodies were laid out on their backs, others were curled up, and three were buried in a single grave. Eleven disarticulated skulls were also found. Five of the skeleton belonged to young adults, aged between eighteen and twenty-five, and four were a little older, between twenty-six and thirty-five. The others were all adults, none over forty-five. They were all male. Of the disarticulated skulls, seven appear to have been buried as bones, suggesting the heads had been displayed, perhaps on stakes, prior to burial. They were lacking their jaws, which might have dropped off as the head decomposed.

A slight problem was found with the skulls in that a number turned up in an old badger sett, but is it not very likely that the badgers collected them. At least four of the heads had been cut off while the flesh was still on them, and so were probably from people who had been beheaded. Cut marks on the bones of some of the skeletons and skulls confirmed this impression. This is a higher percentage than usual – far fewer beheadings were seen at three execution cemeteries excavated in Surrey (Staines, Ashtead and Guildown) where hanging seems to have been a more usual practice. The executioners in Yorkshire seem to have been somewhat amateurish – they did not despatch their victims cleanly. One young man had suffered three blows to his neck before the executioner succeeded in cutting off his head. A feature of some execution cemeteries is the strange placement of decapitated skulls – sometimes between the legs. In some cases there are extra skulls in graves – possibly heads which had previously displayed before being removed to make way for new ones. For some reason, this seems to have happened more often in Surrey, a county with a particularly large number of known execution cemeteries.[2]

Execution cemeteries differ from other burial sites because of the way in which the bodies have been treated, and because of the types of trauma that are seen. Sometimes the bodies are laid in strange positions, like those discovered at Sutton Hoo, close to the famous burial mounds. Thirty-nine 'sand bodies' - so-called because all the physical remains of the bodies had disappeared into the acid sand, leaving just an impression of where they lay - have been found there, dating from between the eighth and eleventh centuries,

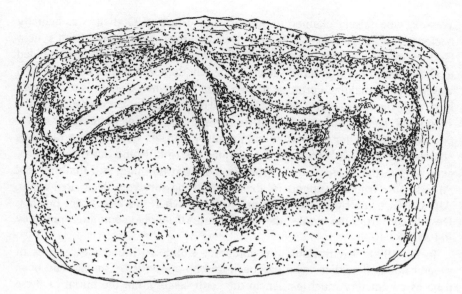

Figure 14. Sutton Hoo sand body

as well as the post-holes of a probable double-post gallows (Figure 14). Some of the dead had been buried face down, two were kneeling, and some had been beheaded. A kneeling burial was also found at Hinchingbrooke near Huntingdon, face-down in a pit. Another execution victim was found at Stonehenge, and has been dated to somewhere around the end of the sixth century. This man, aged between thirty and forty, had been beheaded. Like other sites, Stonehenge lies on a hundred boundary, and other burials found there may also have been execution victims. Graves of execution victims are sometimes multiple – two or three together. One pit was probably dug to take the bodies of several individuals executed on the same day. Graves were not always oriented east—west like normal Christian burials, but were dug at all sorts of angles, often in a ring around the central gallows.[3]

The Guildown cemetery in Surrey near Guildford may hold the evidence for a particularly famous case of murder, which took place in 1035. At this time, king Canute (or Cnut), a Dane who had seized the throne of England in 1016, died. There was an immediate attempt by the descendants of the Anglo-Saxon kings to retake the crown. Alfred Aetheling, the heir presumptive, landed in England with some Norman mercenaries. The *Anglo-Saxon Chronicle* records the events that followed. Alfred was trying to reach London, but as he approached Guildford, he was met by Earl Godwin of

Wessex, who falsely claimed to support him. But Earl Godwin was actually backing Harold Harefoot, the new Danish king of England, Cnut's heir. Godwin took Alfred and his men to Guildown, a hill from which he pretended to show Alfred the wonderful views of the kingdom that would be his. Alfred was said to be making a promise to be a good king when Godwin's men seized him and his men and tied them up. Then Godwin decimated Alfred's supporters. Decimation was an old Roman punishment for mutinous troops – one out of every ten men were summarily killed, as noted in the previous chapter. But Godwin's form of decimation was to kill nine out of every ten, according to the *Anglo-Saxon Chronicle*. The next morning, still thinking that Alfred had too many supporters, the Earl had the survivors decimated again. Alfred was taken by sea to the monks of Ely, where his eyes were put out. Despite care from the monks, the unfortunate Alfred died soon after, probably in February 1036.

In the 1920s, excavations in a garden at Guildown found the remains of several hundred soldiers who had been tied up and killed. The site had been used as a cemetery much earlier, in the sixth century, but the burial of these soldiers was dated to around 1040. The excavator immediately suspected that these were the remains of Alfred's men. There was no church or churchyard nearby, making this a very unusual form of burial for the eleventh century. Was it another judicial execution cemetery? But many of the bodies were laid in triple graves, and showed evidence of dying with their hands tied behind their backs. Signs of injury and mutilation were noticed on the bones – heads, arms and legs cut off, one with his spine broken, and others buried face down. The grave cuts were too small to accommodate the bodies properly – they had been crammed in together or laid on top of each other.

It seems very likely, therefore, that these remains belong to Alfred's decimated mercenaries, mercilessly cut down and carelessly buried by the ambitious and ruthless Earl Godwin.[4]

Vikings in Britain
The Viking age saw quite a number of murders, as might be expected, and evidence for some of these has come to light. However, in one case, modern forensic archaeology has proved one story false. At Hadstock in Essex, there was a local legend concerning a piece of leather found attached to the church door in 1791. Later, in 1883, a label attached to this scrap claimed that it was the skin of a pagan Viking who had been caught robbing the church. He had been flayed and his skin nailed to the church door as a stern warning to other raiders. Recently, a tiny portion of the leather was sent to Oxford University

Figure 15. The filed teeth of a Jomsviking

for DNA testing. Sadly for the legend, it turned out that it was not the skin of a rampaging Viking, but that of an ordinary cow!

Another account of a flayed Viking comes from Worcester. It is said that, in 1041, king Harthacnut sent a tax-collector to the city, but the local citizens were having none of it. They murdered the tax-collector and nailed his skin to the door of the cathedral. Harthacnut's attempt at retaliation failed – the troops he sent to raid the city found that all the people had fled to an island in the Severn, where they mounted a spirited defence. The town was sacked, but the Danes were force to leave without exacting the king's revenge.

In June 2009, on the Ridgeway near Weymouth in Dorset, a mass grave of at least fifty-four individuals was discovered by workmen. They all appeared to be male, and executed some time between 910 and 1030, according to the radiocarbon dates. The bodies had been dismembered, with separate piles of skulls, ribs and legs arranged in the pit. It was a disused Roman quarry on the parish boundary. Most of the dead men had been aged between about eighteen to twenty-six, though a handful were older, and all had been killed at the same time with a sharp blade, probably a sword. They had been hacked to death, each needing several blows to dispatch him. There were no traces of personal belongings or clothes, so they had probably been stripped naked before burial. Some of the skulls are missing – probably taken to display on stakes.

Their teeth (those of one individual had been filed with stripes, possibly as a sign of courage) were analysed for information about their origin (Figure 15). The answer that came back was that they were from Scandinavia. These men were Vikings. In fact, it has been suggested that they were a special 'hit squad' of Jomsvikings, named after their stronghold on Jomsborg in the Baltic. Even among other Vikings, they held the reputation of being the most brutal and horrifying band. One contemporary chronicle records the presence of such a group in England at the time, led by a man called Thorkel the Tall.

The theory suggests that they were ambushed and executed by the Anglo-Saxon locals at some point during the reign of Aethelred the Unready, between 968 and 1016. Elite killers, these men would never have surrendered or stood down from a fight. They may have been raiding as a reprisal for the Saint Brice's Day massacre – 13 November 1002, when Aethelred had ordered the killing of all Danish men living in England, itself a reprisal for Danish raids on British shores. Something that supports this idea is the fact that, unusually, they were beheaded from the front, rather than through the back of the neck. The Jomsviking code demanded that its followers meet death face on – they would see the blow coming but never flinch.

The Anglo-Saxon killers then hacked the bodies to pieces, venting some of the frustration and rage that had built up over decades of raiding, pillage, rape and murder committed on English villages by these fearsome Viking raiders. For once, they could strike back.[5]

Evidence for the Saint Brice's day murders may have been found in Oxford, underneath St. John's College. Nearly forty young men had been killed and thrown into a ditch at a date between 960 and 1020. One had his head cut off, and five more had been stabbed in the back. Other skulls had been crushed, though it is not clear whether this happened before or after death. There may also have been an attempt to burn them. Tests of collagen in the bones showed that these men had originally come from the north of Europe, and there was evidence to show that they were mostly big, robust men. Other Danes had fled for safety to a wooden church in Oxford, but this was burned down by the local residents. There were also report of massacres taking place in Gloucester, Bristol and London.

Sometimes, it seems that slaves were killed to accompany their masters into the grave. Slaves were an accepted part of Anglo-Saxon society, although it was nothing like the kind of slavery we associate with the black slavery of more recent centuries. Saxon-period slaves had some legal rights, and could possess or sell their own products. Slavery was not necessarily a permanent condition – slaves could be freed by their owners and a number of wills record this. They could buy their freedom, and sometimes churchmen bought freedom for slaves. People could also sell themselves or their children into slavery, often temporarily, as a way of avoiding starvation. The slave owner had a legal duty to care for and feed their slaves, which might be the only way to ensure the survival of one's children in hard times, of which there were many. There is some evidence of slaves being forced unwillingly to accompany masters into the grave from Humberside, Kent and Surrey – skeletons are found twisted or unnaturally crammed as if they had been forced down into the grave alongside a body laid out more formally.[6]

This is something that is more usually associated with the Vikings, rather than the Saxons. There is a famous account by an Arab traveller in the tenth century, who witnessed a Rus (Russian Viking) funeral of a chieftain. A slave girl 'volunteered' to join the chieftain in the afterlife. There were ten days of feasting, during which she was given a great amount of alcoholic drink. The chief's longship was prepared, and the chief laid out in new clothes in the ship with his weapons, grave goods, and the meat from two horses. The slave girl was brought to the tents of the men of the band, each of whom had sex with her. She seems to have been in some sort of alcohol or drug-induced trance, and had visions. She was put aboard the funeral ship where she was given more drink and used by six more men, and then placed on the bed of the chief. There they held her down and an old woman stabbed her to death. The ship was then set ablaze. A similar ritual may have taken place during the funeral of the woman buried in the Oseberg ship – the body of a second woman was also found in the grave.

A more recent excavation has found further evidence of the killing of slaves at the funeral of their masters. On a Norwegian island, seven skeletons laid in three graves were found by a farmer. At least three of the dead had no skulls, each buried next to a complete skeleton. The graves were between 1000 and 1200 years old. While the graves were excavated without archaeological precision, it has been possible for the bones to be analysed scientifically. Isotopes in the bones were measured, and it became clear that the headless bodies, and a dog buried at the site, had eaten a diet mostly of fish, while the bodies with heads had dined on beef and drunk milk. It is thought that this represents a significant variation in social status between the two groups of bodies. Those who had access to meat and dairy products were richer, more powerful people. The DNA analysis showed that people buried in the same grave were not related to each other. It is therefore possible that the headless, mutilated bodies were those of slaves, killed to accompany their rich, beef-eating masters to the halls of Valhalla.[7]

Another possible example comes from Anglesey. In a ditch around a Dark Age village, a number of bodies were carelessly thrown in and covered with stones. There were two men, one with his hands tied behind his back, a woman and two children. They were buried at a time when two Viking warlords were trying to seize Anglesey. The records say that 1,000 were murdered, and 2,000 taken away as slaves, during a raid in 987. The settlement where the bodies were found was an important defended place that the Vikings would have used as a base for their raids. The unfortunate people whose bodies were dumped so unceremoniously had possibly been enslaved by the Norse raiders and slain by them during their occupation.

Loot from raids and battles has been found in many places in Britain and Europe. The famous Staffordshire hoard of gold and decorations from weapons and armour, the West Yorkshire hoard, the Cuerdale and Silverdale hoards of Viking 'hack silver' (silver objects literally hacked in pieces for their bullion value), the Vale of York hoard and many others less well known attest to the amount of loot collected by various raiders during .the Anglo-Saxon period. The Cuerdale hoard included over 8,600 pieces, with jewellery, ingots and many coins. The coins came from the Viking kingdoms in eastern England and from Scandinavia, but also from Byzantium, Islamic countries, the Papal States, northern Italy, France and Wessex. This collection was buried around 903–910, in the Ribble Valley, and discovered in 1840. There have been several theories about how and why it was buried, but the dates coincide with the period when the Vikings were expelled from Dublin. The Vale of York hoard was buried in a silver-gilt decorated bowl and consisted of 617 coins, pieces of jewellery and hack silver. Some of the coins came from as far away as Samarkand, and they date the hoard to 927–928. The bowl may have been intended for use in a French church or monastery and been stolen during a raid. In 927 King Athelstan, who was uniting England under his rule, had taken York from the Vikings and seized its wealth, which he shared out among his men. Perhaps one of the York Vikings managed to smuggle his loot out of the city before Athelstan could take it and buried it for safety, but was never able to come back to retrieve it.

Hoards are regularly found in Sweden and Denmark, but others have turned up in the Netherlands, France and Norway. French, Irish and British coins and jewellery appear in the Swedish hoards. The massive hoard found at Roermond on the River Maas dates from the ninth century. There were 1,134 coins and more than twenty-six other silver objects, all discovered during gravel extraction works. It was probably buried in some sort of container, as the finds were fairly close together, and not scattered by the river, although other deposits of the same date have turned up in the vicinity before. Most of the coins were French in origin, but one came from Mercia in England. The other objects included mounts and buckles from sword belts and harness, and a spur. They would have belonged to a wealthy warrior. It is possible that the hoard was hidden by a local worried about imminent Viking raids, or indeed was buried by a raider intending to come back for it.[8]

Zombies and witches

Some crimes might be committed after death – if the dead person turned into a zombie! Two eighth-century skeletons found in Ireland may have been suspected of being able to return to haunt and terrify the living. Because of this, special measures were taken during their burials. Possibly strangers or people regarded as outsiders by their communities, they were laid in their graves with large stones wedged into their mouths. It is also possible that they could have been rapists, murderers, murder victims or had fallen ill with a strange sickness. Although side by side, they were not buried at the same time, so this is a belief which must have had a certain amount of staying power over time. One man was in older middle age, the other perhaps half as old. The large stone wedged into the mouth of one of the men had been forced in until it had almost dislocated the jaw. The mouth was seen as the conduit for the soul to exit the body, or for evil spirits to enter and bring the body back to life. Presumably, a large stone in the mouth would stop the danger of this happening![9]

Witches were also a problem. Saint Augustine had declared that magic was effective because the sorcerer was helped by demons; this grew into a belief that a pact had been made with the devil. In the seventh century, German laws declared witchcraft a crime. By the eighth century, the church had decided that this was just superstitious nonsense. A document called the *Canon Episcopi* claimed that women who believed they could fly through the sky were simply deluded, and a ninth century French archbishop tried to persuade his flock that witches could not sail ships through the sky, change the weather or steal crops, but nevertheless prosecution and execution of witches continued. King Athelstan in the tenth century supported the death penalty for anyone who caused the death of another by casting a spell, and alleged witches in Scotland who were said to have made a wax effigy of King Duffus in 968 were burned at the stake.

King Duffus started to reign in 961, but died just four and a half years later. He suffered from an illness that his contemporaries did not recognise, and began to waste away. The king's doctors had no answers, but heard of a rumour that meetings were being held in the night at Forres that were intended to end the king's life. Troops were quickly gathered and sent to the town and they captured a young girl. Probably after torture, this girl confessed that she, her mother and a coven of devil-worshippers were working on a spell to end the king's life. She gave away the location of the next meeting, which the troops ambushed. They found a collection of 'hags' who were speaking in a mysterious language and pouring a poisonous brew over a wax image. The witches were arrested and burned to death – and the king got better! Unfortunately, returning to the same area again a short while later, King Duffus was murdered and his body hidden under the bridge by Forres.

A charter in Peterborough Cathedral referring to property of one Wulfstan Uccea tells us that he inherited it from his father who had been given the land by king Eadred in 948 after the previous owner, an unnamed widow, had been executed for witchcraft, and her son sent into exile. The language used in the charter implies that she had been using a wax effigy to cause harm to someone. The woman was drowned at London Bridge, eighty miles away, according to the records – or possibly at a nearer bridge over the River Nene on the London road. This all seems rather unlikely – at that time, sticking pins into an effigy was not a capital offence unless it could be proven that someone died as a result. The researcher who describes this case suggests that Wulfstan and his father may have trumped up the charges in order to gain a valuable piece of real estate![10]

Crime in a North German town

Some criminal evidence has come from the North German town of Hedeby. Around 982, a royal longship was sunk near the town. Excavations in 1979 discovered an oak chest lying on the sea bottom, close to the keel of the royal vessel, but half a metre deeper (Figure 16). How did it get there? The chest was some 5m from the jetty – too far for it to have been accidentally dropped when the ship was being loaded. The chest was very well made, with panels fixed into grooves for the sides, a strong floor board fixed by mortices and nails and a curved lid. There is decoration on the exterior, carved into the wood and it once had a strong iron lock. The sides slope slightly inwards, so that it would have remained stable on a rocking ship.

When it was found, the chest was lying open, and upside down, in the mud of the harbour with nothing but a large granite boulder in it. The lock had been forced off. The chest must have been stolen, the lock broken, and the contents pillaged. Then the chest was thrown overboard from a ship, with a rock from a ship's ballast inside to weigh it down and hide the evidence.

The Hedeby harbour investigations also found a great many coins, mostly early local types, but with some Islamic, Carolingian, German and Northumbrian examples as well. In one small area, nine silver *darāhim* were found. They were apparently struck in Baghdad in 807/8 for the

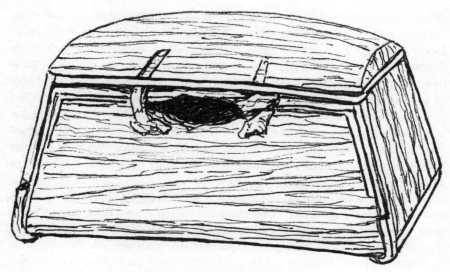

Figure 16. The Hedeby chest

famous caliph Haroun al-Rashid, from whose court came the stories of the *One Thousand and One Nights.* Closer examination of the coins, however, raised some suspicions. They were all identical – the same stamps, the same relationships between back and front, the same diameter and the same weight. All a little too good to be true … and they all weighed just a tiny bit less than real *darāhim.* The metal of the coins was analysed. It was not silver, but instead was composed of lead and tin. They could be seen, on close examination, not to be struck coins, but cast copies.

Another example has also been found in Hedeby, which suggests that the counterfeiter was a local resident, and as the coins did not seem to have gone into circulation, his workshop was probably nearby. Perhaps he was about to be found out, and tried to get rid of the evidence by throwing the coins into the harbour. The coins must have been made after 807/8, but before 900, because after that date, coins were not taken at face value, but weighed alongside hack silver, when the lighter weight would quickly have betrayed their illegal origins. The find site was under an extension of the harbour, whose date gives us a small window for the crime – between 886 and 900! But we do not know if the forger was ever caught.

A human skull was also found in Hedeby harbour, close to the shipwreck and further reports of two skeletons in association with the ship were also made by divers although their positions made it unlikely that they were directly connected with the sinking. One of the individuals was an adult man, the other a much younger adolescent originally thought also to be male. More recent analysis, however, suggests that this was a female. Three different injuries are visible on the right side of the isolated skull's frontal bone, made by stabbing with a sharp object. A knife or similar weapon also punched a hole in the right side of the jaw. Although not fatal, there are no signs of any healing of these injuries, so this person must have died very soon after the attack, possibly from a soft tissue injury elsewhere on the body. How, when or why this attack occurred is unknown. Was the victim a free person or a slave? Were they part of a ship's crew or someone from the town? Was it murder, or an act of war?

Smuggling was probably a common crime in Hedeby. At the time, it was one of the most important Viking ports, and ships would have arrived there from Greenland, Iceland, Scandinavia, Russia, Northern Europe, Britain, Ireland, and the Mediterranean – even perhaps from the Viking settlement in Newfoundland. Sited at the base of the Jutland peninsula, it connected the North and Baltic seas via a river and a sea inlet. It consisted of small houses laid out in a crowded grid of streets leading down to the jetties and harbour. Most people only lived to about thirty or forty, and many of them suffered from a number of serious diseases, including tuberculosis. A Spanish Arab traveller said it was a large but poor town, whose inhabitants ate fish and threw their unwanted babies into the sea rather than have to feed them. He said that both the men and the women wore eye make-up, and that their form of singing was a rumbling sound worse than the growling of a dog!

The town was twice sacked in the eleventh century and was eventually abandoned, leaving its remains to be rediscovered by archaeologists, although much information was probably lost when Nazi archaeologists dug the site in the 1930s to find ideological evidence for Aryan supremacy. More modern excavations have found a vast amount of artefacts and many structures associated with the town's Viking heyday.

All sorts of goods would have passed through the town – some legitimately traded, others the spoils of pillage and looting. Some items were particularly sensitive, and regarded as contraband. The Franks passed regulations against the export of arms and weapons to the peoples of the Baltic. A merchant carrying arms or breastplates was liable to have his whole stock seized.

A number of swords found across the Viking world bear a signature welded into the blade, carrying the name ULFBERHT in damascened iron wire (Plate 4). The reverse side of the blade usually has a geometrical pattern worked on it. It was thought that Ulfberht was a Frankish swordsmith, working somewhere in the region of the Lower Rhine, but a recent study suggests that Ulfberht was more probably the name of an abbot or bishop who oversaw an arms manufactory. The swords were regarded as good quality weapons, so much so that copies with forged signatures also appeared. There are around 166 known Ulfberht blades, but only sixteen of these come from the lands of the Franks. At least 144 of them, in contrast, have been found on foreign sites, particularly in Norway. Did the swords travel as booty, or in ransom payments – or as contraband?

One Ulfberht sword has been found in a grave at Hedeby in 1906. The body had been laid in a wooden coffin, but only the iron nails remained to show its shape. Inside, with the bones, was the sword in its scabbard on the right side, and a knife on the pelvis, possibly originally attached to a belt. The grave can be dated, by the shape of the sword hilt, to between 900 and 950. The inscription of the blade could only be seen through an X-ray scan, as it is obscured by the remains of the scabbard, and then only a possible 'B' and a more definite 'RH' could be identified. So some mysteries are unanswered – was the dead person a legitimate traveller from the Frankish lands carrying his own, legally acquired, sword? Was he a raider who gained the sword in booty stolen from the Franks? Or did he buy the sword as contraband in Hedeby?[11]

A graveyard in the Swedish town of Birka has also produced some evidence of crime. The Hemladen mound cemetery contained the grave of a woman otherwise intact, with brooches dating it to between 850 and 975. The skull in this undisturbed grave was found lying by the body's arm. Was she executed for a crime? But then why was she buried with her jewellery, including a string of pearls, her knife and sewing kit, an antler spoon and some wooden vessels? Bizarrely, a pig jaw had been placed where her head should have been. Was she suspected of being a witch? Perhaps her head was cut off after her death to stop her spirit haunting the living.

Another grave, containing a person in a strangely bent position and with the head removed, was found under a terrace that had once held a longhouse. This was a double male grave dating from the late eighth century. One of the men was buried with a spear, a shield, a set of arrows and an unworked elk antler. Was the person whose head had been removed a slave, killed to accompany his master to the afterlife, like the examples considered earlier in this chapter? In Viking thought of the time, a slave would have been just another personal chattel, to be disposed of in the same way as his other possessions.

In 1996 an early eighth-century burial mound was excavated; several bodies were found and it has been suggested that this was the grave of the exiled Danish king Harald Klak Halfdansson, who had been buried with his murdered cup-bearer and master of horse. The town, sited on the island of Björkö, in Lake Mälaren, lay within the ramparts of a hillfort, with jetties and harbours lining the shore. It was an important trading settlement and also contained a medieval royal estate. It is surrounded by thousands of burials mounds.

Religious crimes

The rise of Christianity in the Dark Ages was accompanied by another sort of crime – heresy. The evidence for this type of crime rests solely on the surviving documents of the period. One example is found in the letters of Saint Boniface written to the Pope in 745. The saint told the Pope that he had found two heretics in Germany, named Aldebert and Clement. He asked what he should do about them. It seems Aldebert was a man originally from France who had set himself up as a living saint. He claimed that angels had given him important eastern relics with which he could perform miracles. Somehow he had persuaded some bishops to consecrate him (possibly through bribery) and he set up chapels dedicated to himself, and used his own nail clippings and hair as holy relics which he bestowed on his followers. He also claimed to know in advance what anyone wanted to say in the confessional, and absolved the penitents without hearing their sins.

Clement was Irish. Clement's faults were that he refused to accept the teachings of the saints, especially Augustine, Jerome and Gregory, would not obey decrees of the church synod, and put himself above church authority. While a bishop, he fathered two children and supported the Old Testament rule that a man can have many wives and marry his brother's widow if he wishes; he taught his congregation that they also could do these things. He also claimed that Christ went down into Hell to free all the souls imprisoned there.

The Pope's punishments were prescribed. Adelbert lost his status as a bishop and was ordered to do penance. Clement also lost his Episcopal status and was excommunicated. Why was Adelbert treated more leniently than Clement? It may be that the Pope thought that Adelbert was insane or had been deceived by demons – this is hinted at in his letter. This despite the evidence of planning and greed shown by Adelbert's actions! Clement, however, was thought to have been quite sane and that his heresies were deliberate. Therefore he was the more dangerous of the two in the eyes of the church.[12]

Clement's views on marriage bring us to a consideration of some of the moral crimes noted in the Dark Ages. Marriage was not a sacrament in the early church; it was a contract made between two people that could be blessed by the church if they wished. Nor was bastardy seen as the shame it became in the later Middle Ages. Many of the great real or legendary figures of the age were bastards, or were said to be – Arthur, Charlemagne, Charles Martel, and of course William the Bastard, Duke of Normandy. This came to worry the established church, especially in cases where the inheritance of land or money was concerned. A British synod of 786 stated that only legitimate children could inherit estates, and that a man should confine himself to just one wife and a woman to just one husband. But it took a long time for the idea to catch on. Welsh laws allowed people to enter trial marriages for seven years and, in Scotland, a year's trial marriage was allowed right up to the sixteenth century.

The church's attempts to impose moral controls on their congregations were somewhat undermined by the behaviour of the churchmen themselves. Pope John XII turned the church of St John Lateran in Rome into a brothel; he was eventually tried for perjury, simony, sacrilege, murder, adultery and incest, and deposed in 963, but his successor, Leo VIII, was little better. He was not even ordained when he became Pope, and died in the act of adultery!

CHAPTER 5

Medieval Crime

Medieval law

The conquest of England by the Normans marked the start of gradual change in the administration of law. The Norman system was based on the holding of land by lords who, while owing fealty to the king, could operate almost independently in their own estates. However, the Anglo-Saxon legal system survived, with modifications. Sheriffs (the old shire reeves) were now appointed by the king directly; hundred courts continued to hear petty cases, and a Court Leet was established to hear purely local affairs. This court was presided over by a Constable, whose duties included keeping the peace in his district. The Constable could not judge cases, but had to keep a factual record of each case. He would find the evidence for the judges to consider in making their verdicts. By 1285, with the Statute of Winchester, each hundred was to have two Constables. In addition, there were watchmen, local volunteers who carried out patrols at night, mainly to deal with vagabonds, strangers and other undesirables, although their presence may well have been a deterrent for criminals.

This system of policing was to continue right up to the nineteenth century for much of the country; it was often inefficient and subject to corruption and intimidation, but it was all there was. In most places, the only real protection against crime was the unofficial 'neighbourhood watch' of people keeping an eye out for misdemeanours and passing information to each other.

Each manor had its own court and towns had borough courts. William the Conqueror also separated church courts from secular and royal ones. By the twelfth century, members of the clergy could be tried in the king's courts, and the church could not judge land or debt cases between clergy and lay people. They were restricted to matters of canon law and some civil law cases. Most criminal cases were heard by the manor and borough courts. The lord of the manor held the power to decide the case – for example, in Oxford, the university chancellor, in effect the lord, could pass judgement on any offence except murder or theft (so they could hear cases on poaching, seditious meetings, loitering after dark, or prostitution). Manor courts were profitable for the lord, who could claim the fines or withhold land from tenants. The sort of matters they dealt with included small debts, damage caused by straying animals, trespass, and assaults that did not involve bloodshed.

Cases of serious crime were heard by the justices, who travelled from place to place on a more or less regular basis. It was the duty of the sheriff to arrest criminals and keep them until the justices arrived. He could also raise a posse to help keep law and order, and he presided over the shire court, which heard cases that could not be heard fairly in manor courts – where one manor lord was in dispute with another, for example. Some sheriffs were notorious for using fraud and extortion to line their own pockets, such as John of Oxford, who was the Sheriff of Nottingham in the earlier fourteenth century. They had to be careful, though – kings who were dissatisfied with their sheriffs could seize their lands from them.

A prisoner awaiting trial was in very severe danger of losing his life – conditions in the gaols were very poor (Plate 5). Most gaols were simply secure chambers in large castles, and lacked heating or sanitation. Fevers took many prisoners' lives before they could be tried.

The most serious criminal cases were heard in the Court of King's Bench, which sat wherever the king was at the time until it was finally more permanently located in London. Early kings and queens were peripatetic – without mass media, the only way for a monarch to control an entire country was to travel around it and be seen by the people.

Increasingly, the growing towns of medieval Europe developed their own systems of justice. Towns were defined by their charters, which separated them from the feudal system operating in the countryside. Municipal tribunals were set up to maintain law and order, and punishments were meted out in very public ways. In Europe, the beginnings of police forces began to appear. Spain had a volunteer force called the *Hermandades* (Brotherhood) which operated against bandits and protected pilgrims and travellers. In France, a constabulary was in existence by the fourteenth century, although it was more of a military unit than a police force.

The coroner was one of the most important law officers. It was his responsibility to keep records of crimes to enable the justices to prosecute prisoners when they arrived to hold court, and to collect fines and taxes on behalf of the king. The keeping of records was vital — it could take years for the itinerant court to arrive in a district. In London in 1321, there was a lapse of forty-four years since the last court sitting. If cases could not be brought because of a lack of records, much income would be lost to the crown.

Then as now, it was the investigation of sudden death that formed the most important part of the coroner's work. It was a complex procedure which could involve fines from all and sundry for the smallest failure to obey the rules. Inevitably, something would go wrong, and the whole community would be facing a penalty. If someone found a dead body, they would ignore it, or hide it, or even drag it to a neighbouring village so it became someone else's problem. The 'first-finder' was supposed to start a hunt for the killer with the people from the nearest four households, and to report the matter to the bailiff and coroner. The local people had to guard the body until the coroner came to look at it – which could take days. Sometimes, when the corpse began to stink, they buried it until the coroner arrived, but this in itself was regarded as a crime and carried a heavy fine. The villagers of Peasmarsh in 1248 clubbed together to bribe their bailiffs not to tell the coroner, but were found out and had to pay.

The coroner had no medical training or advice to help him. He simply viewed the body and then set up an inquest; at various times this would demand the presence of all the men over the age of twelve from the four nearest towns or villages! The first thing was to find out the identity of the dead person. Norman law presumed that anyone who had been killed would be a Norman (probably because so many Saxons wanted to do just that) unless it could be proved otherwise. If the local community could not prove that the deceased was English, they would face another huge financial penalty. Usually, they had to find two relatives of the deceased to swear that the person was not Norman, even up to 300 years after the Norman Conquest. This fine, called the 'murdrum', was payable even in cases of accidental or natural death. It was deeply resented, especially in times of natural disaster such as the famine of 1257/8 when thousands died, many of them along the roads as they fled the countryside to look for relief in the towns. The discontent in this instance led to the fine being imposed only on felonious deaths after 1260.

Another source of income was a declaration of 'deodand' – the object that had caused the death became forfeit and its value had to be paid to the coroner. Deodands could include murder weapons, of course, but also falling trees, horses, dogs, carts, and mill wheels!

A criminal attempting to escape the posse or hue-and-cry, or who had escaped from the local lock-up, could attempt to claim sanctuary. Local gaols were not often very secure, and the responsibility for guarding and feeding prisoners fell on the local community. Sometimes it was easier and cheaper to let the prisoners escape, despite the inevitable fines. The escapee would usually make for the nearest church, where the law could not touch him for

Plate 1. The Tarpeian Rock (Source: Lalupa/Wikimedia Commons)

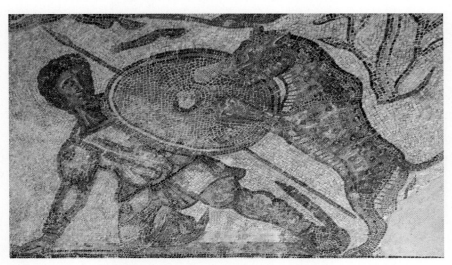

Plate 2. A criminal being savaged by wild beasts in the Roman arena (Source: VillaRomanaLaOlmeda 009Pedrosa de la Vega (Plaenia)Valdavia:Wikimedia Commons)

Plate 3. The ordeal by hot iron

Plate 4. An 'Ulfberht' sword (Source: Martin Kraft/Tarana/Wikimedia Commons)

Plate 5. Medieval prisoner being taken to the lock-up (after Soest 'Nequambuch', 14th century)

Plate 6. 'Market Scene with a pickpocket' by Louise Moillon, early 17th century

Plate 7. Historic buildings at Tortuga – Dry Tortugas National Park Service Digital Image Archives

Plate 8. A ticket for the hanging of Jonathan Wild

Plate 9. Victorian policeman c.1900 (Source: WyrdLight.com/ Wikimedia Commons)

Plate 10. The execution of Katherine Webster at Wandsworth Gaol (published in the Illustrated Police News *1879)*

Plate 11. Ned Kelly photographed in 1880 (Source: National Archives of Australia)

PRISONERS WORKING AT THE TREAD-WHEEL, AND OTHERS EXERCISING, IN THE 3RD YARD OF THE VAGRANTS' PRISON, COLDBATH FIELDS.
(From a Photograph by Herbert Watkins, 179, Regent Street.)

Plate 12. Prisoners working at the treadmill at Coldbath Fields (Source: Henry Mayhew The Criminal Prisons of London, and Scenes of Prison Life *1864)*

forty days. Once inside, or in some cases merely hanging on to the door knocker, he could hope that he could make another escape under cover of darkness, or else he would have to surrender and be hanged, or be made to 'abjure the realm'. Abjuring the realm meant that the coroner would hear his confession and seize all his land and belongings, and then nominate a port to which he had to travel within a set time, before taking the next available boat out of the country.

Some coroners clearly had little sympathy for the malefactors who claimed sanctuary – in Yorkshire, they would nominate Dover as the port of departure, to be reached in an impossibly short time and a coroner near Dover nominated Portsmouth instead. In theory, so long as the abjurer went on foot, as a penitent, he could not be touched, but in practice local residents often took their revenge on known felons or murderers once out of sight of the authorities. Abjurers might also head for Wales, Scotland or Ireland. Cattle raiders from Scotland regularly claimed sanctuary, abjured the realm, went home and crossed back into England for another raid as soon as they could.

Another option for the abjurer was simply to make off into the woods and become an outlaw. An outlaw could be legally killed by anyone, and there was a bounty on their heads of five shillings. The same amount was also payable for the heads of wolves that preyed on stock, and so an outlaw was also known as a 'wolfshead'. A captured outlaw would be hanged, or could enter the king's service as a soldier. Some managed to buy their way out with a pardon and a fine. Only men over the age of fourteen could be declared outlaw.[1]

England's most famous outlaw may or may not have really existed, but it is certain that by the end of the medieval period, any outlaw or highway robber was known as a 'Robin Hood'. The first reference is from the later fourteenth century, although some documentary evidence of earlier claimants does exist. There was a William Robehod whose goods were seized by the prior of Sandleford; this outlaw might be the same as William le Fevere, a member of a criminal gang in Berkshire in 1261. Even earlier, in 1225, the justices of York recorded the seizure of the goods of a fugitive named Robert Hod. At Cannon Hall Museum in Yorkshire is a large ancient bow, which is said to have belonged to Little John, Robin's lieutenant, who was claimed to have been buried at Hathersage. On opening the tomb in 1780 or thereabouts, the bones of a very large man were found, the thigh bone being 28½in long. In 1417 there is a record of one Robert Stafford, a renegade Sussex priest, who roamed the Ashdown Forest under the alias of 'Frere Tuk'.

Church law

In the late twelfth century, St Hugh, the Bishop of Lincoln, pronounced a sentence of excommunication on the daughter of an Oxford burgess. The lady was accused of adultery. St Hugh heard the case in a church and begged the lady to make her peace with her husband and return home – she spat in her husband's face. She remained unrepentant and living separately from her husband until, shortly after, she was 'strangled by the devil' and, as the record rather gleefully reports, went to endure richly deserved perpetual torments. In 1222, just outside Oxford, the Archbishop of Canterbury, Stephen Langton, heard the case of a young Oxford man who had fallen in love with a young Jewess. To win her, he had taken the Jewish faith, going to the lengths of self-circumcision. The archbishop's council excommunicated the young man for apostasy, then handed him over to the men of the much feared Sheriff of Oxford, Fawkes de Breaute. They went outside the bounds of the church property and straight away burned the poor lad to death. Church courts could not impose the death penalty, but they could call on the secular authorities to act on their behalf.

Most of the cases that fell under the jurisdiction of medieval church law would not be considered as crimes in today's world. They are to do with the contemporary and religious sense of morality, or the ritual demands of church practice. Church law also, of course, dealt with cases of wrongdoing by clerics themselves.

More cases of church courts are recorded in the register of Bishop Hamo, a fourteenth-century prelate who became Bishop of Rochester in Kent. Over a period of nineteen months, his courts dealt with 124 cases relating to marriage and morality. Many cases were accusations of fornication or clandestine marriage. Marriage was a somewhat grey area – previously, it had been a civil affair, which might be given a church blessing but did not necessarily need this formal recognition. Weddings were conducted in the presence of a priest at the church door; a bridal Mass might or might not follow, but the marriage contract was otherwise valid if it had been witnessed. By Hamo's time, however, the church was insisting on formal marriage ceremonies, and quite a number of people who had regarded themselves as married found themselves brought to court.

The usual sentence was to be beaten in public, and to abjure from sex until they had gone through a church rite. Banns now had to be published, to prevent marriages between people too closely related to each other, or other reasons that made the union unacceptable. Consanguinity (being too nearly related) was a problem in small villages, and also among the aristocracy who typically restricted marriages to other families of similar status. It is clear that some people continued to flout church rules – there is a record of the prosecution of John Sencler and Agnes Webbe, who had continued to live together despite a previous sentence against them. They were both beaten three times around the church.

Priests were often also prosecuted for moral crimes. Peter of Fangefosse admitted that Juliana ate Denne had been his mistress for years, and the couple had many children as a result. He lost his job. Priests were usually punished with fines, or were sent on pilgrimage. It was not thought acceptable to whip the erring cleric, but their ladies were less fortunate, and had to suffer public beatings. The upper classes were also treated more leniently – a knight in Canterbury who had committed adultery merely had to give alms to a local hospital, but his partner, by whom he had two children, was beaten five times round the church and marketplace, dressed only in her shift.

People accused of crimes by the church were brought before the court by an officer known as a summoner, who also enforced the payment of fines and carried out punishments. The summoner in Chaucer's *Canterbury Tales* was a venal character, who could be bribed to allow people to escape prosecution.[2]

Heresy was a problem for the church, especially in Europe, with sects such as the Cathars attracting many followers. The papacy ordered confiscation of property and imprisonment for heretics, and threatened princes with excommunication if they failed to stamp out heresy in their lands. In 1231, Pope Gregory IX founded the Inquisition. Inquisitors were sent across Europe, to convict and burn heretics. It only took the testimony of two strangers for someone to be arrested for heresy. The courts had to extract a confession from the prisoner, and regularly used torture to do so. Confession led to such punishments as beatings, fines, or penitential prayers. Not confessing, or being unable to prove one's innocence, was punished by life imprisonment or execution, and the seizing of all the accused's property. Once again, it was the secular authorities who carried out the sentences, as the church was not allowed to spill blood. Accused heretics could not bring any defence counsel nor question their accusers. There was no appeal from sentence.

Another crime that came under church law was blasphemy. Punishments took the form of a 'two strikes and you are out' system – after the first conviction, the blasphemer was publicly shamed and fined. The second offence carried a heavier fine, but a third offence resulted in exile, or being sent to be a slave on galleys. Sacrilege, robbery from a church, cremation of the dead, failure to be baptised, and eating meat on the many holy days of the year were all offences which could be punished by execution.

Sexual crimes were common, especially by the later fourteenth century, in the wake of the upheavals caused by the Black Death. For many people across Europe, this terrible plague was evidence that God did not exist, or at least that the church had lost its authority – for if not, why had so many monks and nuns, priests, abbots and bishops, died from the disease? If they were saintly, why were they not saved? Some people embraced a new hedonism, which became apparent in fashion as well as behaviour. Low cut and tightly fitting dresses were in vogue; it was said that ladies laced their bodices so tightly that you could stand a candle on their breasts. Men wore very short jackets and tight pants, with a soft pouch that did little to hide their private parts. Parliament insisted that everyone under the rank of lord should be made to wear longer clothing that concealed their buttocks and manhood, but even priests wore short robes and displayed their male attributes.

Anglo-Saxon attitudes towards prostitutes had been very accepting — indeed, their presence was thought to help society avoid greater evils. English prostitutes were apparently numerous, in France and Italy, as well as at home. A popular place to find a prostitute was at public bathhouses, an amenity brought back by Crusaders, and known as 'stews'. Later kings found it necessary to issue regulations for these establishments, especially those in Southwark, which were mostly owned by the bishop of Winchester. The local prostitutes were called 'Winchester geese'. Other church lords also invested in brothels. Abductions and rapes were carried out by members of the nobility either out of lust, or to force an advantageous marriage if the lady was an heiress or had an important and powerful father who would be forced to support his new son-in-law.

Sexual crimes, particularly sodomy, were rife among the clergy at times. The introduction of priestly celibacy was deeply resented in many quarters and papal injunctions were flouted openly by people such as the bishop of Sens, one Archembald, who evicted the monks from an abbey so that he could install his lady friends there. There are records of monks murdering abbots who tried to reform them, priests passing their livings on to their sons, priests marrying, and priests who had been forbidden to marry turning instead to prostitutes. The bishop of Liege was said to have sixty-five illegitimate children. In Spain, parishioners demanded that their priests kept a mistress, in order to protect their own wives and daughters! Even popes were guilty of sexual misbehaviour, practising nepotism on behalf of their bastard sons, and using convents as brothels. Pregnant nuns were not so unusual. The church authorities issued proscriptions against such practises, threatening expulsion from the church and imprisonment. But when a priest was tried and found guilty by a Church court for sexual offences, he very often got off very lightly, with a just a penance or a fine. Walter Ramsey was sentenced to be whipped three times round Dartford church, and twice round Rochester and Dartford markets, for the sin of fornication, in 1445. The sentence was waived when he agreed to pay a fine and maintenance for the lady and her bastard child.

The selling of relics was a major industry during the medieval period. The vast majority of these were fakes, if not all. Possession of a relic of a saint, or better still of Christ or the Virgin Mary, ensured that a church or abbey could rely on a steady patronage by pilgrims. Relics were believed to be able to effect miracles – such as healing, granting pleas and so on. The pilgrim trade was the medieval equivalent of today's tourist industry, a major source of income for the town or religious institution that held a good selection of relics. Towns and churches purchased relics, had them donated by citizens demonstrating their piety or looking for favours, or they simply stole them from other towns and churches. Whole gangs operated these raids on occasion. The reformer John Calvin was particularly incensed by the relic trade. He pointed out cogently that if all the relics were real, every saint was made up of several bodies, and that the various pieces of the True Cross would fill a ship. He was very sceptical about a board known as the Titulus Crucis, allegedly the board nailed to Christ's cross naming him king of the Jews (Figure 17). There were several relics claiming to be this piece, but the one that survives is kept in the Church of the Holy Cross in Rome. Modern investigations have noted that in fact the inscription is written incorrectly, and carbon dating of the wood puts its origin in the eleventh or twelfth century.

The Turin Shroud was regarded as a fake as early as 1389 by the bishop of Troyes, and carbon dating gives us a fourteenth century date, but it is still claimed as genuine by the church authorities. Other remarkable relics included numerous crowns of thorns, leftovers from the feeding of the five thousand, three of John the Baptist's heads (one from when he was a boy), very large quantities of the Virgin's milk, and lots of baby bones from the Massacre of the Innocents. Chaucer also makes fun of the relic seller's claims in the *Canterbury Tales*, listing many unlikely items in his stock. One relic collector of note was Bishop Odo of Bayeux, half brother to William the Conqueror. He wanted to acquire the relics of Saint Exuperius, and paid a vast sum to the sacristan of the church in which they were kept to dig them up and bring them to him. The sacristan, the story goes, dug up the remains of a peasant who was also named Exuperius, and when challenged by the bishop, swore that these were indeed Exuperius' bones, although he was not qualified to judge their holiness! The bishop, it seems, was satisfied.

Figure 17. The wooden sign claimed to be the Titulus Crucis

Forensic investigations were undertaken on a piece of bone and a fragment of cloth reputedly relics of Joan of Arc, which, it was claimed, were rescued from the river Seine after she was burned at the stake in 1431. It turns out the cloth had been dyed to appear burned, and the bone was from a domestic cat.

The Vatican holds numerous relics in its collections – many of which on investigation have turned out to be from farm animals, but had been certified as genuine parts of various saints. There are two separate skulls of Saint Peter – one in the Vatican, the other at the Cathedral of St John Lateran. Further bones of Peter were said to have been discovered and kept by Pope Pius XII in his chambers. In 1956 an anthropologist found that they included five tibias! The Virgin also had many legs, if the claims of various churches in Spain are to be believed. At one time, Canterbury Cathedral had some of the clay left over from when God made Adam.

The monks of Glastonbury Abbey probably committed a famous fraud with a secular relic. In 1191, after a disastrous fire, and suffering from competition in the pilgrim trade, the monks miraculously discovered the remains of King Arthur and Queen Guinevere in the grounds of the abbey (among a number of other fortuitous relics that turned up around the same time). The lead cross that was said to have been found with the bones bore an inscription: HIC IACET SEPULTUS INCLITUS REX ARTHURIUS IN INSULA AVALONIA; a slightly different

Figure 18. The inscription on the Glastonbury cross

version was drawn by the antiquarian William Camden, but it has subsequently disappeared (Figure 18). There is an account by Giraldus of Wales, who claimed to have been present at the time of the discovery. He said that the monks were told where to dig by the king, Henry II, who had been told of the site by an aged poet. It would have suited the king to find evidence that Arthur was truly dead, as he wished to put an end to Welsh insurgence and, for the Welsh, Arthur was a symbol of independence. So this was a very convenient fraud, both for the king and for the monks!

Rarely, an object that may have been stolen has been recovered by archaeology. In 1976, in a cesspit in Winchester, a 'burse-shaped' (that is, shaped like a hanging purse) reliquary was discovered. The pit was dated to somewhere around AD 925–950. The reliquary was made of beechwood covered in a decorated sheet of a copper alloy covered with gilding (Figure 19). A reliquary was a special case meant to hold the relics of a saint – not something that would normally be casually thrown away into a cesspit. X-ray examination showed that hidden inside the case are small cavities, possibly containing parchment and a tiny stick-shaped object, just fifty by seven millimetres, the nature of which is unknown. The metal casing was embossed with designs of leaves on the back, and the seated form of Christ on the front. There may have been a strap attached, so that it could be carried around.[3]

Figure 19. The Winchester reliquary

Reliquaries could travel quite a lot. They could be carried to places where oaths were being administered, or to the homes of the sick, or in liturgical processions. In the case of the Winchester reliquary, it was noted that the front metal covering had been torn off, although it had then been folded up and placed in the pit alongside the rest of the object. It does not appear that anything was taken from inside. So, was the reliquary stolen, perhaps by someone who mistook the gilded casing for real gold? When he discovered his mistake, did he try to hide the evidence in the cesspit? Why did he not remove the relics, which would have had a value for traders and collectors of such items? Perhaps the enormity of the crime hit him – for this was a crime of blasphemy as much as a crime of property. But perhaps this is just speculation, and the real story was quite different. We can never know for sure.

In 1204, during the Fourth Crusade, the Church of the Holy Apostles in Byzantium, then called Constantinople, was ransacked. The holy reliquaries were stolen, the sacred vessels, icons, imperial regalia, vestments, and contents of the imperial tombs were seized and carried off – not by the Turks, but by the Crusader knights. Some of these items may be seen today in museums in, among other cities, Rome and Venice.

During the Mameluke period, between the 10th and 13th centuries AD in the Middle East, tomb robbing was so prevalent, that it was officially subject to tax as an industry. Unfortunately, tomb robbing continues today, resulting in the loss of irreplaceable archaeological and cultural information in many countries across the world.

Forest law

The Norman lords were very fond of hunting; large areas of the countryside were 'emparked' – designated as hunting grounds. The largest hunting grounds of all belonged to the king. In these areas, they encouraged red and roe deer, and probably introduced fallow deer as well, along with wild boar and game birds. Particular areas were set aside for another introduction – the rabbit. By the early thirteenth century, about a third of all the land in England was royal forest. There are some survivals of these hunting grounds today – Epping Forest, the Forest of Dean, and the New Forest in particular, but others included Sherwood, Exmoor, Clarendon, Windsor, High Peak and Pickering. Much of the land in a hunting forest was open grazing or heath, and sometimes villages and farms lay within the bounds. In other places, people were summarily evicted and their homes burned to make way for the lords' hunting pleasure. The whole area within the boundary, or pale, was subject to Forest Law.

It became illegal to hunt or kill any of the game animals or birds, to enclose any part of the forest, to put up a building, to cut down any trees or scrub, to carry hunting weapons, or to keep a dog except as a guard dog, and only if its claws had been pulled out.

Various officers were appointed to patrol the forest, manage the game, and to prosecute offenders. Foresters policed the area and could arrest people, and agisters collected the fees and fines levied on the local people for pasturing their animals within the pale, which they had to pay when, as sometimes happened, whole counties were enforested. A series of special forest courts heard cases relating to affairs within the area – there was a Court of Regard specially to oversee the declawing of dogs, which was held every third year. A Court of Attachment presided over by verderers (landowners owning privileges in the forest) every forty days to hear indictments for crimes and to hand out fines for small infractions, a Swainmote thrice yearly to try offenders thus indicted, and the Forest Eyre, presided over by travelling royally appointed judges which could pass sentence for the most serious crimes.

Such a crime was committed by Alan of Leverton, clerk of Sherwood Forest, and his page in 1279. These two were accused of taking a doe in the forest with a red greyhound, although the body of the animal was not found, as it was lost in the dark. Alan was sent to gaol for the offence, and his property seized. The page did not turn up for trial, and may have gone on the run. Adam d'Everingham was the Warden of the forest at that time; the position was inherited by his son Robert, who soon lost the job and ended up in prison for poaching deer himself!

Possible evidence for deer poaching in the medieval period turned up during excavations at a site in Kingston upon Thames, now under a big John Lewis store. This area had been used as a cattle market and butchery site, and contained a number of pits full of waste material from carcasses, including many cattle foot bones. Hidden in one of these pits were the remains of a red deer, presumably poached from the royal park of Richmond, and concealed amongst the other, legitimate, bones in the market.

The rabbit, or coney, seems to have been re-introduced into Britain in the twelfth century, although there is some evidence for rabbits during the stone age and Roman periods, but they had died out until the Norman Conquest. At that time, these delicate Mediterranean animals were reluctant to breed in the cold damp northern climate, so special artificial warrens were built to shelter them (Figure 20). Rabbits were rare in our countryside until the eighteenth century. Some of the warrens were immense – one at Thetford had an outer boundary stretching eight miles. Special weeds were encouraged within the warren enclosures, and feed was imported for the winter months. As rabbits commanded high prices for their meat and their fur, it is not surprising that they were a target for poachers. Whole gangs appeared, some armed and with dogs and nets, to take advantage of unwary warreners. There is a record of a canon at Blythburgh who made a business of training and leasing out dogs to other poachers, including his fellow canons. In 1442, three of the canons appeared in court, caught in the act of poaching with their trained greyhounds.[4]

Rabbit warrens were sometimes enclosed by moats as well as fences. A number of warrens have been excavated, especially the form known as a pillow-mound. These oblong earthworks often enclosed stone-lined tunnels and chambers for the rabbits to inhabit. There is a large concentration of such pillow mounds on Dartmoor. In some places, homes were built for the warreners too, such as the 1590s 'folly' at Rushton, Northants.

Figure 20. A medieval rabbit warren after a manuscript illustration

Common Law

The term 'common law' dates from 1154 when Henry II created a system of law based on custom and precedents that was intended to unify legal practice and judgments across the country – a common code. The jury system was reinstated, and judges were sent from the royal courts to deal with disputes and cases around the realm. Their decisions were recorded and were referred to by other judges dealing with similar issues, so that what was agreed in one county would form the basis for an agreement in another. The church was not altogether happy with this system, which took power away from the church courts. This led to a schism between the king and the archbishop of Canterbury, Thomas à Becket, which in turn resulted in the murder of Becket in the cathedral. National outrage at the murder set Henry's law reforms back considerably.

One offence under common law was called petty treason. This was defined as an act against a superior by an inferior. In earlier times, petty treason covered a lot of possible crimes including cowardice in battle, forging the seal of a lord, committing adultery with the lord's wife or daughter, and plotting against the life of the king or his ministers. A hermit called Peter of Wakefield was brought before King John in 1212 because the king had heard that the hermit had predicted that evil would befall him. Peter further prophesied that the crown would pass to another head on Ascension Day in 1213. John sent the hermit to be imprisoned at Corfe until after the fateful date. Having survived the day, John ordered Peter to be dragged by horses to Wareham where he and his son were hanged. The Treason Act of 1351 tightened up the definitions of treason, and regarded petty treason as aggravated murder in cases such as a wife killing her husband, a servant killing his employer, or a priest or clerk killing a senior clergyman. These offences were seen as worse than murder, because they threatened the hierarchical structure of society, something which was seen at the time as divinely ordered. Treasonable criminals forfeited all their property to the crown, and it was thus in royal interests to expand the definition of the crime, something the lords, who would otherwise profit from land and goods seized in felonious judgments, opposed. Another form of petty treason had been counterfeiting, but under the 1351 Act, this became high treason instead. For both petty and high treason, the penalty for the guilty was death – men were hanged and women burned.

Many different types of other crimes are recorded; a study of fourteenth-century Paris gives us a general picture of the medieval criminal city. Paris was affected by the Hundred Years' War, leading to influxes of migrants and refugees, and former soldiers. Most of the criminals were servants, farm labourers, and journeymen craftworkers. Many of the accused had several occupations, often unrelated to each other. Most were not originally from the city. The list of crimes committed included treason, moral crimes, arson, fraud, forgery, adultery, rape, assault, sorcery, slander, robbery, breaking and entering, receiving stolen property or the selling of it, and murder. Many murders were committed in the process of robbery, while others occurred during quarrels or feuds.

There were many thieves – persons suspected of theft made up over half of those arrested. Many seem to have been habitual offenders, confessing to multiple crimes. A large number of thieves specialized in robbing travellers at inns and taverns, taking their belongings while they slept. Most stolen items had a fairly low value, as were things stolen in the workplace or in market thefts. These were things easily sold on and hard to identify once they had passed through other hands. This also applies, of course, to thefts of money.[5]

Until the middle of the fifteenth century, house-breaking, or burglary, was not treated as a separate offence, but as an aggravated theft. After the 1450s, burglary was treated as an offence in its own right, and carried a penalty even if nothing was taken, because the intent to steal existed.

On the local level, many crimes were associated with standards and rules of craft production. Particular laws related to the production and sale of food and

Figure 21. Punishment of a baker

drink. Quality standards and pricing regulations were enacted, especially in England for bread. The Assize of Bread of 1203 was codified in 1266. From this time, bread had to be labelled by the baker, so that underweight or poor quality loaves could be traced to their maker (Figure 21). Each baker had his own seal which was stamped into every loaf. Prices were set by weight, the aim being to ensure that everyone could be able to afford this staple food. This did not entirely stop fraud – some bakers in fourteenth-century London were selling bread made from flour mixed with dust or chalk, and one even put pieces of iron into the loaves, to make them seem to be of the proper weight.

Another staple, ale, was also subject to regulation. Ale-conners were appointed to test beer for quality and price, and to report all infractions to the court leet. Before the introduction of hops, ale had a very short shelf-life, and was made in many small local or domestic breweries. The ale-conner therefore had to try a great deal of ale, often rather bad. Contrary to what one might imagine, it was not a popular job, and it was sometimes necessary to force people into the job. The public saw ale-conners as unwelcome representatives of authority.

The wine trade was another source of much fraud. Wine was often deliberately mislabelled, or mixed with inferior quality vintages. By 1419, the law required wine to be labelled with its region of origin and in London, taverns were required to store wines from different countries separately.

Anyone found selling bad or fraudulent wine would be forced to drink all of it! They could be fined, or placed in the pillory. The same was true of dairymen who sold bad milk. Another form of punishment was to force a bad brewer to wear a barrel, or for a baker to have all his loaves strung around his neck.

Expensive imported spices were often adulterated with ground-up brick, nutshells, weed seeds and other materials. Spices, especially pepper, were very expensive but necessary to give flavour to an otherwise bland diet (and sometimes to disguise the flavour of meat or fish that was beginning to go off, a constant problem in an age without refrigerators).

Smuggling, particularly of wool, began to become a major crime in the later medieval period. A duty had been placed on the export of wool in 1300, which rose rapidly during the Hundred Years War as the crown became short of money to pay for the troops. For the first time, a Customs service was set up, initially just in the major ports and only to collect the tax. In Sussex, the only dutiable port was Chichester. Merchants from Sussex and Kent found it much more profitable to carry out their trade from the Cinque Ports such as Rye, where there were few or no officials but sometimes they got caught – several merchants were tried in Rye in 1357 accused of smuggling goods through Pevensey.

It was not only people who were sometimes brought to court for crimes – a variety of animals, birds and insects were recorded as defendants in various cases. Animals were prosecuted for causing injury or death – some were pardoned, some were excommunicated by church courts, and others received the death penalty. Pigs were particularly subject to prosecutions. In Falaise in Normandy, a pig was convicted of murdering a small child in 1386. She was hanged from the village gallows, and her six piglets were acquitted of being accessories to the crime because they were so very young and had been given a bad example by their mother!

Crimes were not only committed by domestic animals or the lower classes. In the fourteenth century, members of the gentry were prominent members and directors of large criminal gangs. The Folville family of Leicestershire, led by Eustace Folville, was a long established minor gentry clan, that may have fallen on hard times. In 1326 Eustace and his brothers, along with other local landowners, ambushed Sir Roger Bellere and murdered him. The Folvilles escaped justice and were declared outlaws. Between 1327 and 1330 they were roaming the region, committing robberies and murders. They seem to have made an alliance with another gang, the Coterels, based in the Peak District and the northern part of Sherwood Forest between the late 1320s and early 1330s. The Folvilles were, on occasion, employed by apparently respectable people, including churchmen and monks, as mercenaries. In 1331 they were employed by monks from Sempringham Priory and Haverholm Abbey to destroy a rival's water mill, for a fee of £20. Like most of the Folvilles, the Coterels never faced trial for their crimes. In fact, later they gained important civil and military positions. The Coterels were a wealthy family; the three brothers who founded the gang were supported by numerous religious foundations and local lords. They preyed upon travellers, demanding ransoms, and undertook commissions to attack churches and manors. They engaged in robbery, extortion, kidnapping and murder, and pillaged widely, including the estates of the Earl of Lancaster. Efforts to arrest James Coterel failed because he was tipped off in advance by one of his clients, the Prior of Lenton. Their reputation grew to such a level that all they had to do was to send a victim a letter demanding money and he would pay up.

Other knights were involved in similar forms of crime, and their thefts were on a much greater scale than those of the lower classes. The lords Simon de Montecute and Ulfrid de Beauchamp carried off a hundred trees from the woods of the abbot of Glastonbury, killing one of his men in the process. No-one was safe – Sir Henry Beaumont, travelling to Durham with his brother the bishop and two cardinals, was abducted and the cardinals were robbed by a gang of gentry. Sir Henry and his brother were taken to the castle at Mitford, seat of his kidnapper, Sir Gilbert de Middleton, where they were kept until a ransom was paid. In other cases, people were abducted and forced to sign charters handing over land and estates.

A favourite way for these knights to avoid justice was to volunteer to serve in royal armies. Members of the Folville and Coterel gangs served in the king's wars in Scotland, as did Simon de Montecute.[6]

Witchcraft was not in itself a crime in England, unless there was a death brought about by spells or sorcery. However, some unusual burials may represent a local reaction to witches. The body of a teenage girl found in Hoo, Kent had been decapitated, with the head laid beside the rest of the skeleton. The burial was in unconsecrated ground, under a holly bush. The site director believes that the decapitation indicates that this girl may have been seen as a witch, although she may have committed some other type of crime, or had committed suicide.[7]

An even more macabre burial was found in Piombino, Italy dating from the fourteenth century. The cemetery in which this body was found may have been dedicated to witches or criminal women. The body of a twenty-five to thirty-year-old woman was found to have seven nails driven through her jaw and another thirteen around the skeleton that pinned down her clothing. The woman was buried without a coffin or shroud in a shallow grave. Another woman was surrounded by seventeen dice. This is an unlucky number for Italians, and women were forbidden to play dice games. However, in this case the graveyard was in consecrated ground, and the excavator has speculated that these women were from influential families who could use their connections to have them buried by the church.[8]

A violent era

The fourteenth century was one of the most violent eras in the history of Britain – one calculation is that it was ninety-five per cent more dangerous than the present day. Ten times as many homicides took place – between 36 and 52 people per 100,000 were killed in London each year in the first half of the century, compared to 25.9 per 100,000 in New York City in 1993, and just 9.3 per 100,000 for the USA as a whole in 1992. Everyone carried a knife, and quarrels easily got out of hand. The fourteenth century was a dreadful time. The climate deteriorated badly, leading to crop failures and murrains among cattle and sheep. As a result, people starved. Then in 1349 the Black Death arrived. The battle for survival was sometimes very vicious.

One of the most violent towns seems to have been Oxford. Between 1297 and 1322, thirteen murders were committed by students at the university. There were riots and battles between the townspeople and the students and staff of the colleges. A three-day riot began as a pub brawl in 1355. A group of students went to an inn near Carfax, but took exception to the poor quality of the wine there. They complained to the innkeeper, who answered them back rather robustly. The students threw the jug of wine at his head. The locals took up the side of the innkeeper, armed themselves with bows, and went out to attack any students they could find. It turned into a whole series of running battles in the streets, with university buildings set on fire and the death of six members of the university.

There was little correlation between alcohol and murder, however. Most people drank ale (as the water was notoriously unsafe), which was quite weak, and wine was a drink for the wealthy rather than the common people. Drunkenness as a crime does not appear until the later Tudor period.

The most popular day for committing a murder appears to have been Sunday – thirty-eight per cent in London with another twenty per cent on Monday. In Oxford, Saturday was the most perilous day of the week – twenty-nine per cent of murders were committed on Saturdays. Modern murders are also most often committed at weekends – a combination of getting paid on Friday, drinking over the weekend, and having to spend more time with the family! In medieval times, there was no such thing as a weekend, but people did get some time off on Sundays and saints' days.

Again, as today, most murders were committed in the evening and at night, and more frequently in the summer than in the winter. Most murders were committed by men, although the cities saw more female killers, such as Juliana, the concubine of a chaplain. She was in bed with the chaplain when a man, John de Maltone, entered the room and knifed the chaplain in the belly. John ran with Juliana to a nearby church, where they confessed to being accomplices in the murder.

Murder of children was relatively rare, with the occasional case of infanticide, and most recorded cases of child murder happened during the course of robberies. Many robberies and burglaries seem to have been extremely violent, even sadistic, particularly in rural areas. Torture was used to make householders reveal where they had hidden their valuables, and burglars came equipped with knives and axes to kill or maim their victims.

Some murders were commissioned. In 1301 John of Weldon was asleep when Reginald Porthors and Ralph le Chapman broke into his house and murdered him with a hatchet. They then stole ten shillings, and returned to their employer, Lord Ralph Porthors. The posse from the neighbourhood followed the murderers but were denied entry to his manor. The lord then assisted the murderers to escape. Warrants were issued for the arrests of all three, but it seems clear that Lord Ralph would not have faced justice – nobles almost always got an immediate royal pardon.

However, most murderers seem to have been otherwise respectable tradesmen, as were most of the victims. Servants were also often murderers, and prostitutes were often accused. Members of the clergy also appear in the records as killers.

The murder weapon of choice was the ubiquitous knife or dagger, carried by everyone. If no knife was available, a staff or cudgel was used. Very few murders ended up with a successful prosecution. Only some thirty per cent even ended up with a trial at all.[9]

The medieval period was nothing if not imaginative in devising punishments for crime. Public humiliation, with or without physical pain, was popular. We have mentioned the pillory, and punishments such as being forced to wear a barrel for selling bad ale or wine.

Women in particular might be sentenced to the thewe, a type of pillory reserved for them. This was the punishment meted out to Alice de Salesbury in 1373; she had kidnapped and disguised the young daughter of a London grocer, John Oxwyke, to use as a foil for begging. Alice was only sentenced to stand at the thewe for an hour as the child was returned unharmed!

Brandings and public whippings were carried out, particularly in towns, and imprisonment was beginning to be used as a punishment, rather than just as a holding measure. Archaeologists working at Lincoln castle have found what they believe to be an underground prison there. Robbed out walls suggest cells that existed before the newer prison was built in the eighteenth century. Small lock-ups existed for short-term prison sentences, particularly in market towns. The area under the stairs to the upper hall in the Titchfield Market Hall, rebuilt at the Weald and Downland Museum, was probably used as a lock-up, and in 2013 a fourteenth-century prison was discovered in Middle Row, Faversham, Kent, during the laying of a new water main. It was a circular structure, about 15 to 20m in diameter, whose entrance was possibly via a trapdoor in the ceiling. There is a record of just such a structure in the town known as the Whitehouse gaol and cage, a 'deep hole or cage with heavy oaken planks across the top'. Later, two rooms were built over the top, and this structure combined the functions of guildhall and gaol.

The ultimate penalty, of course, was death, usually by hanging. Gallows were erected in many places, usually somewhere prominent, by roadsides, or at the edges of towns. The gallows was intended to be a visible deterrent to crime. The actual structures rarely survive, but their presence is often preserved in place names, such as Gallows Gate, near Torquay in Devon, Gally Hills in Surrey and Doncaster, Yorkshire or Gallows Hill in Wiltshire and Lancaster. Medieval hanging was a slow death – the 'long drop' gallows, causing the neck to break, was yet to be invented; instead people were left to dangle while they asphyxiated, a process that could take a very long time.

A number of excavations and studies of gallows sites have been undertaken in Europe. Some of these were at places which held more ancient remains, such as prehistoric barrow mounds, and are surrounded by the graves of the executed criminals. These burials were typically carelessly carried out, with bodies in odd positions, and often with their hands or legs still bound. Sometimes, the postholes of the gallows trees have also been found. At Alkersleben in eastern Germany, some seventy bodies have been found at a site on a hill overlooking the road to Nuremberg. One individual had been strangled with an iron chain. Details of the bodies and the way they were buried are shedding light on medieval execution procedures. Some bones were found in a mixed-up jumble, evidence that the bodies had been gibbeted for long enough for the skeleton to fall apart. Records tell us that at Augsburg, up to thirty criminals at a time were left hanging from the gallows there, and then afterwards just tossed into small pits.

In medieval Germany, criminals could be broken on the wheel. The unfortunate victim was first given over to a torturer who broke their legs, arms, hands and feet, and then their limbs were threaded through a large wheel that was hoisted up in the air on a pole. They would hang there in agony until they died. In fact, some people actually survived this awful fate, and earned a pardon.

Beheadings were also common in Europe, and during in the medieval period a sword was the weapon that delivered the fatal blow. Not all executioners were good at their jobs – skulls show wounds on the back of the head or the back where the headsman had missed his target. Executioners could also make a good living quite apart from the fees they earned at a hanging. They also worked as butchers and for fellmongers (dealers in animal skins), cut off the hands and feet of poachers and other criminals, and undertook brandings. On top of all that, they could sell souvenirs and body parts of the people they had executed – human fat, brains, fingers and other body parts that were much sought after for the making of magical remedies and charms. Despite their usefulness, however, executioners were never popular members of their communities![10]

CHAPTER 6

Early Modern Crime

A time of change

The period from the end of the Wars of the Roses in the late fifteenth century to the reign of Queen Anne in the early eighteenth century saw some of the most fundamental changes in British religion, politics and society. The country was still reeling from the effects of the Black Death, which reduced the population by at least a third, and then the bloody wars between the rival dynastic houses of York and Lancaster. Wars with the French and Spanish were set against a background of the dissolution of the monasteries, the Reformation, and the break from Rome. In the seventeenth century, religious and political schisms led to the English Civil War, the execution of the king, the Commonwealth and subsequent restoration of the monarchy, and wars with the Dutch. At the same time, new lands were being discovered, and as the religious arguments raged, science was beginning to gain a place in the way people saw the world. All these events, and more, affected the types of crimes that were being committed, and the forms of policing and punishment that were needed to deal with them.

By the start of the seventeenth century, the population was on the rise again, and society was more complex than in the medieval period. The waning power of the aristocracy after the Black Death had created a situation in which a powerful middle class could rise – made up of merchants, yeomen farmers and lawyers – for whom law and order was seen as an essential prerequisite for prosperity, both personal and national. Prices rose faster than wages, and the acquisition of the previous monastic estates by courtiers and speculators created hardship in the countryside for many of the lower orders. Poor harvests added to the problems. Many people lost their landholdings and became vagrants, and vagrancy became the new *bête noire* of the governing classes. Whilst not everyone became a villain, bands of vagrants posed a threat to order in a number of districts, and the perception of the problem may well have grown out of proportion to its reality.

There were many beggars on the roads and a large number found their way into the towns; some of these turned to crime – organised crime began to be recorded. The population of London rose from 60,000 in 1520 to 500,000 by 1700, many of whom were displaced peasants, refugees from various religious and political conflicts in Europe, soldiers and sailors released from service who did not want to return to the countryside, itinerant traders, carters, and so on – a mobile and thrusting community.

There was no proper police force except for the constables, who were locals serving a one-year term, and the nightwatchmen, and there was a lack of holding facilities – early in the Tudor period, the Mayor of London had to order each area to build a prison house for beggars and vagabonds detained in their streets. Long term correctional prisons did not begin to appear until 1576. Houses of Correction, where the inmates were put to work, were often called 'Bridewells', after the first one in London, founded in 1553. This first institution was intended to house homeless children in the City, and to punish vagrants. There were also no facilities for relief of the poor and homeless, a function that had once been at least partially undertaken by the religious houses.

In the countryside, it was the justices of the peace, usually local landowners, who oversaw most criminal prosecutions, acting as judges at the sessions held once a quarter and imposing penalties. Minor cases and some religious infringements were still heard in manor and church courts. Serious cases went to the assize courts. There was no overall system, and the mechanisms of law varied from county to county. Jury trial figures for the county of Essex during the reign of Elizabeth I show that theft and burglary were the most common serious offences there, followed by murder and witchcraft. Some cases, of course, went to higher courts – treason and offences to do with the outlawing of religious practices. These included new crimes – the saying of the Mass, for example, or refusing to attend Mass, depending on the dominant religious complexion of the period.

Laws against vagrants, or 'sturdy beggars', included draconian punishments. A law of 1531 recommended that a vagrant should be tied naked to a cart's tail and whipped until he was covered with blood. Poor Laws were enacted, dividing vagrants into those who needed care, and those who were regarded as lazy or venal. The latter were to be punished and returned to the parish from which they originally came. In 1547 the Vagrancy Act dictated that beggars should be whipped, branded and forced into work. A number of strict new laws became known as the Bloody Code – many more crimes now carried the death penalty. Other physical punishments were used, as were punishments designed to humiliate the wrongdoer. The stocks joined the pillory as a feature of many towns and villages.

The mass of people in towns took what pleasures they could, with bear baiting, cockfights, and much drinking. One result of the dissolution of the monasteries was to make brewing of beer, rather than ale, more common in ordinary homes and taverns. There was a sharp rise in drunkenness as a result – beer is stronger than ale — and for the first time, public drunkenness became a crime.

Convicts to the colonies

From the 1620s onwards, another new form of punishment was introduced – transportation – and merchants formed syndicates to exploit this profitable trade. Estimates vary, but between 50,000 and 120,000 convicts were transported to North America until the American War of Independence. Merchants contracted to take the convicts by ship to Canada and New England, or to the West Indies. English convicts, but also the Irish and Scottish poor or defeated soldiers were transported. Cromwell sent thousands of Scottish soldiers to the Americas during the Civil War. On arrival, the transportees were sold into bondage, usually for a term of up to seven years, as indentured servants. The Scottish sent their own vagabonds too – a transport was commissioned by Edinburgh merchants to take a cargo of 'idle and debosht persons' to Barbados. In 1666 it is recorded that the Edinburgh authorities were attempting to send another cargo of such people to labour-hungry Virginia with its tobacco plantations. Conditions could be hard – one source claims that of the first 300 deportees, only four were still alive after four years. Many ran away or committed suicide. Some rebelled and were executed.

One who did not survive was the victim of a murder that happened near Annapolis in Maryland. Digging in a seventeenth century cellar, archaeologists came across the body of a boy. Analysis of his bones showed him to have been in his mid-teens, and of European origin. His teeth and spine showed evidence of disease and hard labour. He may well have been an indentured servant, or even a convict transportee. He had been buried in a small pit and covered with fragments of broken bottles and pots, and ash from a fireplace. Lying on his bones was a broken milk pan, which seems to have been used to dig out the grave (Figure 22). A coin of 1664 and a piece of glass marked with the date 1663 suggest that the boy died some time before 1675.

At that time, colonial laws were passed forbidding private burial of indentured servants, precisely to stop owners from hiding their abuse of these

Figure 22. The grave of a possible indentured servantboy in Annapolis

people. The actual cause of death is unknown, but the boy's right wrist was broken, as if he had tried to protect himself against a beating. It seems the burial was done secretly, to avoid the discovery of the crime.[1]

It is claimed (among others by Benjamin Franklin) that it was these unfree, indentured servants who provided the basis for the success and development of America in later periods, and that they made up as much as half of the colonial immigration.

Another destination was Tangier, where men and women were sent to support the royal colony as forced labour, to build the defences. There is a record of Margaret Summerton, who was whipped for trying to raise sedition among the Tangier convicts in 1663.

Everyday crimes

The scale of day-to-day crime and punishment can perhaps be illustrated by the assize records for Ewell, a small community in Surrey, during the reign of Elizabeth I. In 1569 Thomas Tyckner, a labourer, stole a horse worth twenty-six shillings and eight pence – he was sentenced to hang. In 1586 Richard Clenche stole a sheet worth eleven pence; he was sentenced to a whipping. The next year Priscilla Turpyn stole clothing and was remanded as she 'pleaded her belly' – that is, as a pregnant woman, sentencing had to be deferred. In the same year, Lionel Gest, a gentleman, along with two others committed highway robbery, making off with a gold chain, a gold ring, a sword, a pistolet, £34 in cash, and a whole list of clothing from John Turner; Gest was sentenced to hang, but his accomplices were not caught. In 1588 the local constable was fined for allowing a local innkeeper to escape custody.

During the period, large numbers of local people were accused of recusancy – failure to attend church. In 1609 Peter Porte was whipped for stealing a tenpenny piece of boxwood. Sheep stealing was a common crime, as was petty larceny. What is interesting to note is that even when the value of stolen goods was high, the court often only found the accused guilty to the extent of ten pence – worth a whipping, but not a hanging. There was, on average, only one hanging every five years from this community. A surprisingly large number of not guilty verdicts were entered, despite the presence of witnesses. There were also some more serious crimes, including burglary, which was treated more stringently than robbery. John Rowse was sentenced to hang for taking his daughters from their bed and drowning them. It seems that through bad management and bad luck, he had lost all his fortune, and could not bear the thought of his children living in penury. He was hanged at Croydon in 1621 'where he died with great Penitency and Remorse of Conscience'.

Charles Godden was a labourer who stole a pair of garters worth two pence, two pairs of hose worth two shillings, a silver-gilt ring worth three shillings, and one shilling in cash; he tried to claim benefit of clergy but on examination, was proved to be unable to read, and so was sentenced to hang. Benefit of clergy was a medieval leftover – the civil courts were unable to prosecute clergy, who could prove their status by being able to read. By the Tudor period, all the accused had to do was to read the beginning of Psalm 51, a verse that was easy to memorise. It seems to have become regarded as a way of letting off first-time offenders lightly. Perhaps Charles Godden was given a different verse to read! Another labourer who broke into a house, stole clothing and a larger amount of money was granted the benefit of clergy, as was a yeoman who attacked a man with a dagger, inflicting wounds from which he died the next day. Robert Hardinge faced numerous counts of stealing cattle and sheep over several years, but though confessing, was given benefit of clergy too. He was clearly not a first-time offender – perhaps he could bring other influences to bear on the court.[2]

A study of the records for Sussex during the later Tudor period shows that the proportion of women to men accused of theft increased during the later sixteenth and early seventeenth centuries, although the types of theft they engaged in were different. Women rarely stole horses, or robbed people on the highways, but they did burgle houses, cut purses, and commit larceny. Women also tended to join mixed gangs and rarely worked alone. They tended to steal items for which they could easily find a market – clothes and household items. Misogynist literature of the time castigated women for their slyness, envious natures and underhand ways. The canting language used by the underworld of the period has fewer terms for specifically female crimes than for male or unisex ones, but there are some that suggest that a section of criminal activity was thought to be female dominated, such as stealing from lodgers, stealing clothing left to dry on hedges and so on. It was thought by some that women were better at picking pockets (Plate 6) and shoplifting, as their many layers of clothing made it easier to conceal stolen goods. There were couples who worked together, but in these cases it was usually only the man who was charged with the crime, as the social *mores* of the day regarded the male of the household as the responsible individual in law. Women supported male thieves and robbers too, bringing them food, and hiding them from the law officers.

Small thefts were often dealt with without recourse to the authorities – the victim might go with some friends to the home of the suspect and recover the stolen items, perhaps administering a beating or extorting extra compensation from the thief. Such cases are recorded in a number of places, in rural Wales and elsewhere. Many people would have been reluctant to go to law – they would face a time-consuming process that would take them away from their work, and there would be expenses and inconvenience. Some would have been afraid in case the thieves or their friends took vengeance upon them. And then there was the problem of investigation – with no police force, it was the victim and his friends who had to take on the duty of finding the villain and proving his guilt, not always an easy thing to do. Local knowledge of victim and offender counted for a great deal, but was not always enough to make an arrest or extract a confession. Sometimes people undertook investigations in order to avoid being in trouble themselves, for example if they had inadvertently bought stolen goods.

In Wrexham in 1676, two butchers bought thirty sheep from a pair of brothers called Thomas, only to have the real owner, Mr Phillips, turn up and accuse them of the theft. They were forced to obtain a warrant to search for the real thieves. Eventually, the son of one of the butchers found the Thomas brothers in Shrewsbury, after a considerable amount of time and effort. In another case Hugh, a butcher in Llanrwst, was accused of stealing sheep that he claimed to have bought from a man called Evans. Hugh was an established dealer with witnesses to his legitimate trade, but there were no witnesses to his deal with Evans, who could not be found, and although Hugh had been nowhere near the scene of the crime, he was nevertheless convicted of theft.

Markets were good places in which to sell stolen goods, as were alehouses. Few people made close enquiries about where the goods had come from if they were presented with a bargain. This was an area where women were prominent in crime – as stallholders and alehouse keepers with premises where stolen goods could be fenced — as well as committing thefts themselves. Women also often acted as pawnbrokers and received stolen items, paying in cash, kind or drink for them.[3]

Evidence of a fraud has been found at the Museum of London. In 1912 in Cheapside, a hoard of five hundred pieces of jewellery was discovered, probably the stock of a local tradesman. Investigations have revealed that the hoard, buried during the Civil War at some time between 1640 and 1666, could have belonged to Thomas Sympson. Sympson's family was known to have been suspected of receiving stolen goods taken from Gerrard Pulman, a fellow jeweller who had been murdered while travelling to Persia in 1631. Among the gems hidden at Cheapside, the Museum has discovered fake balas rubies – pieces of rock crystal that had been carefully cut, and then dyed red. These fakes could have been passed off as the real thing for up to £8,000. Little is known about the workings of the jewellery trade at the time – it was a very clandestine business, as traders and workmen were afraid of being robbed or threatened by criminals.

Royal and noble murder

There were many murders and assassinations among the aristocracy in this period, such as the murder of Mary Queen of Scots' husband Lord Darnley in 1567. The twenty-one-year-old had been staying at lodgings in Edinburgh, convalescing from an illness, probably syphilis. The queen visited him there on that evening and then returned to Holyroodhouse. At two in the morning, gunpowder that had been packed into the cellars below Darnley's rooms exploded and destroyed the house. The next day, Darnley's body, and that of his servant, were found in the garden next door – with no signs of burns or bruises. People immediately believed they had been strangled before the explosion. The Earl of Bothwell was suspected, as was Mary herself, but the truth has never been established.

Another notorious murder took place at Calverley Old Hall in Yorkshire, of which the Tudor hall and chapel still survive. In 1604, Sir Walter Calverley was taken by a fit of insane rage, and ran through the hall. He murdered two of his sons and tried to kill his wife, who was saved when his knife skidded off the metal stays of her corset. She fainted, and Calverley thought he had succeeded in murdering her. He set off on horseback to find his youngest son, who had been taken out by his wet nurse, but the horse tripped over a rabbit hole and fell on top of Sir Walter. His distraught servants caught up with him and bound him, and he was sent first to prison in Wakefield and then to York. He would not enter a plea, and was then tried for contempt of court. His punishment was to be pressed. This form of execution involved laying the condemned man down with a heavy oak slab on top of him. Stones were then piled on top of the slab until the prisoner was crushed to death. The story goes that an old retainer was present and, affected by Sir Walter's cries, piled more stones on the slab as quickly as he could, to end the torture more quickly. The servant was hanged for interfering with the course of justice.

Religion, treason and the scourge of witches

When Henry VIII broke with the Catholic Church in the 1530s, the scene was set for more than a century of religious dissent and the criminalisation of matters of belief. A number of important people were executed for failing to support the religious stance of the ruling monarch – Protestantism under Henry and his son Edward VI, Catholicism under Mary, and a return to Protestantism under Elizabeth, followed by the rise of more extreme forms of non-conformism in the seventeenth century. Under Mary, some 280 Protestants were burned to death for the crime of heresy; Elizabeth was more tolerant of religion, but not of treason. When the Pope encouraged English Catholics to rebel against the queen, they were sought out, tried and executed for this crime, not for their faith. The failure of James I to support the Catholics to the extent that they hoped led to the Gunpowder Plot of 1605, when a group of conspirators hoped to blow up the king, along with other influential lords, at the Houses of Parliament.

This period also saw the large-scale persecution of people accused of witchcraft across Europe. Before the fifteenth century, witchcraft was seen as a relatively minor offence, based on self-delusion or superstition, which had no place in a Christian society. People turned to witches for help with ailments and domestic problems, in lieu of other forms of help. Even the church authorities did so – in Thatcham in Berkshire in 1583, the churchwardens sent for a 'cunning woman' to help them find the thief who had stolen the communion cloth from the church. However, papal condemnation of witchcraft began to grow and the practice was strongly outlawed by 1484. The Inquisition was given the power to persecute witches, and two inquisitors in Germany produced a book in 1486, the *Malleus Maleficarum,* or the *Hammer of the Witches*, describing their beliefs about the practices of witches, how to identify witches, and how to try and execute them.

It is believed that half a million people were subsequently condemned to death across Western Europe. Belief in witchcraft and its powers was widespread, and few were prepared to oppose the Inquisition's actions. There was no Inquisition in England. Queen Elizabeth's religious tolerance also extended to witches – only if the bewitched person died was the death sentence to be invoked, and all other charges were treated as lesser offences. In 1604 however, James I revised the law to make all and any witchcraft liable to the death penalty. Nevertheless, very few witches were tried or executed in England, partly because English law did not allow the accused to be tortured. The tortures of the Inquisition led to people confessing not only their own crimes, but crimes allegedly committed by their families, neighbours and workmates, who in turn, when tortured, added more names to the list. Many of the accused in England were acquitted or simply fined. Less than 500 executions took place between 1550 and 1685, although in Scotland the number was three times higher. In the same period, there were 50,000 witch trials in Germany and, between 1625 and 1635, some 6,000 people were burned at witches in Bamberg, Mainz, Cologne and Würzburg.

A notorious witch trial occurred in 1441. Among the accused was the duchess of Gloucester, along with her personal clerk, her chaplain, a physician/vicar from her household and a woman named Margery Jourdemayne, known as the 'witch of Eye next Westminster'. Margery had 'form' – she had previously been imprisoned for sorcery. It is possible that Margery was a purveyor of love-charms and other philtres to the ladies of the royal court. The duchess claimed that Margery had previously supplied her with potions to encourage the duke to marry her. The affair began in midsummer when the duchess, Eleanor, was told that three of her servants had been accused of a conspiracy to harm the king, Henry VI. Henry's heir was the duke of Gloucester, and it may be that Eleanor's clerk had cast her horoscope to see if she would become queen; the implication was, of course, that as this could only happen if the king died, there could have been a plot to kill him to make sure of a favourable outcome for the duchess. Further indictments accused Eleanor of more dabbling in the black arts with this end in view.

Apprised of this, Henry commissioned his own 'reading', which was more favourable; his council charged the duchess' men with conspiring to kill the king using necromancy. The clerk was publicly humiliated and made to swear to give up all sorcery; the physician was imprisoned in the Tower on a charge of heresy and plotting to do away with the king. Roger, the clerk, implicated the duchess, saying that she had egged him on because she wanted to know her future. Eleanor was brought before a church court and charged with witchcraft, heresy and treason; she was then imprisoned at Leeds Castle to await a further trial. During the church court trial, Eleanor implicated Margery, saying she had sought the witch's advice. Margery was arrested. In

October, the duchess was brought back to Westminster for a second church court hearing, and was charged with trying to bring about the death of the king by sorcery. Clerk Roger brought to the court a number of 'magical' objects and images, possibly made of wax, which he said Eleanor and the others had been using.

Eleanor's defence was that although she admitted using witchcraft, it was in order to bring about her pregnancy, so that she could give her husband an heir. She denied treason, but her physician and Margery both accused her of being the instigator of the plot. Margery was found guilty of heresy and witchcraft, and was burned to death. Within a day, the physician was also dead, possibly as a result of suicide.

Eleanor was found guilty of sorcery and witchcraft, but acquitted of heresy and treason. Her marriage was pronounced null and void as she had admitted using witchcraft to bring it about. Nevertheless, she was given a generous pension and allowed to live, supervised, in some comfort until her death. Her husband was never implicated in the plot, but he lost his political power and position. Roger the clerk was dragged on a hurdle to Tyburn, where he was hanged, drawn and quartered, and his head was set up on London Bridge, with the other parts of his body being displayed in various towns as a warning to would-be heretics. The chaplain, John Home, who had a reputation as a brawler, was arraigned on lesser charges of having known of the conspiracy, but not of being part of it. He was acquitted after several spells in prison. He is commemorated by a brass in Hereford Cathedral where he was buried in 1473.

None of the people accused was of poor birth or lacking in education, which is why this particular affair became such a scandal. Two ambitious women, one a noblewoman, the other from landed yeoman stock, who were both intimate with the affairs of court, and three educated men of the cloth, had all, it appears, taken witchcraft seriously enough to endanger themselves. But it was not the making of potions or the casting of horoscopes that led to their downfall – after all, the king himself believed in the stars. Rather it was the smell of treason and heresy that brought the harsh reaction of the authorities down on them.[4]

The Pendle witches case of 1612 was based on the claim that thirteen witches had brought about the deaths of some seventeen people in the Pendle Forest area of Lancashire. They were said to have sold their souls to familiars and accomplished the deaths by making clay effigies of their victims which they then burned or crushed. The area was described as lawless and wild in the early seventeenth century, and people clung to Roman Catholicism, or were, at best, reluctant churchgoers.

One of the accused witches, a woman known as Demdike, had long had the reputation of being a local healer or 'cunning woman'; her granddaughter Alizon Device one day met a pedlar, John Law, and tried to buy some pins from him. He refused – perhaps because he mistrusted her or because he was unwilling to stop and unpack for such a small sale. As he walked away he fell, possibly having suffered a stroke, but got back to his feet and managed to reach a local alehouse. Some days later, Law laid accusations of witchcraft against Alizon, who with her mother and brother was summonsed to appear before the Justice of the Peace. Under pressure, Alizon confessed to having sold her soul to the devil and caused John Law to go lame.

Her mother Elizabeth only admitted that her own mother, Demdike, had a mark on her body that could have been left by the devil. Alizon then named Anne Whittle, known as Chattox, from another local family reputed to dabble in witchcraft. She accused Chattox of murdering four men and her own father, John Device, and claimed that the Chattox family had demanded protection payments from the Devices in return for not harming them with witchcraft. By the time they were arrested, both old women – Demdike and Chattox – were over eighty years old and blind, and both confessed to being in league with the devil. They further accused others, including Chattox's daughter Anne.

A meeting of friends and supporters of the Demdike family was held at their home, Malkin Tower – suspicious of this, the magistrates ordered the arrest of a further eight people who had been present and charged them with witchcraft. A trial was held at Lancaster Assizes, hearing testimony and evidence from a number of witnesses, including the nine-year-old sister of Alizon, Jennet Device, who testified against her sister, brother and mother, telling the court that her mother and her brother spoke to familiars in the form of dogs. She also claimed that several of the other accused had been present at the Malkin Tower meeting, despite their denials. Nine of the accused were found guilty at Lancaster, and one at York Assizes. All were hanged except for one who died during the trial, and one who was acquitted.

An account of the trial was published by Thomas Potts, the Assize Court clerk in 1613. Recently, engineers working near Pendle Hill discovered the ruins of a seventeenth-century cottage apparently buried under an earth mound. Inside the building was a sealed room with the skeleton of a cat bricked into the wall. Despite the presence of a Victorian kitchen range and pottery, it has been speculated that the building might originally have been the notorious Malkin Tower. This is unlikely to be the case, however, as this building is not old enough to be the house that Demdike's family had lived in for several generations, and it seems that in fact this is simply a small abandoned farmhouse!

The worst period of witch-hunting in England took place in 1645 with the persecutions carried out by Matthew Hopkins, who called himself the 'Witchfinder-General'. He accused thirty-five Essex women of witchcraft, nineteen of whom were hanged at a mass execution in Chelmsford. Nine other unfortunates died in gaol. The general lawlessness of the Civil War period seems to have led to an increase in persecution.

Accused witches in Europe were unlike those in Britain. Many more were male, and many were well off, while in England, most of the accused were women of lower birth aged over fifty. Many prosecutions were initiated by private people who might have seen a way to either get their hands on useful property, or to take revenge against someone who had insulted or offended them.

To identify a witch, there were several methods and procedures available and, without torture, these were essential for a successful prosecution. 'Pricking' involved finding a 'devil's mark' on the skin of the accused and sticking a knife or a pin into it. It was believed that if the person were a witch, they would feel no pain. Some professional 'prickers' were said to have used retractable blades to make it seem that the accused was in league with the devil. Another method was 'swimming' – the theory that a witch could not sink into water, especially if it had been blessed. The accused was bound, with her thumbs tied to her feet, right to left and left to right. A rope tied around the waist allowed the innocent to be pulled out before they drowned. This practice was deplored by both the civil courts and the church, but went on in rural districts.

'Watching' involved placing the witch on a stool and observing them for hours or even days to see if a familiar imp or creature would appear, coming to their aid. Finding familiars, or wax images, or implements associated with witchcraft in the person's home also provided evidence, along with the testimony of those claiming to have been bewitched. Witches were also examined to see if they had a 'devil's teat' with which they suckled their imps or familiars (Figure 23). The 'familiars' were usually the domestic pets of these poor, lonely old women – their cats and dogs and rabbits.[5]

There were ways to protect oneself against a witch. One popular English method was 'scratching'. If you scratched a witch deeply enough to draw blood, the enchantment would fail but this seems to have been a purely folk practice, frowned upon by many in authority. Another method was to make up a 'witch bottle'. Many of these have been found, often under hearths or doorsteps. The

Figure 23. A witch and her familiars from a 17th century woodcut

contents are usually urine, pins (often bent) and sometimes, pieces of cloth or hair. An example found during excavations in Reigate in Surrey dates from the early years of the eighteenth century. The corked bottle contained nine bent pins and some urine. The belief seems to have been that the urine would either 'stop' the urine of the witch, or fool the witch into believing that the bottle contained the person being bewitched. The bent pins would then trap the witch inside the bottle. Bending the pins seems to be an idea which harks back to prehistory – swords were often bent or broken to accompany a funeral, so that the spirit of the 'killed' weapon could travel along with its owner to the afterlife. In the same way, the bent pins would be able to attack the witch in the spirit world.[6]

Evidence of probable witchcraft practices has come from Cornwall, near the home of archaeologist Jacqui Wood. During an excavation to construct an experimental furnace, she came upon a buried clay floor from the Mesolithic period. At a later date, some small pits had been dug through this platform, and filled with strange items. The feathered skins of swans lay beneath piles of pebbles and birds' claws. Another larger pit was also lined with swan feathers and fifty-five eggs, some close to hatching. The bodies of magpies had been laid next to these. Carbon dating placed the pits in the period around 1640, a time when there was strong persecution of witches in Cornwall. Jacqui Wood has speculated that these pits were offering to St Brigid, the Christianised form of the Iron Age goddess of childbirth.

In a nearby pool, she found medieval pins, bits of fabric, leather and shoes, finger-nail clippings and hair, as well as part of a cauldron. Some of the fabrics must have belonged to high status people – they included brightly coloured silks and wool. The pool and another close by were lined with white quartz, and may have been thousands of years old, suggesting that this had been a place of magic for many generations. Further pits have also been found, containing odd items. One was lined with the skin of a black cat, on which were its teeth, claws and whiskers, and twenty-two eggs. In another was a dog skin, dog teeth and a pig's jaw. These last pits were much more recent – the dog pit was made in the 1950s. Did witchcraft continue here?

Piracy on the high seas

Piracy was nothing new in Early Modern Britain – pirates had been raiding the coasts and shipping since Roman times. One pirate of the era was a woman – Gráinne O'Malley. She was born around 1530, daughter of a shipowner and trader. After the death of her husband in the 1560s, she set up a base on Clare Island on the west coast of Ireland and took over a castle that her husband had taken from the Joyce clan.

Soon the city of Galway began to send complaints to the council in Dublin that her ships were stopping traders, boarding them and demanding money or their cargos in exchange for safe passage into Galway harbour. They were using strong-arm tactics, and even murder to extract their protection money. Gráinne recruited mercenaries from Ireland and Scotland, and began plundering in the Western Isles, as far south as Waterford and around northern and western Ireland. Castles and strongholds of the clans along the coasts were also attacked. She was a wealthy woman in her own right, having inherited ships, lands and stock from her father, but she seems to have relished her piratical activities.

There are many legends and stories about her exploits – how she abducted the grandson of Lord Howth because she was refused entry to his house when she came to pay a courtesy call, forcing the lord to promise always to keep his gates open and to set a place at dinner for an unexpected guest. She seized Doona Castle in revenge for the killing of her lover and followed the owners, the MacMahon clan, when they went on a pilgrimage, killing those responsible for her lover's murder. She was accused of stirring up revolts in the west of Ireland, seeing off all attempts to take her base by force. But English power was eventually too strong and in 1593, when her sons and half-brother were captured by the English governor of Connacht, Gráinne sailed to

England to beg for their release. She met the queen at Greenwich Palace and it seems the two women got along well together. Elizabeth agreed to free the prisoners as long as Gráinne promised to stop her piracy and rebellions. The queen also agreed to remove the English governor, but Gráinne's demands for the return of cattle and land allegedly stolen by the governor were not met and, before long, the governor himself was reinstated. Gráinne returned to piracy and rebellion. She died, probably, in 1603, the same year as Elizabeth. Her descendants today include the Marquess of Sligo, whose seat at Westport House contains parts of a castle and a collection of mementos of the pirate queen's life and acts.

Piracy reached new heights with the development of trade and the plundering of the new lands around the world that opened up to European interests in the sixteenth and seventeenth centuries. French, Dutch and English pirates raided the Spanish treasure galleons and bases in the Caribbean, and pirates from many nations haunted the routes around West Africa and towards India, China and the Spice Islands. There was a fine line between a pirate and a privateer – a privateer operated under a letter of marque issued by the government that allowed him to prey upon shipping of enemy countries. If caught by the enemy, he was regarded as a pirate and executed as such. The Ottoman Empire licensed the Barbary corsairs in the Mediterranean, who took 466 English merchantmen between 1609 and 1616. Sir Francis Drake was a privateer, licensed by Elizabeth I to harry the Spaniards.

However, some privateers also attacked ships of friendly nations. One such was Thomas Tew, active in the last years of the seventeenth century. He had a letter of marque from the governor of Bermuda, and Bermuda backers provided him with a ship, the *Amity,* to raid French settlements in West Africa. The story goes that he had hardly set sail before he and his crew decided to turn pirate and headed for the Red Sea to prey upon the India convoys. Their first haul amounted, reportedly, to £100,000 in gold and silver, as well as ivory, silk, spices and jewels. A second cruise in a new ship in 1694 ended badly when a Mughal ship fired upon Tew's ship *Fancy* and Tew was killed. Captain William Kidd had received a commission to hunt Tew down, not knowing that he was already dead. Kidd had been part of a pirate crew in his youth that mutinied against their captain; he had later turned more or less respectable, aiding the governor of the island of Nevis against the French. The stories about Captain Kidd are ambivalent – it is not clear to what extent he was a willing pirate or a victim of events and the actions of his crews. He had a reputation for cruelty and certainly knew many notorious pirates, such as Richard Culliford with whom he met up with again in Madagascar in 1698.

Most of Kidd's crew deserted him and went over to Culliford, leaving Kidd to return to the Caribbean with just thirteen men.

Learning that he was wanted as a pirate, Kidd scuttled his ship and headed for New York, where he believed he had influential friends. He was lured to Boston in 1699 but stopped and buried some of his treasure on Gardiner's Island on the way. The treasure was said to consist of a box of gold and two of silver, precious stones and silver tableware. Mrs Gardiner was given a bolt of gold cloth from an Arab ship captured off Madagascar and a sack of sugar, and Kidd asked the family to keep the booty safe for him. His Boston friend betrayed him and he was arrested and tried, the treasure being produced in court as evidence against him. After a year of harsh imprisonment he was sent to England, where the Tory government hoped he would implicate Whig politicians who had financed his voyages. He refused to do so, believing that these old acquaintances would save him. They did not. He was tried again by the Admiralty court, found guilty of murder and piracy, and hanged at Execution Dock in Wapping, the traditional place for the execution of pirates. His body was hung in a cage at Tilbury Point for three years, as a warning to others.

Many efforts have been made to trace the ship scuttled by Kidd in the Caribbean, the *Quedagh Merchant*. In 2007, a shipwreck was found off the coast of the Dominican Republic which is thought to be the famous pirate ship. It was lying in less than ten feet of water. Underwater archaeologists from Indiana University found anchors and many cannons, as well as pottery, weapons, coins, jewellery and other artefacts which seem to confirm its identity.

The pirates set up a number of bases in the Bahamas and Caribbean. Tortuga and Port Royal both began life as pirate ports in the middle of the seventeenth century (Plate 7). French, Dutch and English pirates inhabited Tortuga by 1640, calling themselves the 'Brethren of the Coast'. In 1645 the French governor supplied them with some 1,600 prostitutes, in the hope that this would calm the pirates down. The island changed hands between the French, Spanish and English several times. Around 1670, when it was in decline, the Tortuga pirates found a new employer – Henry Morgan, a Welsh pirate – who hired them as mercenaries for the French but they kept on with their piratical activities, and hid their booty in Tortuga.

Port Royal on Jamaica was founded in 1518; by the end of the sixteenth century, it had become an international pirate centre. Taken by the English in 1655, it grew rapidly. In 1657 the governor invited the Brethren of the Coast to make Port Royal their home port, as part of his scheme for defending the island. They preyed upon the Spanish and gained the status of privateers. They co-operated with merchants who, while trading with the Spanish colonies, also financed the attacks upon Spanish shipping. This was highly profitable for both the pirates and the merchants, and Port Royal became one of the richest towns in the Americas, its profit from privateering far exceeding the value of its legitimate sugar plantations.

Port Royal had a safe harbour conveniently sited on the shipping lanes, big enough to hold many vessels, and well defended. It also became known as the most desperate sink of iniquity in the New World. There was a great deal of debauchery, drunkenness, public disorder and excess. There was a tavern or drinking den for every ten inhabitants of the population of some 6,500 in the later seventeenth century.

As the town eventually gained more respectability, all this changed. Anti-piracy laws passed in 1687 turned Port Royal into a place of pirate execution, at Gallows Point. In June 1692, the town was hit by a massive earthquake, which destroyed most of the northern part. Excavations have revealed buildings and ships from its pirate heyday both on land and underwater. Taverns, markets and houses have been investigated. There was a wide variety of different building techniques in the pre-earthquake town. Some were built of brick, with several floors, multiple rooms and traces of businesses. Plaster and paint were used, as were decorative brickwork patterns. One excavated building seems to have housed a woodturner/cobbler and a tavern, with jugs, bottles and tankards among the finds. Other buildings were simply timber-framed shacks.

Pirate crews often organised themselves along surprisingly democratic lines. The captain and the quartermaster were elected – the captain was the fighting leader, but it was the quartermaster who dictated what prizes to take and where to sail, as well as controlling the sharing out of the booty. There was also a system of compensation relief, as each pirate paid an amount of his share into a common fund to support the injured. Nor were they as bloodthirsty as often supposed – it was more sensible to scare the target ship into surrender, which would happen more readily if the victims believed they would be spared. The image of vast quantities of pirate gold, however, is far from the truth. Mostly their loot consisted of necessities – food, water, clothing, weapons, ship's supplies, and alcohol. Apart from anything else, these items were easier to sell than jewels. The money would be shared out among the crew according to seniority and responsibilities.

Further evidence of piracy has turned up in London's East End. An excavation has found pottery from many countries including China, Germany,

Figure 24. A seventeenth century pirate ship

Portugal, Italy, Turkey and France, with Italian glassware and sixteenth-century bronze coins from Mexico, a cannon ball, and parts of a bear and a tortoise. The pottery was not export ware, and it is thought that it represents artefacts seized by pirates who made port in London and dwelt in the area. At least four privateers are known to have lived within yards of the site in the sixteenth and seventeenth centuries. The area had held timber-framed houses which were demolished in the first half of the seventeenth century and replaced with brick houses, possibly built with the wealth brought back by the privateer captains. The excavations also found remains of the food being eaten in the houses – lots of beef and fish, small amounts of pork and mutton, and some poultry, including turkey.

Marine archaeologists have found the remains of possible pirate ships around the coasts of the British Isles (Figure 24). One off West Cork held coconuts and Spanish pottery. While off the coast of Cornwall, a large armed vessel of the right period has been found that may have been the *John,* which belonged to Captain John Mucknell, the 'pirate king of Scilly', and which was run aground in 1645. As part of a fleet of around eleven ships based in the Scilly Isles, Mucknell preyed on ships in the Western Approaches, possibly supported by Charles I. However, after the king's execution, the Parliamentary forces tracked him down with warships. He ran the ship aground and escaped ashore. After the restoration of Charles II Mucknell joined the Royal Navy, received a knighthood and became a vice admiral.[7]

Another ship found off south Devon could be the remains of a Barbary corsair vessel. Found by amateur divers, it produced hundreds of gold pieces. The corsair ships raided as far north as Scotland, taking people from seaside villages and farms to be sold in the eastern Mediterranean and North Africa as slaves. One estimate suggests that, in 250 years, more than a million people from Europe were captured and enslaved. The fabric of the ship has long since disappeared, but its cargo remained on the seabed. There was a vast amount of Islamic coin struck in Morocco, the latest being dated to 1631–6, as well as jewellery and Dutch china and pipes. Much of the bullion had been chopped up, possibly to share between the pirates. It is thought the ship was a xebec, a fast, light galley rowed by slaves, with cannon at the bow and stern. Only one piece of timber was found, which is thought to be from North Africa.[8]

Smuggling as a major enterprise developed after the Black Death in the fourteenth century. The lack of surviving labour for farming was met with an increase in stock farming, particularly sheep, which required fewer men, and English wool began to command high prices in Flanders and Italy. Exports were taxed as early at the late thirteenth century, and King Edward I set up the first customs service to collect the money. Later, a tax was imposed on wine imports, and on a variety of other import and export commodities and inevitably, people went to some effort to avoid paying the taxes. Mary I also imposed taxes, and the rates kept climbing.

The customs service in its early days had no way of enforcing the tax, but by the fifteenth century, this began to change. At that time, all trade was supposed to come through one of thirteen official ports, and the customs officers were supposed to patrol the stretches of coastline in between. A controller was in charge at each port, with a collector of customs – a two-part system meant to ensure the honesty of the officials; however, they were able to make a charge when they seized smuggled goods, on production of a signed and sealed receipt. It was easy enough to issue a blank receipt and allow merchants to pay them off in return for filling in whatever they chose to declare. So many customs officers became involved in this fraud that a new post was created – the surveyor of customs, one based at each port, to monitor the others.

At least one officer, however, seems to have been exemplary – William Lowe, a 'searcher' at Poole in the mid 1400s. He was supposed to patrol the coast from Sussex, around the Solent and into Dorset on horseback. He managed to seize a large number of illicit cargos, but his greatest success came in 1452, when a Dutch ship loaded with illicit goods for export belonging to merchants from several Dorset towns fell to his diligence. He was much hated by the local merchants, and was even subjected to a knife attack by a wool merchant from London.

There were a host of other minor officials responsible for making sure ships moored where they were supposed to, and did not unload cargo out of sight of inspectors, people who checked the cargo to make sure it contained what had been declared, and people to unpack and weigh the cargos. This did little to stop the illegal export of wool, even when wool smuggling was made subject to a sentence of death in 1661 – by 1700, it has been calculated that 120,000 bales of wool were being smuggled out each year.

Kent was the county most involved in this trade, with gangs of armed men operating the illegal movements of up to 20,000 packs of wool across the Romney Marshes, and over to Calais every year. The smuggling began to badly affect the national economy. In 1671 Charles II set up a Board of Customs and financed customs cutters to patrol the coasts, and then 'riding officers' – mounted men who patrolled the shores and farms. Laws were passed controlling the sale of wool for up to fifteen miles inland. But there were only eight riding officers for the whole of the Kent coasts, to control not just the wool exports, but a rising tide of illegal imports. The smuggling ships could make a profit on both outward and homeward journeys. The navy had to be used to patrol the sea until a waterguard was established. By the end of the century, the number of riding officers had been greatly increased, although their low level of pay made them very susceptible to threats, bribery and corruption, especially as they had to live amongst the smugglers themselves in the coastal villages. Smuggling only got worse in the next century, as we shall see in the following chapter.

The fate of the 'Batavia'

Some crimes were committed far from European shores. In 1629 the Dutch East India Company ship *Batavia* struck a reef off the coast of Western Australia. Some forty people drowned out of the complement of one hundred soldiers, the crew and the three hundred passengers aboard. The rest made it ashore to a tiny island. The captain, Pelsaert, decided to take two of the ship's boats and sail north to get help, leaving 223 people to wait for rescue (Figure 25).

Among the passengers was a troublesome merchant, Jeronimus Cornelisz; as soon as the captain was gone, he decided that he and his gang would captured the rescue ships when they appeared, and in the meantime, he would

Figure 25. The massacre of the survivors of the 'Batavia' (after an illustration from the 1647 Ongeluckige voyagie, van't schip Batavia – *author unknown)*

murder the other survivors. At first, the murders were done in secret, at night or on fishing trips. The soldiers were sent to another island – he had some official authority to do so as undermerchant for the expedition. Then the killings began in earnest.

When Pelsaert returned with the rescue ships, he found that 125 people had been murdered. Some had managed to escape and join the soldiers on the neighbouring island, and with their help, Pelsaert attacked the mutineers and captured Cornelisz, initiated a trial, and executed many of the murderers along with their leader.

Archaeologists from the Western Australia Maritime Museum began to investigate findings of skeletons on the island. Earlier finds had included a teenage girl with a head wound, and two men who had been hit with a sword and an axe. A mass grave was excavated which held the remains of three adults and three children, one of whom was a small infant - the bones and un-erupted teeth from a nine-month-old baby were found in the bottom of the pit.

The archaeologists have attempted to identify these victims. It was known that one woman, Maijken Cardoes, was nursing an infant. Her body was found in a grave that contained the remains of three women that had been massacred. These included members of the family of the expedition's minister. His young daughter had been beaten to death, and his teenage maidservant had been stabbed. The captain's journal of the trial includes the testimonies of how these people had been killed. The minister's wife and six children had all been killed, with the maid, on the same day as Maijken. Many other murders are recorded – the carpenter, the gunner and a sick cabin boy amongst them. Other deaths resulted from sickness.

Speculation about the identities of the other victims in the mass grave suggest that they were Hendrik Denijs, a company official who had been beaten around the head; or Paschier van den Enden, who had been stabbed and had his throat cut; as well as Jacob Hendricxsz, the carpenter, who was killed in the same way. Hendricxsz had a bad knee, which would match one of the skeletons. The third adult may have been Jan Pinten, an English soldier, whose throat was cut on the same day. One of the children was probably the cabin boy, and the last child may have been Hilletgien Hardens, a six year old girl who had been strangled.

Unfortunately, the conditions for the survival of DNA are poor, and so far no usable material has been recovered to help confirm these assumptions. However, it is hoped that lead isotope analysis could lead to the identification of Jan Pinten, who, coming from England, would have a different pattern of isotopes from his Dutch companions.[9]

CHAPTER 7

Crime in the Age of Industry and Empire

Property crime and thief-takers

By the end of the seventeenth century, the speed and scale of growth of towns began to increase and become generally uncontrolled. Urban population levels rose sharply, and with them came more crime, disorder, riots and drunkenness. It was a period of large-scale immigration – from the countryside to the towns, and from strife-torn areas of Europe to Britain. Populations had become more mobile, more fragmented, and thus harder to control. While the revolution in industrial processes made fortunes for some, it also made paupers of a great many people, living in urban slums. Various wars also had their effects, leading some to imprisonment and execution for treason, and turning criminals into soldiers and sailors (and back again).

At the start of the period there was still no provision for organised policing. London in particular, with a population of some 600,000, was rife with crime. In theory, it was opposed by City officials such as Charles Hitchen, who became Under Marshal in 1711, having bought the appointment for £700. Hitchen's own behaviour seems to have been far from exemplary. He is reported to have accepted bribes to free criminals and to have coerced favours from male prostitutes. The Board of Aldermen found out about these activities and suspended him from his post in 1713. It was about this time that Hitchen approached Jonathan Wild, then aged around thirty, who had served prison time for debt. Wild had so ingratiated himself with his gaolers that he was permitted to accompany officers who went out to arrest thieves. Through his marriage to a prostitute who ran her own gang, he became familiar with London's underworld. In 1712 he was released from prison, and went to work as a pimp and a fence before Hitchen offered him a job as a thief-taker – a 'nice little earner' which paid £40 for each arrest made.

The rise in crime, particularly property crime, grew more threatening in the public mind because of the increasing number of daily newspapers that were being produced. Both criminals and thief-takers began to take on the role of media heroes. By 1714, the end of the War of Spanish Succession resulted in unemployed soldiers being turned out onto the streets, and a new crime wave. Despite lacking any official sanction, although Hitchen had recovered his position in that year, Wild opened an office in the Blue Boar tavern, and set himself up as a leading thief-taker.

From his office Wild, London's first organised crime boss, ran a gang of thieves. When their thefts appeared in the newspapers, he would announce that his 'thief taking agents' had recovered the goods, and claimed a reward for their return, some of which went back to the original thieves as their share. His men would 'assist' the authorities in arresting criminals – members of rival gangs or disobedient members of his own crew – claiming the bounty. In this way, Wild avoided the dangers of trying to fence the stolen goods, and could maintain a facade of apparent righteousness. A new law had made the receiving of stolen goods a crime punishable by transportation, making it harder for thieves to dispose of their loot and handing the thieves neatly into Wild's clutches. Wild also took over Hitchen's extortion business, firstly on the disgraced officer's behalf, but later as a rival.

In 1718 Hitchen published a report naming Wild as a criminal boss – Wild retaliated by publishing an account of Hitchen's homosexuality. This was enough to eliminate Hitchen and destroy his reputation permanently. To the public, Wild appeared to be a hero; he encouraged the press to print rousing stories about his battles with thieves, and people began to flock to his office to seek his assistance in recovering their property, despite Wild's introduction of a charge for his 'advice' in addition to any reward payable. He was even consulted by the Privy Council in 1720 to help to find ways to control crime. They adopted his suggestion that the fee for arresting a criminal should be increased from £40 to £140 a head!

Wild eliminated a great deal of the criminal competition in London in this way. To his extortion of public money, he added private extortion, using information gained during thefts to blackmail owners, such as evidence of homosexuality, debauchery or debt. He consorted with smugglers and employed convicts who had returned illegally from sentences of transportation.

His downfall began with the arrest of a housebreaker called Jack Sheppard, who had previously been one of Wild's gang. After a number of escapes, Sheppard was convicted of burglary and sentenced to hang. Somehow, he managed to escape from Newgate Prison's death cell but was rearrested nine days later. The next month, Wild and his men arrested Sheppard's partner, who was tried and convicted for the same burglary. This man, 'Blueskin' Blake, attacked Wild in court, inflicting a knife wound in the thief-taker's throat. Wild had to be taken for treatment by a surgeon, and during the disturbance, Sheppard managed to escape once again, even though he had been chained to the floor. Unhappily for him, he was recaptured a fortnight afterwards, and imprisoned with 300lbs weight of iron chains and shackles. Daniel Defoe wrote about him, his portrait was painted by a noted artist of the day, and upper-class society flocked to visit the prison to see him in his cell. A few days later he was hanged at Tyburn, having become a London celebrity.

Public opinion began to turn against Wild, and early in 1724 he was arrested for attempting to break one of his gang out of gaol. He carried on with his business even while in Newgate, and evidence was brought that he had stolen jewellery during the previous year's ceremony for the Knights of the Garter. One at a time, his gang began to give evidence of his crimes and methods. In the end, it was the theft of some pieces of lace from a woman called Catherine Statham that eventually saw him convicted and sentenced to death.

He attempted suicide before the hanging, but failed. Daniel Defoe has given a detailed account of the hanging on 24 May 1725, commenting on the vast crowd, many of whom had bought advance tickets for the best viewing places (Plate 8). Three other men were hanged that day before Wild, who had taken laudanum and was unconscious, was strung up. Buried temporarily, his body was later removed and sold to the Royal College of Surgeons for dissection purposes. His skeleton was preserved and is still on view in the Hunterian Museum in Lincoln's Inn Fields. A detailed account of some of Wild's dealings may be found in the pages of the Newgate calendar.[1]

The Newgate Calendar[2]
The so-called 'Bloody Code' that enacted laws demanding the death penalty for over 200 different offences was intended to deter people from crime, but it failed. Indeed, the most famous British executioner, Albert Pierrepoint, was to say in his twentieth-century memoirs, that even he did not believe that the death penalty had any effect on crime levels. It was also the case that many cases were commuted, so that only a third of the death penalties given out were actually performed. Nevertheless, during the eighteenth century, more people were hanged in London than in most European cities (Figure 26). In three years during the 1770s, there were 139 executions in London, compared with just thirty-two in Paris.[3] Eventually, the public began to lose their taste for watching the spectacle of people dying, especially when the condemned were guilty of only petty crimes.

Figure 26. Hanging outside Newgate Prison Hanging outside Newgate prison (after an early nineteenth century print)

The Newgate Calendar gives a long list of those individuals incarcerated in London's foremost prison. It is a fascinating window into the lives of Londoners during the period. There are accounts of prisoners great and small, rich and poor, innocent and guilty. John Larkin was hanged in 1700, an Irish schoolmaster who 'committed so many Forgeries and Cheats that he had not Time to confess them all before he died'; John Holliday (aka Simpson) was hanged in the same year, having been found guilty of stealing two feather beds and confessed that while a soldier in Flanders, he had crept into the King's tent and stolen £1,000, as well as robbing churches. Some crimes are shocking – the case of the Reverend Thomas Hunter who had served as chaplain and tutor in the house of a distinguished Edinburgh merchant is one such. Rev. Hunter began an illicit affair with a female servant in the house, but was seen in the act by the two young sons, his pupils. He decided they had to die to save his reputation. He took them for a walk and cut their throats in broad daylight. Spotted by a passer-by, he was quickly arrested and condemned. His only regret, he said, was that he had failed to kill the family's one surviving child, a little girl. His body was publicly gibbeted.

We can have some sympathy for Mary Channel, executed in 1703 at the age of eighteen. A clever, beautiful girl, she was married by force to a man she despised, but whose wealth had mightily impressed her father. Soon after the marriage, her husband died, apparently from poison, and Mary was convicted of his murder. She was burned alive at the stake, even though the judges themselves felt sympathy for her.

Some of the convicted were habitual criminals – Anne Harris, at twenty years old, already twice widowed by the hangman, was so notorious a shoplifter that she had been branded so many times there was nowhere left on her face for further brands, and so she was hanged. Sixteen-year old Roderick Audrey had worked up a successful scam with a trained sparrow. If caught climbing through an open window to steal, he claimed he was merely chasing his pet bird. He was imprisoned in Newgate no less than twenty times in his brief career before going to the gallows.

There are also accounts of people hanged for crimes they did not commit – including William Shaw, convicted of killing his daughter, who was later found to have committed suicide, and Captain John Massey executed for piracy although he had simply been captured by pirates and forced to accompany them until he could inform on them to the authorities. There were female gang leaders, abortionists, heretics, traitors, homosexuals, highway robbers, a female polygamist, smugglers, mutineers, rapists and resurrection men.

The 1752 Murder Act had stated that criminal corpses were to be anatomised, but there was still a shortage. The resurrection men stole dead bodies for sale to the medical colleges for purposes of dissection, and part of the official sentence for many was that, after hanging, they would be dissected. Not all hangings were efficient, however. William Duell was executed in 1740 for killing a woman during a robbery and was hanged at Tyburn. His body was taken to Surgeon's Hall to be 'anatomised'. An assistant was washing the body when it was noticed that it was breathing; Duell soon revived, was returned to Newgate prison, and subsequently had his sentence commuted to transportation.

The case of Mr Duell was not unique, and indeed posed a problem for surgeons. People in comas, or suffering from hypothermia, could appear dead, and the medical science of the day had few methods to confirm death. Surgeons had to use a variety of methods to make sure their subject had actually expired. Once they cut into the body, they were in fact killing the patient, in contravention of the Hippocratic Oath. Most surgeons believed that dissection of criminals was in the public good, but some also made a lot of money out of the process. Hanged convicts at York were often dissected by William Hey from the Leeds Infirmary. His dissections were three-day public events in front of very large crowds. He charged three pence per person on the first day, to view the laying out and preparation of the corpse; during the dissection of Mary Bateman in 1809, a woman executed for murder and witchcraft, he collected £30 from a crowd estimated at 24,000. Medical students were allowed in at a fee of half a guinea a head and tickets for one hundred gentlemen at a cost of five guineas each were sold on the second day to view the dissection proper. On the third day, he dissected the eyes and gave lectures to ladies, having removed the more gory remains. Mary Bateman's dissection was worth over £80 in total. Other surgeons made similar profits in various towns and cities.[4]

Prison as punishment

Newgate Prison was sited next door to the Old Bailey court and included debtors' wards as well as criminal accommodation. Five storeys high, it was extended in the 1720s to hold 150 inmates, and fifteen condemned cells were added. Other London gaols included the Clink, which had existed since 1161 in Southwark, and in the same borough as the Marshalsea prison. Only a small portion of the walls of the Clink survive, and there is now a Prison Museum at the site. The Marshalsea prison predominantly held debtors, as did a few other prisons in London whose traces have now disappeared.

The early eighteenth century saw a rise in the use of imprisonment as a punishment in houses of correction or 'Bridewells', named after the original hospital and prison of the banks of the River Fleet. These institutions housed petty criminals who were usually committed by Justices of the Peace and who had been arrested by the watchmen or constables, or because of complaints made by private individuals, such as the victims of thefts. A very large proportion of the inmates of the Bridewells were women, often newly arrived in the city and without means of support. The prisoners were put to hard labour, usually beating hemp, and many were also whipped as a part of their punishment. By the eighteenth century, the Bridewells were increasingly used to house prisoners awaiting trial.

As with most other prisons, which were run as private businesses, the life of the inmates depended on their wealth. Two of the wards at Newgate were reserved for those who could pay for decent food and accommodation, while all others were put into common wards. Gaolers charged for all privileges at exorbitant rates, inventing charges at will. The right to administer prisons for profit were sold to private individuals and even the royal household. Gaol fever (typhus) was rife in most prisons in Britain, and it was not unusual for a prisoner to die of the disease before they were brought to trial.

By the end of the eighteenth century, the state of prisons was causing some concern; measures were introduced to require regular inspections, money was raised for new buildings, accommodation was segregated, solitary cells were introduced, arrangements were made for work to be provided for prisoners, for religious instruction and basic medical care. Even so, conditions could be unpleasant – Tothill Fields prison in Westminster held 110 prisoners in three day rooms and seven night rooms in 1777, with no proper infirmary. Conditions in provincial gaols were often worse than in London. Prison improvements continued in the nineteenth century, fuelled in part by the notion that prison could reform criminals, specifically through putting convicts to hard labour. More and more people were sentenced to prison, and new prison buildings were built across the country. Individual cells for solitary confinement were introduced, so that prisoners could spend time in reflection on their sins and salvation. Conditions were improved, especially hygiene, to reduce the spread of disease within prisons, and more work was provided to keep the inmates busy.

In recent years, a number of archaeological excavations have looked for traces of the prisons from this era in Britain, the USA, Ireland and Australia in particular. Examples include the gaols of Oxford where foundations and walls of the late eighteenth century rebuild of the castle prison were unearthed. The central structure and its two wings were sited next to the castle motte, and a number of burials were found at the gallows site, including some showing evidence of being subjected to dissection by members of the university. Another Oxford prison, the Bocardo, which was an octagonal building surrounded by a six metre high wall, was built in around 1789.

Lincoln Castle gaol was rebuilt to accommodate the 'separate system' in the early nineteenth century. This was a regime which aimed to keep each inmate remote from any human contact, locked in a solitary cell, allowed no conversation with other inmates, and when brought out of the cell for any purpose, including attending church services in the prison chapel, being made to wear a hood which concealed their identity. According to Charles Dickens, in *David Copperfield*, this had the effect of *'the reduction of prisoners to a wholesome state of mind, leading to sincere contrition and repentance.'* Lincoln is the best surviving example of a 'separate system' prison, with its chapel, cells and exercise yards, and may be visited today.

Pentonville Prison was the first in Britain purpose-built to house the 'separate system' in 1842, with radiating wings from a central hub typical of this style (Figure 27). The human cost of the isolation policy pursued in the 'separate system' was high – large numbers of prisoners went insane, suffered

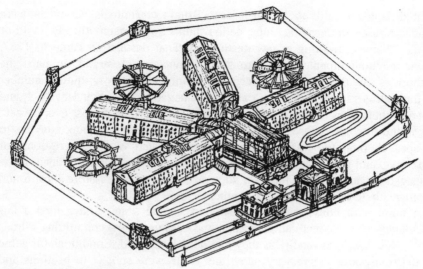

Figure 27. Plan of Pentonville Prison 1840–42, designed to facilitate the 'separate system' (After: Plan by Joshua Jebb, 1844)

delusions or committed suicide. However, it was not until the end of the century that there was a general move towards less stringent prison conditions.

At York Castle Museum, a former prisoners' yard is being recreated; the yard originally had a low wall topped by railings, to allow the citizens to come to stare at the convicts.

An American colonial prison in York County, Massachusetts, succeeded earlier structures in 1729. A stone building was added to on a number of occasions, with a wooden gaoler's house and kitchen for preparing the prisoners' food, and an extra wing. A second storey was added during refurbishments in 1763. This allowed felons to be held separately from debtors. The gaoler was a deputy sheriff, who looked after an average of fourteen prisoners a year, but more just before the court sessions. A total of 1,053 prisoners are recorded between 1788 and 1860, male and female. Burials covered with lime were found at the rear of the buildings. Study of the food remains seems to indicate that it was the gaoler's wife who prepared the meals for the prisoners, and that they ate very similar food to the gaoler and his own family – plain but healthy.[5]

Transportation to the American Colonies as a form of punishment continued through much of the eighteenth century, until the American Declaration of Independence in 1776, when it was made clear that the new

United States would no longer accept Britain's criminals. Convicts were instead housed in decaying ships, called 'hulks', at Portsmouth, Plymouth or in the Thames, awaiting a new destination. That destination came in 1787, when the government decided to send convicts to Australia. In part, the authorities saw this as a more acceptable destination anyway; quite a number of transportees to the American colonies managed to find their way back and re-enter their lives of crime. Ships' captains were bribed almost every week, according to some records, allowing a goodly traffic of returning convicts to escape, despite the many advertisements posted with descriptions of runaways, and the rewards offered for their capture and return. Indeed, some managed to do no more than set foot on American soil before they found another ship to take them back to England again.

A number of convicts were transported several times, and gained a fair knowledge of the American landscape and escape routes, committing crimes in the New World as readily as they had done in the Old. Conditions for some of the transportees were very harsh and some were subject to beatings and misuse, although hard labour in the fields became less common after the start of the importation of black slaves. Even children were sentenced to terms as indentured servants; a common duration period was still seven years. Although called servants, in real terms these people were slaves. The arriving convicts were sold off at the docks, and often either arrived sick as a result of conditions in prison or on the transport ships, or fell victim to new diseases and dangers presented by the strange surroundings. Some masters made sure they extracted the last ounce of work and strength from their workers before their term of servitude expired, setting them to back-breaking tasks such as clearing land of rocks and trees by hand. On the other hand, many settlers resented the arrival of the convicts, who brought not only disease, but crime and dissolution with them, and the transportation issue became one of the triggers for the American War of Independence.

The early days of transportation to Australia, between the 1780s and 1830s, have been revealed by excavations in The Rocks area of Sydney. The first arrivals in 1788 included 717 convicts among some 1,000 passengers. Government and administration buildings and homes were built on the east side of the creek in the bay; convicts were sent to the west side. There was little supervision or control over convict activities in the early days. The convicts moved into the area, built wattle-and-daub huts, and started up businesses and farms wherever they wished. Many businesses and trades became established, although there was also a fairly large shifting population. Forty-two houses have been excavated, and three-quarters of a million artefacts found. By the end of the first decade of the nineteenth century, much more substantial houses were being built of stone by the convict settlers, surrounded by large yards. A wide variety of trades and services is recorded, and there were many children living there, whose toys were also found. Until about 1820 when road-gangs and distant penal stations were introduced, the convict settlement was 'free on the land', with none of the usual accoutrements of a prison. Most of the inhabitants were fairly young, many with useful skills and trades, and with a surprisingly high literacy rate of seventy-five per cent. An account by a surgeon in 1827 tells of the clean, agreeable accommodations, with whitewashed walls, comfortable furniture, pristine tablecloths and gleaming dinner services. There were curtains at the windows, mirrors and prints on the walls, and fine ceramics on the tables including Spode transfer-printed wares and Chinese export porcelain.

The houses were not arranged in ordered streets, but set up wherever the owner wished, most facing the sea, and the houses were frequently extended in an unplanned manner. New rooms were tacked on as the need arose. The artefact distribution suggests that many rooms lacked a defined purpose, being multi-functional, inner and outer rooms being accessed only through each other. The yards held cisterns or wells, and gardens – by 1800 the people there were growing peas and beans, turnips and cabbages, mustard, watercress and radishes, and also introducing English weeds such as dandelions, clover, chickweed and nettles. Lemon, apple and peach trees were planted. The yards were surrounded by privet hedges or paling fences. Cows, sheep, pigs, dogs and chickens were kept.

Many women earned money by doing domestic chores or through cottage industries. Margaret Byrne was probably a seamstress – some of her sewing equipment had slipped between the floorboards, to be discovered beneath, along with a number of the marbles her children had played with.

Food remains show that forty per cent of the meat eaten was mutton, twenty-five per cent beef, and the rest pork, goat, chicken or fish, with large numbers of oysters. Tea, coffee, sugar and cheese were also available. There was also plenty of evidence for alcohol consumption, including the remains of what may have been an illicit still.[6]

Somewhat later, conditions for convicts in Australia became much more regulated, and indeed brutal. Work on road gangs meant constantly toiling in heat wearing heavy leg-irons, and receiving up to fifty lashes a time for transgressions. Notorious harsh penal stations were set up in more distant locations such as Port Arthur in Tasmania for repeat offenders or 'hard cases'. About twenty per cent of the convicts were women, and for these, factories were created in order to put them to useful work. One of these was the Ross Female Factory in Tasmania, where the nursery has been excavated. About 12,000 female convicts were sent to Tasmania between 1803 and 1854. The women were put to work making convict uniforms, while their children were confined to the nursery. The regulations stated that the mothers were officially only allowed to have contact with their children while breast-feeding them. At three years old, the children were removed to an Orphan School in Hobart, some seventy miles away.

Evidence from the archaeological excavations has produced some lead cloth seals, fragments of cloth, thimbles, buttons, pins and needles in the nursery. These finds suggest that the Superintendent, Dr Swarbeck Hall, thought to be a strict disciplinarian, might have allowed the women to do their work in the company of their children, in contravention of the regulations. It also seems that, on completion of their sentence, the Governor assisted the women to find work near to where their children were being kept. This offers a glimpse of a more humane regime than official records suggest, a level of kindness that was never formally recognised.[7]

Near Cork in Southern Ireland, a fort from the Napoleonic era was converted in 1847 to a prison, during the peak of the Great Famine. Levels of public disorder caused by the famine had led to a government need to contain more prisoners. The gaol was designed to hold prisoners who were to be transported to Bermuda and Australia. As well as convicts, political prisoners were held there. The death toll at Spike Island prison was high – over 1,000 in its thirty-six-year history. The prison was purpose-built, its architecture reflecting current thinking on penal incarceration. An archaeological project begun in 2012 is studying how the artefacts can illuminate the relationships between the prison warders and the convicts, the health and fitness of the prisoners, and the labour to which they were put, toiling to build the naval docks and military structures which still survive today.

Most smaller towns and villages in Britain had a lock-up – a place to hold prisoners awaiting trial, or for short-term incarceration for minor offences. Many of these buildings still survive. One of the few to still exist in London is in Cannon Lane, NW3, which dates from 1730. Another fine example is in Bradwell-on-Sea. This was built in 1817, of red brick, and cost £3 10s. 9d. It could hold six prisoners inside, with a further five places outside attached to the pillory beside the door. The pillory has a number of rings, one of which is sited low enough to accommodate child prisoners. There is also a whipping post attached to the door jamb.

Other forms of punishment included fines, branding, the pillory, and whipping. Branding was first done on the face, but later on the thumb, with a T for a thief, an F for a felon, or M for murderer. Punishment was designed to make public the shame of the criminal and every town had its pillory and whipping post. Time spent in the pillory was generally fairly short – an hour or so – but even so, the rain of missiles thrown by the crowd sometimes proved fatal, and pillorying proved to be a source of riot and public disorder and the practice was progressively discontinued. Whipping, which actually remained a legal punishment until 1948, was now carried out behind prison walls rather than in public. As with executions, the public appetite for these spectacles was waning.

The new police
As the nineteenth century began, fewer crimes were punished with the death sentence – only the most serious offences were still capital crimes after 1861, although sections of society, particularly the established church, continued to robustly defend the death penalty. Executions now took place inside the prisons, attended by officials and a chaplain. In 1790 burning was abolished, and in 1820, the last sentence of drawing and quartering was handed down, although in the event the convicts (the Cato Street conspirators) were merely decapitated.

The problem of policing remained; the system of constables and watchmen was clearly insufficient, especially in the rapidly growing industrial towns and larger cities. In 1749, the author and magistrate Henry Fielding founded a force of six officers, who became known as the Bow Street Runners. Unlike Jonathan Wild and his ilk, the force was formally attached to the Bow Street magistrates, and was paid from government funds. On the authority of the magistrates, they gathered information and arrested criminals; the men were trained for the work so that they were familiar with the law. Later, mounted officers were added to the force. Under the direction of Fielding's blind brother John, a register of crimes was compiled, and information about crimes, stolen goods and wanted felons was published – a move that led to the founding of the Police Gazette. To their earlier duties was added the role of street patrols as a step towards crime prevention. By 1797 there were sixty-eight men in the force. Similar groups began to be set up across London from 1792. By the 1820s, however, they were in decline, with suspicions of corruption leading to a public loss of trust in their honesty, and the force was disbanded in 1839.

Horrors such as the Ratcliffe Highway murders in 1811 fuelled the desire for better policing in the capital. In 1829 the Home Secretary, Sir Robert Peel, passed the Metropolitan Police Act, founding London's first official police force, which superseded the Bow Street Runners, magistrates' constables and the river police. They moved into headquarters at Scotland Yard, close to the Thames. In 1839 the separate City of London Police force was set up. The 'Met' had an initial complement of 895 constables, 88 sergeants, 20 inspectors and 8 superintendents. Seventeen police divisions were created covering a seven mile radius from Charing Cross, with others following later. Recruits had to be under thirty-five years of age, healthy and strong, at least 5ft 7in tall, able to read and write, and with good characters. By 1874 there were nearly 10,000 police officers in London. The County Police Act of 1839 allowed the establishment of similar forces across the country.[8]

The Metropolitan Police carried no weapons, but attacks on officers led to the issue of firearms, which were only to be used at the discretion of senior officers. Cutlasses were issued to some officers involved in guard duties.[9] They wore a distinctive blue uniform to distinguish them from red-coated military police, which consisted of a blue tailed coat with a high collar to prevent the officer from being garrotted, white trousers in summer, dark ones in winter, and a cane-reinforced top hat which was strong enough to stand on. White bars on the sleeves of the coats helped to distinguish police officers from naval personnel. Officers were given a rattle with which to call for assistance, and a truncheon, while senior officers carried swords. A whistle replaced the rattle after a while. The coat was replaced with a tunic in 1863, and the archetypal policeman's helmet was introduced (Plate 9).

It was a terrible murder that led to the creation of a detective department in 1842. In April of that year, Daniel Good, a Wandsworth coachman, who lived in the stables where he worked, killed his common-law wife, dismembered her body and tried to dispose of the pieces by burning them. A little later, he stole a pair of trousers from a pawnbroker, who informed a constable. PC Gardiner went to Good's house to conduct a search for the stolen trousers. PC Gardiner saw something that he first thought to be the body of a pig or goose, but then realised was a female torso, partially burned. Good made a run for it, locking the constable inside the stable.

The Metropolitan Police searched everywhere for the murderer for ten days, but he had escaped to Kent. It was there that a former constable from the Wandsworth District recognised him, having read about the case in the local newspaper. Good was arrested, tried, and executed at Newgate in May.

The whole business was very embarrassing for the police. A murder suspect had got away from them, and was only caught by the lucky chance of a civilian, albeit ex-police, being alert. The press had a field day, pillorying the police force. The response of the Police Commissioners was to set up the first centralised detective force in the country, consisting of two inspectors and six sergeants, with a small number of constables.

The detective branch's remit was serious crimes, particularly murders. The freedom of movement that detectives enjoyed, as opposed to constables following a prescribed 'beat', enabled them to investigate and pursue criminals more effectively. They used informers and contacts in the criminal underworld. They also undertook political inquiries, fraud cases, protection duties for diplomatic and political figures, private investigations for individuals, and surveillance of possible foreign terrorists. The detective force provided a rich seam of material for novelists such as Charles Dickens and Wilkie Collins, whose sympathetic portrayal of the officers did much to create a very positive public impression.[10]

Improvements to policing in the city took time to have an effect in more rural districts. Highway robbery, petty theft, and assaults were common and hard to deal with when miles of countryside and forest offered sanctuary to criminals. For example, the majority of Surrey crimes that were successfully prosecuted were those which occurred in the South London districts, rather than those in more remote parishes. Two famous and much reported murder cases in Surrey did result in convictions. The first is commemorated today by a headstone set up in Thursley churchyard.

In 1786, a sailor, whose name was never discovered, stopped at the Red Lion pub in Thursley. He fell to talking to, and buying drinks for, some men he met there, and offered to help them on their way across the Devil's Punchbowl, a well-known local valley, towards Hindhead and the road to Portsmouth, where they claimed to have berths waiting them aboard ships. The young sailor's body was found naked, mutilated, and almost decapitated, where the robbers and murderers had pushed him down the side of the Punchbowl. Locals had seen the crime, and the felons were soon taken up. They pleaded guilty at the assizes in Kingston upon Thames, executed, and their bodies tarred and displayed on the gibbet for many years at Hindhead.

The second notorious Surrey case took place in 1817. A customer entering the Godalming shoemaker's shop of Mr George Chennel found the elderly housekeeper lying with her throat cut on the floor, partially blocking the door. Calling in some neighbours to help, the customer and several others climbed the stairs and discovered Mr Chennel's body in his bed, his throat almost severed through, and with bruises suggesting that he had put up a fight in his defence. From the temperature of the bodies, the witnesses believed that the assaults must have been committed on the previous night. A hammer found next to Mr Chennel's body appeared to be one of the murder weapons.

The magistrates were informed straight away and began an investigation. Suspicion fell upon Mr Chennel's son, also George, who was arrested at his home a little distance away on suspicion of being involved in the crime. He claimed to have been drinking in a nearby public house that night, although he had disappeared for a short period between nine and ten o'clock. He was said to have been a dissolute character whose habits had greatly distressed his father. The coroner's inquest the next day found that the murders had been committed by 'a person or persons unknown'.

Suspicion also began to fall on a man called Chalcraft, who had been employed by the elder Mr Chennel as a carrier, was a known associate of the younger Mr Chennel, and who also had a bad reputation. The magistrates worked to put together sufficient evidence to arraign Chalcraft and the son, until eventually they were brought to trial in 1818 at Guildford Assizes. The two men were charged with both murders, their motive being the not inconsiderable property owned by Mr Chennel senior. The evidence against Chalcraft rested on the fact that, on going to Mr Chennel's house the morning after the murder as would be usual, he apparently failed to notice the dead housekeeper, although he would have had to step over her body, and that he told the neighbours that Mr Chennel was murdered upstairs before his body was found. A search of the younger Chennel's goods found two one-pound banknotes, one with bloodstains on it. The son claimed they had been a gift from his father the previous morning, but witness said that in the evening of the same day he was unable to pay a bill of a few pennies. However, after ten o'clock in the evening he went back into the pub and spent profusely. Witnesses had seen both men in the street together at half past nine, despite their claims that they had not seen each other that evening. Much further evidence was produced, including bloodspots on clothing, remarks made by the accused, their characters, their finances and their associates.

The trial was lengthy – a very full account of it can be found in the pages of the Newgate Calendar. The jury brought in a unanimous verdict of guilty, although both men continued to protest their innocence; Chennel in particular was noted for his apparent indifference towards the crime and to the sentence. On the day of execution, they were taken from Guildford to Godalming, through immense crowds who had gathered along the roads, and hanged on a gallows set up in a field north of the town. After an hour, their bodies were cut down and handed to two surgeons for dissection. The procession set off through Godalming and stopped at the house of the victims, where the bodies of the hanged men were brought inside. The surgeons opened the bodies for dissection there, in the kitchen, on the spot where the housekeeper's corpse had been found. 'Thousands' of people rushed in to see the event. Later, evidence came to light that Chalcraft may have been implicated in an earlier murder at Petersfield, and that both may have been involved in one at Farnham, where the murder weapon was found to be one of Mr Chennel senior's working knives.[11]

These cases were unusual in that the penalties were enacted at the place of the crime. Normally, Surrey murderers would be executed on the roof of the gatehouse of the county gaol in Horsemonger Lane, Southwark. Gibbets were at one time a common sight in the countryside, set up at crossroads or other well-frequented places, where the sight of the decaying corpse of a hanged felon might serve to dissuade others from a life of crime. One such stood by a lane on the edge of Saxilby Moor, near Doddington, holding the remains of a man called Thomas Temporell (or Tom Otter), who had been executed in 1806 in Lincoln for the murder of his young wife on the day of their marriage. He had been forced into the marriage by the parish authorities because the young woman claimed he was the father of her unborn child. Neither man nor wife were literate – the parish register shows their marks instead, and the witnesses were parish constables. After the ceremony the pair went towards Lincoln, and later along the road to Saxilby, but the next morning the body of the wife was found in a ditch. Temporell was arrested, tried and hanged, having confessed to the crime. He already had a wife and child living in Southwell.

His body was taken to be hung in irons on a thirty-foot-high gibbet close to where the body had been found; the occasion was celebrated by the locals who erected stalls and made merry at the site. The gibbet stood until 1850 when it was blown down in a storm, having been weakened by souvenir-hunters cutting pieces off. The remains of the gibbet were eventually taken by a local doctor to be made into a chair. A part of the iron gibbet cage is now preserved at Doddington Hall.[12]

Many 'Gibbet Hills' can be found across the country, as well as in the US and Canada; a few have replica gibbet posts still standing, such as Combe Gibbet in Berkshire. Gibbet irons are also preserved in a number of places, including in Quebec, Kingston in Jamaica, Leicester, and Rye in Sussex. No two are exactly alike, having been made by a local blacksmith as occasion demanded.

There are also many places which record the presence of a gallows, as mentioned earlier, from the famous site of Tyburn Tree (Figure 28), near Marble Arch to Gallows Hill, Barnard Castle, and Gallows Hill, Salem, Massachusetts.

In 1992 archaeologists in Williamsburg, North Carolina, found the remains of a large triangular gallows about a mile away from the town's gaol. It was

Figure 28. Executions at Tyburn from a seventeenth century illustration

intended as a copy of the famous Tyburn 'Triple Tree', with each arm eleven feet long, to accommodate mass hangings. It was sited in a very visible place with easy access. Many artefacts dating from the eighteenth century were found at the base of the structure, including coins. The researchers believe that this was the gallows upon which up to thirteen members of the crew of the pirate Blackbeard were hanged in 1719. The famous pirate himself had died the year previously in a battle with HMS *Pearl*, and the Navy vessel had sailed back into harbour with Blackbeard's head hanging from the bowsprit. There are no records of the trial and executions, and it is unclear how many of the accused were actually hanged, or where the executions took place. One theory suggests some of the men had received a Royal Pardon.

In the 1980s, archaeologists found the burial of a man nearby at the former Customhouse Point. He was buried face down between high and low water marks, a local custom for the disposal of buccaneers and pirates. Local legend says Blackbeard's head was displayed on a stake nearby.

Pirates and smugglers

Piracy continued to be a problem well into the eighteenth century. Two of the most infamous were women – Anne Bonny and Mary Read. A certain Captain Charles Johnson (who was probably, in reality, Daniel Defoe) wrote a number of accounts of pirates of the day in 1724, entitled *A General History of the Robberies and Murders of the Most Notorious Pyrates*. According to this document, Bonny was born illegitimately in Ireland around 1698. Her father, to avoid a scandal, pretended she was a child of a relative, and dressed her as a boy. The family emigrated to South Carolina; teenage Anne was a problem child, reportedly badly beating a would-be rapist and murdering a maid with a knife. She was promiscuous and frequented taverns, and, when this began to affect his business, her father disowned her. In 1718 she married an impecunious sailor and left with him for Nassau in the Bahamas, where her husband James Bonny acted as a 'grass' for the governor, informing on pirates for the bounty.

Anne continued drinking and being promiscuous, and fell in love with a notorious pirate, Calico Jack Rackam. She left her husband and joined Rackam's crew. Although she dressed as a woman most of the time, when Rackam attacked a ship she donned breeches and armed herself with a brace of pistols.

It seems that Rackam attacked and took Mary Read's ship in the Caribbean, and took Mary prisoner. Anne tried to seduce her, thinking she was a man, presumably because Mary had also taken to wearing men's clothes. Mary admitted her true gender and the two women became friends. Mary had also been born illegitimate and had been dressed as a boy, for similar reasons to Anne. Mary had joined the Royal Navy at the age of thirteen as a 'powder monkey', one of the boys who ran between the powder magazine and the guns to bring ammunition to the gun crews during an engagement.

There were often a number of women aboard naval ships – some legitimately as wives of the warrant officers, but a number also in disguise. They joined for a number of reasons – to follow husbands or lovers who had been press-ganged, to escape from a stultifying home life, to experience the freedom and adventure only available in that era to men, or for sexual satisfaction. Some were very successful in avoiding the exposure of their true gender. Mary Anne Talbot joined the Navy in 1792 to follow her lover. When he died at sea, she remained with the crew as 'John Taylor' until wounded and captured by the French. When released, the Navy tried to press her back into service, at which time she finally revealed her true identity.

Mary Read then joined the army in Flanders, but resigned when her lover threatened her secret. She married him, but he died soon afterwards. She then took to wearing men's clothing again and sailed for the West Indies on the ship which was captured by the pirates. Believing her to be a man, they urged her to join them. A hard-drinking, cursing, aggressive person, no-one suspected her of being female, until she revealed herself to Anne and Rackam. The two women fitted in with the rest of the crew, undertaking the same tasks and fighting side by side. The cruise was a very successful one, and Anne and Mary led their own raids against schooners.

Some time later, one midnight, vessels from the Governor's fleet crept up on the pirate ship. Anne and Mary saw the danger and called for help, but most of the crew were dead drunk, and only Rackam was sober enough to open fire with a swivel gun. This was met with an explosion of gunfire from the official vessels and most of the pirate crew fled belowdecks. Rackam decided to surrender, but the women were not having it. They shot at the governor's men and brandished their cutlasses. Without support from the rest of the pirates, however, they were soon overpowered. Rackam was tried and condemned, and asked to see Anne before he was hanged. She berated him for his cowardice, blaming him and the other men for their capture, saying 'If you had fought like a man, you need not have been hang'd like a dog.' Ten days later, at the Admiralty Court in Jamaica, she and Mary pleaded not guilty, but were sentenced to be hanged. The executions were postponed, as both women had become pregnant (probably for this purpose). Mary died in prison, but Anne disappeared. It is believed that her father spirited her away to Charleston, where she later married and went on to live to a ripe old age.[14]

The myth of pirate treasure is, in most instances, just that – a myth. When pirates got hold of money, they usually spent it on prostitutes, rum or more prosaic needs. A persistent story, however, relates to Blackbeard's ship, the *Queen Anne's Revenge*. In 1996, a wreck was found in shallow waters off North Carolina. The finds that have been recovered are suggesting that this wreck was Blackbeard's famous ship, which ran aground in 1718.

Work is being carried out on the identification, cleaning and conservation of the finds, including the long six-pounder cannons and other objects unidentifiable under a thick crust of corrosion. No treasure has yet been found. Edward Teach, aka Blackbeard, was probably born in Bristol around 1680 (Figure 29). Fetching up in the West Indies, he is first recorded in Nassau in 1716, as part of the crew of a pirate called Benjamin Hornigold. He seems to have become master of his own sloop under Hornigold's direction, and the two raided shipping around the Bahamas. The capture of another pirate ship, the *Revenge*, brought the pirate fleet to three, with Teach now captain of the new prize. Hornigold's reluctance to attack British ships led to a break between the two men and their crews.

Teach continued to raid shipping, taking a 300-ton, armed French slaver and merchantman, *La Concorde* from St. Malo, in 1717. Teach took over this ship and renamed it *Queen Anne's Revenge*. More ships and crews were added to his fleet over the next few months, as he attacked vessels across the

Figure 29. Blackbeard (after Benjamin Cole's illustration in A General History of the Pyrates, *1724*

Caribbean. He regularly ransacked these ships, but there are no records of any deaths or injuries being suffered by their crews, who were usually set ashore soon after. Early in 1718, naval vessels began to combine in a search for Teach, whose fleet was now very large. Teach named himself commodore, and in May 1718 took his force to blockade Charleston, stopping and raiding every ship that tried to enter or leave the harbour, holding several prominent citizens hostage. He demanded medical supplies in return for their lives. These were provided and the hostages released.

Then Teach heard of the imminent arrival of several men-of-war sent from England to capture pirates. He took his fleet north into a concealed inlet in North Carolina, where *Queen Anne's Revenge* ran aground on a sandbar, possibly deliberately as it was too big to navigate those waters. The ship was stripped and Teach abandoned most of his crew, in the hope of a royal pardon which had been issued for those pirates who surrendered before a certain date. He was granted this in June. But he returned to his piratical ways and was finally overcome in a battle in November on 1718 with ships commanded by Lieutenant Robert Maynard of HMS *Pearl*. Maynard hung Blackbeard's head from the bowsprit and sailed back to collect the reward.

The finds made in the wreck included many turtle bones, some sprinklings of gold dust, a signal gun, loaded cannons, lead shot, scrap iron and glass in bags which was probably used as shrapnel shot, medical equipment and window glass. A sword hilt has also been recovered, as well as slave manacles, objects engraved with a fleur-de-lis and African glass trade beads, which may relate to the ship's earlier existence as a French slaveship. All the finds date from the period just before 1718. There are no definitive pieces of evidence, but the size of the ship, its location, and the large amount of armaments point to its being Blackbeard's flagship. Further ongoing work including analysis of biological remains may help to confirm this, if some of these prove to have an African origin.[14]

Another form of maritime crime that was rife in the eighteenth and early nineteenth centuries was smuggling. Right across the southern coastal counties of England, smuggling began to be a major industry. Vast quantities of spirits and other goods were illegally imported (the price of gin being so low that it was claimed some Kentish villagers used it for cleaning windows). Up to fifty per cent of all the brandy drunk in England was said to have been smuggled. In some places, smuggling was the only employment for most of the population – in the Scilly Isles, for example. The stimulus for the massive increase in illicit trade was the level of taxation and excise duty. The government was in urgent need of money to fund the war against the American colonies and their French and Spanish allies, and raising taxes on imports became an essential part of national economic strategy. Some commodities, such as tea, were carrying such heavy rates of duty that they were unaffordable for most of the population, and the tax on salt was especially hard to bear for fishing communities who needed salt to preserve their catches. The machinery for collecting the taxes was cumbersome and inefficient – and enterprising people soon saw ways to get round the officials. The multitude of small fishing and trading boats and ships around the coasts of Britain, Holland and the Low Countries, and France, with their experienced crews, their vessels and their intimate knowledge of the coasts were well-placed to engage in contraband activities. Knowledge of the massive profits to be made encouraged many erstwhile colliers and fishing boats to join the 'trade' – most commodities could be sold on for between 200-400 per cent profit.

These men were ably supported by the rural populations inland. This was a time of great rural poverty. Enclosures of common land, especially woodland, had forced many people to the edge of starvation. They could no longer pasture a cow or two, or keep a few pigs, or gather fuel to supplement their diets or keep them warm. Much woodland, which had previously been a source of extra food and materials for the poor, was being destroyed for shipbuilding and charcoal burning to fuel the iron and gunpowder industries.

The profits to be made helping to 'run' smuggled cargo to the customers in towns vastly exceeded what could be earned legitimately – perhaps equalling a week's wage for a night's work — and hundreds of men and women became involved in moving and hiding the cargos.

Shares might be sold locally to finance a trip, involving whole communities; people with a vested interest in the goods such as publicans and wine merchants might also put up the money to fund the venture. In the South-East, London and other urban areas merchants became involved in the financing of smuggling to a greater extent than in the more remote parts of the West Country. There is a strong suspicion that other individuals also put up the money as a form of speculation, some of whom may have been very highly placed and outwardly respectable citizens, not only in the coastal towns but also in the cities. Foreign suppliers might also finance trips to ensure the market for their gin or brandy, in some cases providing their own vessels for the job.

Large gangs were operating in parts of the country by the mid-eighteenth century – in East Sussex, in Suffolk and elsewhere — some of which were hundreds strong and renowned for their violence.

Agents across the Channel arranged for the cargos to be embarked, to be carried to a rendezvous and transhipped to the waiting smugglers' small and nimble fore-and-aft rigged boats and ships, from places such as Lorient, Calais, Dieppe, Roscoff and Vlissengen. The French government encouraged the trade, which provided export income. Efforts were made to pack the goods into smaller containers than those used for legitimate trade, because the exporters were well aware of the means by which the goods would be distributed once they were landed in England. Small barrels or half-anker tubs weighing about half a hundredweight each contained tea or spirits, slung in roped pairs that could be carried by one man, or slung across the back of a mule or pony. The spirits were supplied over-proof, to save space, and were to be diluted and flavoured when delivered. Over time, more and more ingenious ways were employed to conceal cargos – false bottoms, tobacco disguised as ropes and so on.

As the trade developed, larger ships were employed, often designed to very high standards, and usually much better built than the vessels employed by the revenue agents. Many were armed with small cannons. The smugglers were faster, stronger and better seamen than the typical revenue crews, and they had stronger motivation to succeed. The only other defence the authorities had was the shore-based riding officers, who stood little chance of being able to intercept a cargo being landed, or to be able to face-off a large number of

Figure 30. Graffito on a ship on a wall at Brighstone, Isle of Wight

armed men, although some brave souls tried, and in some cases lost their lives doing so.

Gangs, sometimes of several hundred men and women, with 'tub-men' who carried the barrels and packages, accompanied by guards, would move the contraband off the beach as quickly as they could to waiting ponies and horses to start the trek inland. Many hiding places were used to conceal contraband – caves, dunes, and tunnels were used, such as the one at Hayle in Cornwall which ran for several hundred yards and can still be seen. Tightly sealed barrels could be submerged with a floating marker or in a known location for later recovery. Other hiding places included table tombs in churchyards, like those of Chale and Niton, and the belfry of Freshwater church on the Isle of Wight. In the village of Brighstone, south-west of Newport, a number of houses have carvings scratched into the chalk walls, depicting sailing ships and other symbols (Figure 30). Local legend says these indicated safe houses where smugglers could offload their goods.

The roads and lanes used to bring contraband up from the south coast were dotted with farmhouses and cottages with secret cellars, and some towns were notorious as centres for the collection and distribution of smuggled silk and tobacco, brandy and lace, with the locals actively protecting the smugglers from the revenue men. Dorking's caves were probably used to hide goods brought over the hidden tracks that crossed Holmwood Common, and the town was the scene of a trick that trapped revenue men in a pub yard, allowing the smugglers and their goods to escape.

Various attempts were made by the government to control the 'free trade', including the introduction of more and more severe penalties and some temporary tax cuts, but with minimal success. In Cornwall, attempts to prosecute smugglers often failed – no Cornish jury was going to convict fellow countrymen on behalf of the distant and 'foreign' government in London! All that happened was that matters grew ever more violent. Millions of pounds of revenue were being lost. A series of wars reduced the number of troops available to combat the smugglers, and of course raised demand for smuggled goods.

The wars against Revolutionary France between 1792 and 1815 provided even more opportunities for the smuggling community, coupled with the activities of spies from both sides. Napoleon was desperate for money to pay his troops, and the transfer of gold across the Channel was assisted by the use of 'free trade' shipping. Patriotic smugglers used their connections to pass information to the Royal Navy and helped French aristocrats to escape the Terror; others assisted French prisoners of war to escape and return home.

New, faster, revenue cutters were commissioned, and began to have an effect. The victory at Trafalgar in 1805 cleared the seas of much French shipping, and permitted more resources to be transferred to the Revenue Service. The Channel Islands closed their free ports, cutting off a major source of supply for the smugglers of the West Country. Napoleon declared Roscoff to be a free port in an attempt to encourage the smuggling to continue in Brittany; for him, this was an important avenue for both profit for French suppliers, and for his spies to gain information from 'perfidious Albion'.

The construction of defences against a French invasion along the south-east coast, such as the Martello towers and the Royal Military Canal, made smuggling more difficult, as did the co-ordination of the revenue forces and the increase of officers' pay. At the end of the war, the Martello towers were used to house squads of preventative men in the Waterguard division. Blockades of the coast substantially reduced the amount of smuggling, as did the introduction of a comprehensive coastguard service. The rise of Methodism in the West Country began to erode public support for illegal trade too, and with the development of the tin and other mines in that part of the country, there was more legal work available for local people. Smuggling became a more clandestine and dangerous business. The introduction of a free trade system in the 1840s as a result of the burgeoning industrial economy effectively destroyed the profits of the 'free trade', and it largely died out.

One last avenue for profit remained for the old smugglers – they began to write and publish a series of luridly exciting tales of their former lives and activities, which became immensely popular and in no small way helped to found the tourist industry of Devon and Cornwall.[15]

CHAPTER 8

Victorian and Edwardian crime

Changes in society

Social changes in the nineteenth century began to alter the public perception of both crime and punishment. Many towns, such as London, had 'rookeries' – ramshackle areas of poor, crowded housing, dissected by dark, narrow alleys, where criminals could be more or less sure of support and concealment. Areas such as Clerkenwell, Pentonville and St. Luke's in London were places the police did not dare enter. People lived in cheap lodging houses or squatted, sometimes several families at a time, in cellars. Violence, drunkenness and prostitution were common features of their miserable lives.

For the first time, people became aware of 'youth crime'. The behaviour of children in public places, even those from middle-class families, was a cause for concern. There was noise, vandalism, bad language and even violence committed by gangs of children in parks and in the streets. By 1898, the word 'hooligan' began to be used in the press to describe packs of teenagers with distinctive clothing and haircuts, forcing people off pavements, swearing and brandishing sticks and clubs. In Manchester during the 1870s and 1880s, gangs of 'scuttlers' roamed with home-made weapons and engaged in mob fights, with perhaps up to 500 youths involved, egged on by girls as young as fourteen. They took over music halls, and rival gangs decked out in 'gang colours' of scarves and caps fought each other with sharpened belt buckles and knives.[1]

Further evidence of youth misbehaviour in parks has been collated by Ruth Colton at the University of Manchester. Conceived as civilising places, urban parks were also places for young people to 'hang out' and get into trouble. Groups of youths would swear at other park users, fish illegally in the ponds and steal fruit from the trees. Excavations in Whitworth Park in Manchester have found the remnants of games such as marbles, but also remains of food and alcoholic drink containers, at a time when eating and drinking in the parks was forbidden.

Nevertheless, crime rates started to fall from the 1840s onwards (annual crime statistics had been published since 1810). Crime statistics in London for

155

1856 show that 18,000 of the 73,240 arrests made were for drunkenness, 4,303 for prostitution, 2,194 for assaults on the police, 6,763 for common assaults, 7,021 for larceny and 8,160 for unlawful possession of goods. There were probably many more unreported crimes, but these figures compared well with those of a half century earlier.[2] One reason for this may have been Britain's commercial and industrial success in the period, outstripping the French, Germans and Americans. There was a general rise in national wealth, and the ordinary working man began to be seen as less of a threat and more of an asset to the middle classes (unless they were seduced by political factions such as the burgeoning labour and trades union movements). Urban skilled workers felt themselves to be more empowered; there were more opportunities available, more steady work was to be found, and, as a result, living standards for many improved. There was, of course, still a level of society that was unskilled, casually employed, or criminally minded – but there was a growing gap between them and the majority of working-class people.

Respectability was the keyword; respectable homes, respectable appearances, even respectable entertainment. Philanthropic institutions and individuals provided reading rooms, educational classes, sporting venues, clubs for young people, and so on. Public houses began to adopt the glass, brass and polished wood décor that we now think of as typical, with bright lights and an air of sophistication. Music halls and magic lantern shows, exhibitions and performances all served to wean the poorer individuals away from the criminal element and their squalid environment towards the aspirational values of the middle classes.

The 1870 Education Act provided free schooling for all children, providing them with literacy and other skills, preparing them for their working futures, and removing them from the streets. Improvements in housing, sewerage, water supply, rubbish collection – all these reduced the necessary background of deprivation and squalor that characterised crime in the late eighteenth and earlier nineteenth centuries.

Urban developments began to sweep away the worst of the rookeries and slums, especially because of the provision of new wider roads for the increased traffic and railway lines into the centre of towns and cities that cut through the problem areas. The criminal gangs that had relied on these districts were broken up as a result. Of course, new forms of criminal organisation took their place over time; some criminals found it more pleasant to utilise the railway system to move out to live respectable lives in the suburbs and commute into the city to commit their illicit activities.

The focus of policing changed too. Rather than chasing down known criminals, they were to concentrate on preventing crime by regulating the behaviour of the working class (Plate 9). New offences such as 'loitering with intent' were introduced, and police were used as inspectors of markets, public houses, meeting halls, and even the homes of the poor. They were to patrol the streets and reprimand any behaviour they thought to be contrary to good order. Arrests could be made on the spot for 'nuisance' crimes such as playing a musical instrument in the street. This heavy-handed morality was superficially effective. Street crime declined, and even the crowds at the Great Exhibition behaved themselves, with only a dozen arrests for pickpocketing.

The change in the forms of crime committed included a replacement of the gangs with networks of criminal contacts, and indeed contacts with the police. A degree of professionalism entered the criminal world, including the use of 'fences' to move stolen goods, and the corruption of hotel and domestic staff to pass on information about likely targets for theft and robbery. Racketeering began to flourish in the form of organised crime networks engaged in black market activities, extortion and control of prostitution. It was a notable period for a rise in crimes involving fraud.

One such case, recorded in the archives of the HSBC Banking Group, took place in Bridgnorth, Shropshire in 1889, and was particularly scandalous because the criminal was a respectable woman.[3] Miss Eliza Jane Scoffham, a teacher, went to the local branch of a bank to pick up a chequebook on behalf of a Mrs Blaythwayt, a friend who had previously lent her money; she carried a letter of introduction from Mrs Blaythwayt as identification, and the clerk handed over the item without a qualm (Figure 31). Miss Scoffham then went to a room above a confectioner's shop, and sat practising the forging of Mrs Blaythwayt's signature. She then returned to the bank with a signed cheque for £210 (approximately £20,000 today) and asked for the money in gold. The clerk readied the money, but then became suspicious and turned away to make enquiries. It seems that for this visit the fraudster had dressed as a nurse, and put on a wig, a disguise which clearly did her no service. Miss Scoffham grabbed the package of gold and ran out, but the cashier chased her and caught her as she made for the railway station.

Fraudsters working on a larger scale were more likely to get away with it. There were some major embezzlements in the late Victorian period – over a million pounds from one bank in 1882 and several millions from Baring Brothers Bank in 1897. It was in the interests of the banks to keep such crimes hidden, so as to maintain public confidence; the perpetrators, being of the 'respectable' classes, were not viewed in the same way as 'common'

Figure 31. A copy of court sketches made during the trial of Eliza Jane Scoffham

criminals. They were guilty of betraying their class and letting the side down, but were not seen to be as demonic as the criminals on the streets.

Less exalted burglars and robbers had to learn new skills, as complex safes and ever more intricate locking systems were devised and manufactured. New avenues for crime and evasion of police included the railway networks. Confidence tricksters, pickpockets, female blackmailers and illegal gambling rings set themselves up in the railway carriages.

The Great Train Robbery of 1855 is said by some to be the first modern criminal venture. It was carefully planned in advance, down to undertaking a rehearsal on the train to make sure everything would go to plan. The London to Paris express was carrying bullion in the form of gold coins packed in sealed boxes inside steel safes — £12,000 was to be stolen from the gold put aboard the train at London Bridge Station. A railway guard was bribed and one of the gang succeeded in gaining employment with the railway company. Lead shot was prepared to put into the boxes so that the theft would not be discovered immediately, and copies of keys were made, tested and refined to open the safes.

The heist went off successfully, and it was not until the boxes were opened at the Paris bank that the theft of the gold was discovered. French and British police made hundreds of arrests and spent many months investigating the crime without a result, despite the offer of a substantial reward for information. Each country claimed that the robbery must have taken place in the other country's jurisdiction. It was rivalry between members of the criminal fraternity that eventually broke the case. A man called Edward Agar was arrested for passing a false cheque after police had received a tip-off. Sentenced to transportation to Australia for life, Agar was sent to Pentonville and then to a prison hulk at Portland. During this time he discovered that his partner, Fanny Kay, had not received the £7,000 that another criminal and ex-railway employee, William Pierce, was supposed to have given her. That amount of money would be worth more than half a million pounds today. Fanny told the governor of Newgate prison of her suspicions about Pierce, and the governor told the investigator for the railway company, who went to see Agar.

Agar then told the full story. It had been Pierce who had conceived the plan for the robbery, using his knowledge of the system gained through his employment. Further members of the gang were recruited from within the railway company. When they heard that a substantial shipment was due to be made, Agar and Pierce bought first class tickets to Folkestone. Agar slipped into the guards van with the bribed guard, while Pierce went to the first class carriage. Agar immediately set to opening the safes and boxes and exchanging the gold for the lead shot they had carried on in bags under their greatcoats and in their luggage. At Folkestone they left the train and took another to Dover, where they had some refreshment and then caught a third train back to London. They shared out the gold between the members of the gang, melting some of it down.

With Agar's testimony, the four other members of the gang were arrested and brought to trial early in 1857. Two were sentenced to fourteen years penal transportation – Pierce, the instigator, received only a two-year sentence for larceny.

All this took place at around the time of the end of the transportation system; in 1853 the colonies told the British government that they would no longer accept convicts. These developing societies had begun to achieve the confidence that would eventually lead to independence, and they resented being seen as the dumping ground for Britain's shame. With nowhere else to go, prisoners languished in the various hulks offshore until a new programme of prison construction could provide them with housing. Transportation as a penalty was replaced with penal servitude with hard labour in this country.

The first murder on the railways occurred on 9 July 1864. Thomas Briggs, an elderly banker, boarded a first class carriage on a North London Railway train bound for Hackney. When the train arrived at Hackney, two bank clerks entered the now empty carriage and saw bloodstains. They called the guard who inspected the carriage and found a walking stick, a bag and a beaver hat. The train was taken to Chalk Farm, and the carriage detached and sent to Bow for examination. The items found within the carriage were handed to the Metropolitan Police. Meanwhile, the driver of another train spotted something on the track between Hackney and Bow. He stopped his train and got out to investigate. There he found the unconscious, bleeding body of Mr Briggs. Though taken to hospital, Mr Briggs died the following night.

The press seized on the murder and reported every gory detail. An article in the Daily Telegraph reported that

As news of the murder spread a feverish fear emerged. It was said that no-one knew when they opened a carriage door that they might not find blood on the cushion, that not a parent would entrust his daughter to the train without a horrid anxiety. That not a traveller took his seat without feeling how he runs his chance.

The police identified the stick and bag as belonging to Mr Briggs, but the hat was not his. A label testified as to its maker, whose business was in Marylebone. Mr Briggs' gold watch and chain, and his spectacles, were missing.

Evidence began to accumulate. A jeweller gave a description of a German man who had brought a gold chain into his shop. A cabman identified the hat as one he had bought on behalf of his daughter's ex-fiancé, a man called Franz Muller (Figure 32). Shipping lists showed that Muller had sailed for New York on 11 July. Two police officers were sent to New York by steamship, reaching the city on 5 August, three weeks before the arrival of Muller's sailing vessel. On arrival, Muller was arrested and searched – he had Mr Briggs' gold watch on his person, as well as the murdered man's hat. On 3 September, Muller was extradited back to Britain for trial, sentenced and hanged.

A positive result of this case was the introduction of the communication cord in railway carriages, to alert staff to incidents in the carriages.[4]

Other social advances also introduced new opportunities for crime. The ability to use portable electro-plating equipment allowed forgers to 'silver' coins from base metal copies, and a whole range of specialist tools became available for the burglar – skeleton keys, lock-picks, gimlets and so on. Forgery of antiquities also became more common, with the new technologies enabling the copying of ancient artefacts, especially coins. The rise of a relatively affluent lower middle class in the suburbs gave many more opportunities for the house-breaker. The introduction of the penny post created another new set of crimes to be attempted – the forging of postage

Figure 32. Franz Muller, photographed c.*1864*

stamps, and 'fishing' – the practice of attaching a weight and bird lime to the end of a piece of string to stick to letters inside pillar boxes so that they could be pulled out. The introduction of postal orders in 1881 was a particularly attractive reason for this crime – they were easily negotiable by the thieves.[5]

Crime and detection – the public appetite
Trials were increasingly referred to the police (magistrates') courts for minor offences, under a system of summary jurisdiction. The system was inexpensive and fast; eighty per cent of cases were tried in magistrates' courts by 1911, compared to sixty-six per cent in 1857. Only serious cases requiring a jury were referred to the Crown Courts. This had its problems. The lay magistrates were overwhelmingly from the middle classes, with the prejudices against the poor and the working classes that were typical of the age. No training was required, and all the old attitudes of social status and expectations remained in place.

More and more prosecutions were brought by the police rather than by private individuals and, as they hired barristers for the prosecution, so the accused began to require barristers for the defence.

The focus of punishment had moved from revenge and the infliction of judicious suffering to a desire to discipline, correct and reform the wrongdoer. Public executions came to an end, not least because they were occasions for public riots and disorder. So popular had some hangings been that Thomas Cook ran excursion trains to them, and Charles Dickens was among 30,000 people watching a hanging in 1849. Executions became the focus for political speechmaking too, and before long it was deemed necessary by the authorities that all hangings should take place behind closed prison doors. Some of these closed execution chambers survive, such as that at Bodmin Gaol.

Public appetite for sensationalist stories about crime did not disappear, however. The most notorious publication (and voted the 'worst newspaper in England' in 1886) was the *Illustrated Police News,* founded in 1863. With a price of one penny, this newspaper carried lurid stories and pictures of crimes and bizarre events, not only in England but abroad and across the Empire. It had a regular circulation of between 100,000 and 150,000 copies, with 'special' issues being even more popular. The editor, George Purkess, commissioned artists to record crime scenes, and commented that on several occasions he had been complimented by criminals on the excellent portraits of themselves that he had published.

The Victorian era also saw the rise of fictional accounts of crime and detection. Stories were often published in serial form. Perhaps the first truly popular tale came in 1841 with the publication of Edgar Allen Poe's *The Murders in the Rue Morgue*. Charles Dickens introduced both criminals and detectives into his works, such as in *Bleak House*, Wilkie Collins wrote the famous mystery *The Woman in White*, and many other less well known novels became extremely popular. In 1887, the most famous detective of them all was created by Arthur Conan Doyle – Sherlock Holmes. Holmes' methods of detection foreshadowed the forensic approach of modern crime detection – an emphasis on material clues rather than testimony, and on the gathering and analysis of physical evidence, such as various types of cigar ash, to identify criminals.

Great strides were made in the development of the forensic sciences in the later half of the nineteenth century. Several cases were landmarks in the use of scientific means of detection, a theme that Doyle often used in his stories and novels.

The case of Sarah Dazley is an example of advances in the detection and identification of poisons. Daughter of a barber, who died while in prison for debt and a mother who was known for entertaining a number of gentlemen, Sarah, who had been born in 1819, was a pretty girl with many admirers. In

1838, she married and had a child who died within a few months. Her husband was distraught, not only by the loss of his son, but also by the promiscuity of his wife. Then, suddenly, in 1840 he died.

Within weeks, Sarah began to see a labourer called William Dazley and four months after the death of her first husband, she married him. They moved away to the village of Wrestlingworth, where they lived with her first husband's fourteen-year-old sister Ann Mead. Soon, William was to be found drinking alone and very heavily. One night, on returning home, there was a violent row, and William hit Sarah. Sarah turned to one of her admirers, William Waldock, and told a long story of marital abuse, which most of the village treated with disbelief.

Shortly after, William Dazley fell ill, with bad stomach pains and vomiting. A doctor was called, and William began to get better. A few days later, young Ann was surprised to find Sarah making up pills in the kitchen, which she believed to be sweeteners to make the doctor's medicine more palatable. A neighbour saw Sarah throwing away some pills and substituting others in the bottle but, when challenged, Sarah claimed that far from being better, William was worse, and that she did not think the doctor's pills were any good, so she had got some others from a village wise woman. William noticed the difference in the pills and refused to swallow them. Trying to help, Ann took one of the pills herself to encourage William, and he agreed to take the medicine. In short order, both Ann and William became terribly ill; William ran out of the house and vomited into the pig pen. The next morning a pig that had eaten the vomit was found dead.

This time, both William and Ann survived. But Sarah continued to dose William with her pills, and in September 1842 he died. A few weeks later, Sarah announced she was going to marry Waldock. The village took Waldock to task and persuaded him to break off the engagement. They also took their suspicions to the local coroner, who ordered that the body of William Dazley be exhumed and a new post-mortem be held.

The inquest was held in the Chequers Inn where Dazley had often drunk. White arsenic was found to be present in his gut. A warrant for Sarah's arrest was issued, but she had taken off and headed for London. A police officer followed her there and she was arrested, loudly proclaiming her innocence.

The bodies of her first husband and child were also exhumed and examined. Poison was found in the child's body, but the results from the husband's remains were inconclusive. Sarah now claimed that it was Dazley who had poisoned her first husband and child, and that she had poisoned Dazley in revenge. No-one believed her and when her trial began in 1843, she changed her story, saying the poisoning of Dazley had been an accident. Two chemists gave evidence that they had sold poison to Sarah, and Waldock testified that Sarah had threatened Dazley's life.

She was found guilty and sentenced to death at Bedford, with a crowd of 12,000 coming to watch her hang.[8]

It was advances in the detection of arsenic that brought about Sarah's downfall. Arsenic was the poison of choice for many murderers of the time – tasteless, easy to put into food, and its symptoms were similar to those of food poisoning, cholera and dysentry. There would be vomiting, stomach pains, diarrhoea and cramps. It is naturally present in the human body in microscopic amounts and it was commonly available to use as rat poison. Death can occur either quickly with a large dose, or more slowly if small doses are administered over a longer period of time. Inhalation of the vapour or absorption through the skin are eventually as fatal as direct ingestion. James Marsh noted that arsenic remains in the body even after death and can be detected in the hair and bones, and he devised a chemical proof for the presence of arsenic in 1836.

The Marsh Test involved adding fluid obtained from the body to sulphuric acid onto a piece of zinc. With no arsenic present, hydrogen will be produced, but in the presence of arsenic, arsine gas will be produced. If this gas is lit and a piece of glass is held over the flame, arsenic will be deposited on the glass. This test can identify amounts as small as one-fiftieth of a milligram.

In 1851 the Arsenic Act was passed by Parliament. Under its terms, only those known to the pharmacist could buy the poison, and their names were recorded in a Poisons Book. Arsenic could no longer be sold as an innocent-seeming white powder – it now had to be mixed with indigo or soot, to avoid accidental use in place of salt or sugar, and to make life for the would-be murderer much harder.[7]

A pioneer of scientific methods of investigation was Dr Alexandre Lacassagne, a university head of a department of legal medicine, who was called upon by the city prosecutor of Lyon to examine a body that had been exhumed. The remains had been buried for four months, after having been found in a sack in the River Rhône. An autopsy had failed to identify the deceased, but it was believed that it might be the body of Toussaint-Augustin Gouffé, a Parisian widower. Gouffé had gone missing towards the end of July, and his brother-in-law had reported this to the police, but no trace had been found.

Then, 300 miles away and three weeks later, the body turned up in the River Rhône. A broken trunk with a shipping label from Paris was found in nearby woods shortly afterwards.

The first autopsy found some similarities to the description of Gouffé – such as a missing tooth – but the heights were different, as was the colour of the hair, and the age. The first autopsy estimated the age of the deceased at between thirty-five and forty-five, while the missing man had been nearly fifty. Gouffé's brother-in-law failed to recognise the corpse when he viewed it.

In the autumn, the head of the Paris Sûreté, Goron, received an anonymous piece of information. He was told that shortly before his disappearance, Gouffé had been seen in a bar along with a known confidence trickster, Michel Eyraud, and his 'moll' Gabrielle Bompard, and that these two had left Paris the day after Gouffé had gone missing. The shipping label on the trunk was tracked down – it had left the Gare de Lyon in Paris on that same day, and the trunk had been heavy enough to have contained a body. Surely the body found in the Rhône was the missing man, despite the autopsy results.

The exhumation was subsequently carried out, and the second autopsy began. Dr Lacassagne was horrified by the condition of the remains. Bones had been misplaced, the sternum had been destroyed, internal organs removed and placed in a basket, and the top of the skull removed not with a saw but a hammer. Add to that the effects of several months' burial, and it was obvious the doctor faced a formidable task.

He began by assessing the age of the deceased – as the skull was so damaged, he examined the pelvis, the coccyx and the teeth and jaw. The state of the teeth led him to revise the original age estimate upwards – to between forty-five and fifty – and he could also surmise that the man had been a smoker. He then turned to the man's height. He took advantage of the new science of anthropometrics – a statistical analysis of bodily dimensions – based on studies by one of his own students, Rollet. Once again the original measurement was revised upwards. Now it matched the records of Gouffé's tailor and his military service record.

There was still the matter of the hair colour. Gouffé had chestnut-coloured hair, but the corpse had black hair. Repeated washing of the hair from the corpse revealed that it was indeed chestnut – it had been stained by the effects of the putrefaction of the body. Tests proved that this was a natural event – no hair dye had been used. The hairs from the body and the hairs from Gouffé's own hairbrush, when viewed under a microscope, were of identical thickness.

Further detailed examination of the corpse showed the presence of an old ankle injury and probable gout. The right leg was weaker than the left, and a renowned surgeon who studied these for size and weight confirmed that the whole right leg was less well developed. Investigations into Gouffé's history turned up the fact that the man had injured his right leg when he was very young, breaking the ankle, which had never properly healed. His shoemaker confirmed that he always adjusted the right shoe to accommodate the slight distortion that had resulted. His doctor also added his medical records, revealing a history of leg problems, including gout.

Monsieur Goron had a replica of the trunk made and displayed. Twenty-five thousand people visited it in the Paris morgue in the space of three days, and one was able to identify it as having come from a shop on the Euston Road in London. The shop still had the original receipt – it had been bought by Michel Eyraud a few weeks before the disappearance.

By now, Eyraud and his lady friend were on the run. Agents from the Sûreté followed their trail across the Atlantic, through the US and Canada, until in 1890 Eyraud was seen in Havana, and the Cuban police were notified. Bompard was tracked down in Vancouver, where her new lover persuaded her to turn herself in.

Now the truth began to emerge. Monsieur Gouffé was a prosperous man, a man of habits, but also one who enjoyed sexual adventure. He always went to the same bar on a Friday night after taking the cash from the office safe. Eyraud heard about this and prepared the scene. In Bompard's apartment, a rope was passed through an iron ring in the ceiling above the lady's bed, and Eyraud himself hid behind a curtain at the end of the bed with the end of the rope.

Bompard went to the bar and picked Gouffé up with the offer of sex. She brought him back to the apartment, disrobed and slipped on a dressing gown. Sliding the sash of the gown around his neck in apparent play, Eyraud was able to take the ends, attach them to the rope, and haul, hanging their victim quickly. But a search of his pockets was a great disappointment – his takings were not there. He had already put the money in a safer place.

They put the body in a sack and then in the trunk, and the next day took the train for Lyon. They stayed with the trunk overnight in a guesthouse, and the next day hired a carriage. At the point where the road met a cliff over the river, they dumped the body out, believing it would sink. Unfortunately for and unknown to them, it snagged on a bush. They smashed the trunk with a hammer and dumped it in the woods.

Eyraud went to the guillotine, and Bompard received a twenty-year prison sentence. The execution was a massive public event – street vendors were even selling miniature copies of the trunk, complete with a tiny metal corpse inside.

Dr Lacassagne's meticulous approach, his willingness to employ new methods, and his readiness to consult a number of other experts, mark him as one of the pioneers of medical forensics, and raised the bar for investigations

Figure 33. Katherine Webster and Julia Martha Thomas (After: Illustrated Police News, 12th July 1879

not only in France but across the world.[9] His analytical methods have also been the foundation for modern archaeological study of human remains.

A notorious British murder in 1879 demonstrated the public fascination with ideas of 'criminal types', and with crimes committed by people who failed to behave in ways that society expected of them. Mrs Julia Martha Thomas was a widowed teacher who lived alone in Richmond, Surrey. She was a rather eccentric character in her mid-fifties, who liked to travel and to dress as if she was of a higher social class. This desire to give an impression of better circumstances also led her to want to employ servants, but her difficult personality meant that she could rarely keep a maid for any length of time. An acquaintance of Mrs Thomas recommended to her a woman who she had employed temporarily to do some cleaning while her usual servant was ill. Based on this recommendation, Mrs Thomas hired Katherine Webster but failed to look into Webster's background. Had she done so, she might have discovered that Webster, née Lawler, was an Irishwoman with a long criminal record who had served several prison sentences for larceny and theft in both Ireland and England (Figure 33).

The employment was unsatisfactory on both sides. Mrs Thomas complained about the standard of Webster's work, and Webster found her employer to be overly demanding. Eventually, Mrs Thomas gave Webster her notice, telling her that her employment would end on 28 February. However, Webster persuaded her to let her stay until the end of the weekend; on Sunday 2 March, Webster came back late to the house, having been in the pub. Mrs Thomas was angry, as she had thus been made late for church, as she told another member of the congregation. After the service she went home around 9pm to have the matter out with her servant. There was a violent argument, during which Webster threw her employer down the stairs. She followed the body down and made sure of Mrs Thomas' silence and death by choking her until she was still.

Webster then decided to dispose of the body. She used a razor, kitchen knives and saws to dismember the body, and then boiled the pieces in the kitchen copper. She burned some of the bones in the hearth. For the next few days, she cleaned the house, answering the door and acting as if all was normal when tradesmen called. Meanwhile, she was packing Mrs Thomas's remains into a bag and a hat box. Not all the parts would fit – she had to throw one foot on to a rubbish dump in Twickenham, and she buried the head under the stables of the nearby pub.

On the Tuesday, Webster went to see some old friends in Hammersmith, wearing a silk dress that had belonged to her victim, and carrying a black bag. She took her friends for a drink in a pub in Barnes and, while they were drinking, she slipped out and threw the bag into the Thames. She then recruited her friends' son to help her carry a box the next day from Mrs Thomas' house to Richmond railway station. On the way, while crossing Richmond Bridge, the box was dropped into the water.

It was found the next day about a mile downstream by a coalman who alerted the police. The contents, when examined, proved to be a disembowelled torso and two legs, one without a foot. Then a foot was found in Twickenham, and it was apparent that the two finds were connected. The doctor misidentified the remains as those of a young woman, and at the inquest, an open verdict was recorded.

Webster remained at Mrs Thomas' house, and took her identity as well as dressing herself in the unfortunate woman's clothes and jewellery. She made an arrangement to sell off the furniture to a local publican, who wished to furnish his pub. On 18 March, the van turned up to move the furniture, and finally the neighbours' suspicions were aroused. The removers identified Webster as 'Mrs Thomas' and the neighbour realised that there had been a deception. Knowing the game was up, Webster fled back to Ireland. The publican called in the police who searched Mrs Thomas' house. They found bloodstains, fatty material behind the copper, and burned finger bones in the grate. Information was sent to the Royal Irish Constabulary, who identified the woman as one they had arrested previously. She was apprehended, taken into custody and brought back to England for trial at Richmond.

There was massive public horror and interest when the matter was referred to the Old Bailey. Despite attempts to blame a number of others for the crime, including the innocent publican, an old lover, and her friend in Hammersmith, as well as attempting to avoid the death sentence by saying she was pregnant, Webster was found guilty. On 28 July she finally confessed to the murder, and was hanged the next day at Wandsworth Prison, the executioner using the new long-drop method (which resulted in death from the breaking of the condemned person's neck, rather than slow strangulation) (Plate 10). A massive crowd waiting outside cheered as the black flag was raised to indicate that she was dead, and an effigy of her soon went on display at Madame Tussaud's.[10]

The reasons why the case aroused such public notoriety centred around the Victorian assumptions about the nature of women and the place of servants. Servants were supposed to be obedient and to know their place, and women were thought to be passive and weak. That a woman could carry out these dreadful acts, apparently without remorse, then take her employer's place and to try to implicate innocent people, went against all that society thought should happen. Of course, she was also Irish, at a time when English society regarded the Irish as brutish and even sub-human.

Accounts of her physical appearance were seen as indicative, after the event, of her inherent criminality. She was a strongly built woman, described as repellent and sinister-looking with 'obliquely set eyes', a feature which one commentator claimed was often found in murderers and should have been seen as a warning as to her character.

There was much interest at the time in the study of physiognomy – the study of facial appearance. Some believed that there was a 'criminal face' that could identify potential wrongdoers. Among these was Sir Francis Galton, who created composite photographs from police mugshots to try to identify those features that showed criminal tendencies. An earlier Italian criminologist, Cesare Lombroso, had made a list of suspicious characteristics, including pointed heads, heavy jaws, and thin beards. Darwinian theories had taken hold, among which were the inheritance of physical attributes, and this was extended to the idea that psychological traits such as criminality could also be inherited. Webster's appearance, it was felt, proved this theory. As a forensic technique, physiognomy (and its cousin, phrenology, which claimed to assess a person's character by feeling the bumps of their head) has long been discredited, but it was one of the new ideas being tested in the period.

A strange postscript to this case has occurred. A house close to that of Mrs Thomas was bought in 1952 by Sir David Attenborough. In 2009 he acquired the site of the now derelict pub for redevelopment. In October 2010 workmen found a skull in the yard of the building. This was radio-carbon dated and the results suggested it was at least a hundred years old. An archaeological approach to the recording of the find enabled identification of the stratigraphy in which the skull lay. This put it into the Victorian period, as it lay on some Victorian tiles. Low collagen levels indicated that the flesh had been boiled away, and there was evidence of a fracture and possibly asphyxiation which was the probable cause of death. As Mrs Thomas had no traceable relatives, DNA analysis could not be used to prove that this was her skull, but the coroner felt that the identification was reasonable, and in 2011 recorded a new verdict of unlawful killing.[11]

An Australian outlaw

Modern forensic science has also been put to use to identify the remains of a notorious nineteenth century criminal. In 1929, construction work began on a new school at the site of the old prison in Melbourne, Australia. It was known that executed criminals had been buried in the prison yard, with markers on an adjacent wall. One marker bore the initials ' E.K.'. The bodies were exhumed and reburied at another prison. A further group were moved in 1937. These were all placed in mass graves. In 2002, another body was found, missed by the earlier diggers.

There was great excitement at the idea that among these remains was the body of Australia's most famous outlaw, Ned Kelly (Plate 11). Son of an Irish convict, Kelly was in trouble with the law from an early age, but his life of crime truly took off in 1878 when a constable arrived to arrest his brother. The constable then claimed that the family had attacked him; the brothers made off into the bush, and their mother was arrested and sentenced to three years in gaol for attempted murder. Ned and his brother Dan joined up with a couple of other ne'er-do-wells, and the Kelly Gang was formed.

They killed three constables in the autumn of 1878 and a reward of £500 each was offered for their capture, dead or alive. In the December of that year they took twenty-two people hostage at a sheep station and robbed a bank. The next February they took over a police station, locked up the constables, stole their uniforms and in these disguises robbed a bank. They moved into the hotel next door and took sixty people hostage. Kelly issued a long statement about the injustice of the law and court system. By now the reward had quadrupled. When the gang fled, aboriginal trackers were brought in to trace them.

In 1880 they once again took over an inn, holding many hostages, and tried to derail a train carrying police officers coming to arrest them. This failed and the inn was surrounded. The gang had made themselves metal armour from parts of ploughs, and Kelly slipped out of the inn in an attempt to outflank the police. The armour did not cover his legs – the police shot low and brought him down. One of his gang was killed in the shooting, and brother Dan and another member took poison. Kelly was the last survivor and he was hanged in November 1880 at Melbourne.

New archaeological excavations uncovered the mass graves, but the last and largest grave was not where it was supposed to be. It finally appeared in February 2009, a hundred feet from its supposed position, possibly carelessly relocated during drainage work in the 1960s. There were twenty-four coffins containing the mixed remains of fifteen men. Work began on sorting them out.

Meanwhile, it seems that Kelly's skull had been removed in 1937 and not re-interred with the rest of the bones. It had passed through a number of hands until it was placed in the museum of Old Melbourne Gaol, from where it was stolen in 1978. It was returned in 2009, with no record of how it had come to light.

X-rays, CAT scans and photographs of the skull were taken and studied and compared to existing photographs of Kelly and to the plaster death mask taken after his execution. Although it was an exact fit, this was not conclusive because another death mask also provided a good fit – that of Frederick Deeming, an executed serial killer.

The next step was to recover mitochondrial DNA from the bones in the grave and from the skull. This was compared to mtDNA from the living great-grandson of Kelly's sister. One set of bones matched – but not the skull. The bones also showed evidence that matched Kelly's injuries – lead pellets and marks of gunshot wounds to his leg, arm and foot were found.

So who did the skull belong to? There are no known living descendants of Deeming to compare the DNA with, so this remains a mystery. And Kelly's skull? A fragment of cranium was found in the jumble of bones and could be a match. It carries saw marks, as do some of the cervical vertebrae, evidence of post-mortem dissection. Where the rest of the skull is remains yet another unsolved question.[12]

Frederick Deeming was born in Leicestershire in 1853. After running away to sea, he became an habitual criminal. In 1882 he moved to Australia, and was soon in trouble with the law. In 1887 he disappeared while on bail. He was in South Africa in 1888-9, where he was involved in a diamond mine swindle, and then may have gone to Birkenhead. In later 1889 he was in Beverley, living under an assumed name. He married the young daughter of his landlady in 1890, despite being already married. A month later, he disappeared again. Later it was discovered he had visited his four children and first wife in Birkenhead, announcing that he was off to South America. He swindled a local jeweller and, as soon as he arrived in South America was arrested and extradited back to England. He spent nine months in gaol. On his release he went to Rainhill, near Liverpool, where he took a house under another assumed name and was visited by a woman thought to have been his first wife, with her children, telling neighbours she was his sister. Shortly afterwards, he found it necessary to have the kitchen floor lifted because of problems with the drains.

He then married a third woman, Emily Mather, in September 1891 and took her with him to Australia. On Christmas Eve or Christmas Day, he murdered Emily and buried her under cement in one of the bedrooms of the house he had rented. He left the property and the owner tried to let it to a new tenant, who complained of a terrible smell. Emily's body was found; her head had been severely battered, and her throat had been cut.

Deeming, under yet another alias, had sold off his wedding presents, gone to a marriage bureau seeking another wife, and swindled another jeweller. He moved through a number of new names and young ladies, but was arrested in March 1892. At about the same time, police in England had found the decomposing bodies of a woman and four children at the house in Rainhill. One child had been strangled – the other victims had suffered cut throats. They were identified as Deeming's first wife and children.

Deeming tried to plead insanity at his trial, to be suffering from syphilis, and to have visions from his mother's ghost which had urged him to commit the crimes. Nevertheless, he was found guilty and hanged in May 1892.

Even before his hanging, speculation was rife about his movements in late 1888. It is possible that he was in England at this time – one source claims he was in Hull prison, but another source claims he was in South Africa. A fellow prisoner in Melbourne Gaol recounted that Deeming made a confession to him during their incarceration together. Even today, some are still willing to entertain the notion that Deeming was the man he claimed to be in prison – Jack the Ripper.

From Victorian to Edwardian

The police forces facing the new challenges of the nineteenth century were themselves developing and changing. The 1842 Parish Constables Act was intended to increase a police presence in areas liable to unrest, associated with labour disputes and agricultural shortages, but the constables were ineffective, largely because the rate of pay was too low to attract effective applicants. Rules for constables, their duties and the way they lived even when not on duty were onerous. Their beats could involve walking twenty miles a night in all weathers, with no sitting, leaning or refreshments allowed, they often had to provide portions of their own uniforms, and these had to be worn even when not on duty – all for as little as three shillings a day, minus deductions for rent and pensions.[13] The acceptance for the necessity of the police forces was slow – by 1850 only thirty-six counties had a force, and there were only 12,000 policemen to cover the whole of England and Wales. Many people regarded the idea of a police force as somehow 'unEnglish'.

Local authorities objected to the expense involved, and there was no real leadership from government about policing, until in 1856 a Police Act set up a system of inspection and auditing, and compelled each county to set up a police force. As a result, 239 forces were inaugurated, although there were no national standards of pay and conditions. An inspectorate was designed to check on the efficiency of the local police provision. The National Criminal Record was established in 1869, followed in 1877 by the formation of the Criminal Investigation Department. Innovations such as the telegraph system now enabled forces to alert each other about criminal cases and to share information necessary to make the pursuit of criminals more effective.

The immediate result was a fall in street crime and a reduction in the amount of recorded violent crime. A middle-class public, initially suspicious of policing, fearing a military-style force on Britain's streets, now began to be supportive of the police. By the end of the century, 243 forces existed across Britain, with some 46,000 officers.

Prisons, too, were changing. Various pieces of legislation eroded the power of country magistrates, and in 1877 the Prisons Act brought all the penal establishments under the control of the Home Office. Many small local prisons were closed at this time because they were uneconomic. The 'separate system' was abandoned, but was replaced with a much harsher regime of hard labour. The mood had switched from reform to deterrence, although rehabilitation was still a stated goal. Punishment such as the treadmill and the crank were used, as well as repetitive tasks such as picking oakum. The treadmill was a revolving machine worked by prisoners who in effect climbed a continuous stair for ten minutes at a time, with five-minute breaks in between (Plate 12). The crank was a box structure filled with gravel and fitted with a handle that had to be turned to stir the gravel a set number of times in a day – in one instance, 10,000 turns had to be made before breakfast. The box was fitted with a mechanical counter to enable the prisoner's effort to be monitored. Both types of punishment were exhausting, pointless, and in the case of the treadmill, sometimes dangerous. Women and children were often set to picking oakum – pulling apart old ships' ropes to recover the hemp, which could then be reused. The ropes were stiff, covered with tar, and the work quickly blistered the hands of the inmates. Working hours could be very long – up to fifteen hours a day in summer, and thirteen hours a day in winter.

Across the world, new archaeological interest has arisen about these prisons and the lives of those incarcerated within them. As many are pulled down and replaced by more modern institutions, evidence is being gathered through excavations to record and preserve the details of the prison regimes and conditions endured by convicts in the past couple of centuries. Among British prisons which are or have been studied are Reading Gaol, where Oscar Wilde was imprisoned, the Millbank Penitentiary, and Lincoln and York gaols. Irish sites include Spike Island and Roscommon. Several sites have been studied in Australia, and in New Zealand, for example at Mount Eden Prison in Auckland. In the USA, most efforts have been concentrated on excavation of Civil War prison camps. French sites include the Bastille and overseas penal settlements such as the Iles de Salut, in use from 1852, where Alfred Dreyfus ('Papillon') was incarcerated in 1894.

By 1898, a less arduous regime was introduced. Solitary confinement was now limited to no more than one month at a time, and the use of the treadmill was abolished. Already, by 1895, the treatment of young offenders was being questioned, and the desirability of separating young people from adult inmates was gaining acceptance. In 1908, separate institutions for young offenders were introduced, where they were put to work, but were also given educational instruction. These became known as borstals.

Hangings now took place within the prisons, rather than in public. At Pentonville Prison, a deep, brick-lined pit was used for hangings, covered with a two-leaf trapdoor. Pentonville ran courses to train hangmen, instructing them in the calculations necessary to conduct an efficient hanging and the length of time it took a person to die if their neck was not broken when the trapdoor dropped. Training courses continued until 1960.

Whipping was still in use as a punishment. Birch rods of different thicknesses were required depending on the age of the offender, who was struck a decreed number of times on his bare buttocks.

Living conditions, while improved from those of the preceding century, were still severe – insufficient food, and that of a boring nature, and hard beds to lie on. Bread was the prisoner's staple diet, along with thin gruel containing potatoes, which were often rotten. There was also a punishment diet, consisting of just bread and water for four days out of five, and there were accounts of extreme hunger, and riots caused by the condition of the food. The fortunate prisoners at Dartmoor had the unique privilege of cocoa at supper thrice weekly!

Prisoners had their heads shaved when they entered the prison, were bathed in carbolic, given a rough uniform to wear, and a number was issued to be used instead of a name. One fifteen-minute visit and one letter every six months were permitted. Exercise periods of up to an hour were spent in the prison yard, and daily attendance at chapel was obligatory.

The warders often lived in the prisons and were uniformed. They carried truncheons for protection and were as supervised as the convicts themselves. Not until 1864 were they allowed a half day off a week. Every prison had a chaplain who held services and visited prisoners. Medical officers were also appointed to inspect prisoners on arrival, and to make rounds twice a week.[14]

About thirteen per cent of the total numbers of prisoners in 1908 were female, mostly convicted for prostitution or for activism in the suffragette movement. In 1903 Holloway was designated as a female prison.

By 1911 the Metropolitan Police had 200 police stations in twenty-two divisions across London; these included divisions dedicated to the royal household, to guarding military stations and dockyards, on special duty with the armed forces and government departments, and officers seconded to major department stores, museums and galleries. There was a Central Criminal Investigation Department, a Public Carriage Department, a Training School, Executive and Statistical Departments, and Special Branch, which had responsibility for cases concerned with royalty and political affairs. Unlike other police forces in England at the time, the Metropolitan Police was an 'imperial' force, not subject to control by local councils. In one year of the first decade of the twentieth century, the 'Met' dealt with 178,495 minor offences and 17,910 indictable offences, with proceedings being taken against 14,525 individuals, some of whom had committed several offences. Nationally, in 1901, there were 55,453 trials and 45,039 convictions for indictable offences. The number of lesser offences was much higher – drunkenness alone accounted for 210,342 arrests. In that year 199,875 people were committed to prison, three-quarters of them male, representing fifty-two per cent of the convictions for indictable offences. Fines were levied on twenty-two per cent of those found guilty, and nine per cent were sentenced to a whipping. Reformatories or industrial schools existed for juvenile offenders, guilty of crimes such as stealing rabbits, failing to attend school, keeping bad company and being either outside of, or not under parental control.

Fingerprint evidence began to appear in courts – the first conviction on this form of evidence took place in 1902 when Harry Jackson left his fingerprint on the newly painted window-sill of a house that he robbed. Dr Henry Faulds had tried to get the Metropolitan Police interested in the use of fingerprint evidence in 1886, but they were at that stage dismissive of the idea. In 1892 Francis Galton had published a study of fingerprints, proving their uniqueness to each individual, and finally in 1901 the first fingerprint bureau was set up in Britain.

Recording of crime was necessarily done with pencil and paper in the days before computers. Recently a detective's notebook came up for sale at a well-known auction house. The author was a detective inspector based in Manchester, and in the early 1900s he compiled a list of offenders with details of their appearances, aliases, photographs and convictions. His 'rogues gallery' included burglars, safe breakers, petty thieves, 'brothel thieves' and habitual offenders such as Ernest Bell, aged twenty in 1912, whose criminal career escalated from stealing pigeons (fined £5), stealing a bicycle (twelve lashes), and stealing jellies (five years in a reformatory) to shopbreaking, for which he was sent to prison.

The Edwardian period saw one of the most famous cases of archaeological fraud – the Piltdown affair. In 1912 Charles Dawson, a solicitor and amateur geologist, presented a jawbone and skull fragments to the Geological Society of London. He claimed to have found them in a gravel pit near Piltdown in Sussex, where he had been digging for fossils. He claimed the bones to be those of an early hominid, 500,000 to 1,000,000 years old. The find was attested to by Dawson's friend, Arthur Smith Woodward, keeper of the geological section of the British Museum. Few early hominid remains had ever been found, and it was only in 1907 that the remains of *Homo heidelbergensis* had been found in Germany. None had so far been discovered in Britain, so Dawson's evidence was greeted with much excitement. Later discoveries of a canine tooth and a piece of carved fossil elephant bone were made in 1914 and 1915 at Piltdown. Dawson himself died in 1916 and for forty years, the Piltdown fossils were regarded as genuine.

However, doubts began to grow. New discoveries of fossil human bones from round the world failed to match the Piltdown material and, in the late 1940s, a scientist from the Natural History Museum ran some tests. The fluorine in the teeth could now be dated using newly developed techniques, and the Piltdown specimens were found to be less than 50,000 years old and are now known to be only 1,000 years old. Further tests were then undertaken by scientists from Oxford University. They discovered that the jaw and the skull fragments were from two different species, human and ape. The jaw was probably from an orang-utan, and they were able to see, with the aid of a microscope, tiny scratches where the teeth had been filed down to make them appear more human. The bone fragments had been artificially stained with iron sulphate to make them look ancient. The canine tooth had been stained with brown paint and a steel knife had been used to shape the elephant bone. In 1953, the Natural History Museum formally announced that Piltdown Man was a hoax – but by then, almost all those who might have committed the fraud had died. Dawson is now known to have committed a number of other frauds and he had a collection of very dubious 'finds' which have been analysed by a modern archaeologist. Why he did it is unknown – perhaps he simply longed to make his mark in the scientific world. He certainly achieved a lasting notoriety![15]

Conclusion

This book ends at this point, because the events of 1914 bring us to a point in history where a great deal of social, political, judicial and cultural life was altered forever. The consideration of crime, policing and forensics after this point is a matter for different specialist authors and recorders of true-crime stories, and there is much of vast interest to be read in their works, relating to more recent events and characters, many of whom are still living.

There have been many other crimes committed in the course of human history and still more are being committed today, but increasingly the techniques of forensic archaeology are helping law enforcement and justice agencies to identify victims and clues, and to solve and prosecute cases across the world.

It is a sad fact that archaeology itself is the victim of much crime nowadays, as ancient sites and museums are looted and destroyed in wars and insurgencies. Forensic techniques can occasionally repair some of the damage done by differentiating between real and faked objects, but the sad fact is that once an object is stolen from its original location without record, it is not only the artefact itself that is lost, but all the information that should have been recovered with it. The value of an archaeological find is much greater than its physical entity alone. Its true worth lies in the information it provides about the place in which it was deposited, the artefacts it was originally placed among, the way it was put into the ground, and the purpose behind its deposition. All this information is lost when an artefact is simply wrenched from the earth by illicit treasure hunters or looters who are only interested in profit.

Museums and ancient sites have been destroyed in recent years by bombs and mines, sometimes by accident and sometimes deliberately for religious or political reasons. These can never be replaced; once destroyed, they are lost forever. Archaeology is a non-renewable resource and is all the more precious as a result. We have seen how much new archaeological and scientific techniques can illuminate our history – it would be a crime against the past to lose this evidence now.

NOTES

Chapter 1 (pages 1–20)
1. Payne, S. 2008.
2. Edwards, R., 2007.
3. Kind S, & Overman, M 1972, 12–13.
4. BBC News online, 'The science of searching', 12 Dec 2000 accessed 28 Jan 2014.
5. Roberts C & Manchester K 1995.
6. University of Leicester. *Science Daily*, 4 February 2013.
7. www.searchfoundationsinc.org/Romanov_Children_Final_Report, Feb_09 accessed 26 Sep 2013.
8. Watts-Plumpkin, E, 2012.
9. Sample, I., 28 Jan 2014.
10. Karin F Hoth, Robert H Paul et al. 2006.
11. Wilkinson C 2004 *Forensic Facial Reconstruction* Cambridge: CUP.
12. Pace, E. 2000.

Chapter 2 (pages 21–43)
1. Richardson, M.E.J., 2000.
2. Ruth Whitehouse 1977, 94.
3. G. Maspero 1898.
4. Hürriyet MUĞLA *Anatolia News Agency* 22 Aug 12 *www.hurriyet.com.*
5. *www.the-scientist.com* 18 Dec 2012.
6. *www.britishmuseum.org/explore/highlights/.../aes/.../gebelein_man.aspx* The Times 16 Nov 2012 (pg 10*) 'British Museum exhibit Gebelein Man died "violent death"'* BBC News 16 Nov 2012.
7. Steven E. Churchill et al, 2009.
8. Leake, J. 'We'll have our neighbours for dinner – raw' *Sunday Times* 24 Nov 13.
9. Morris, Alan G. 2012.
10. Wileman, J. 2009.
11. Miller, H 2000 & Waugh, Rob 2012.
12. ORCA, www.orca.org accessed **16 Nov 2012.**
13. South Tyrol Museum of Archaeology *www.iceman.it/en/node/226* 1 Sep 2013.
14. Smuda, C 2011 South Tyrol Museum of Archaeology/Marco Samadelli.

Chapter 3 (pages 44–65)
1. Stavrakakis, Yannis 2012.
2. Camp, John McK. 2013.
3. Conn, Robert 2007.
4. Kelly, Martin A. 2011.
5. Polybius, *Histories Book 6.*
6. Maddock, S & Mahon, P 2006.
7. Alison Taylor is the author of 'Burial Practice in Early England' and 'Cambridge: the Hidden History' (both published by Tempus), and is the Head of Outreach and Editor for the Institute of Field Archaeologists.
8. Kuhnen, H-P 2009.
9. York Archaeological Trust 2011 www.yorkarchaeology.co.uk/headless-*romans/gladiators.html* accessed 19 Sep 2013.
10. Brown, S 'The Roman Arena', *Archaeology Archive,* Archaeological Institute of America 2007 archive.archaeology.org/gladiators/arena.html 19 Sep 2013.
11. Bahn, P 2000.
12. Garoupa, N & Gomez Ponar, F. 2005.
13. Lichocka, B., 2006.
14. *Daily Mail* 4 Nov 2010 http://www.dailymail.co.uk/sciencetech/article-1326292/The-Roman-Del-Boy-Cleaner-finds-ancient-fake-coin-Egypt-spelled-wrong.html#ixzz2bmGHvW9k.
15. Holmes N M McQ & F Hunter, 2001.
16. Conti, C., accessed 19 Sep 2013.
17. Cohen J. 2010.
18. Source: Dr Katie Tucker, University of Winchester.

Chapter 4 (pages 66–85)
1. Stander, H.F. 2009.
2. Buckberry J.L. & D.M. Hadley 2007.
3. Denison, S. 2000; David Keys 2000; Reynolds, A. 2009.
4. Lowther, 1989.
5. *Daily Mail* 25 Jan 2012 'The Viking death squads who got a taste of their own medicine: Mass grave shows how the Anglo-Saxons hit back at invaders' http://www.dailymail.co.uk/sciencetech/article-2091401/Viking-death-squads-mass-grave-shows-Anglo-Saxons-hit-invaders.html accessed 17 Jan 2014.
6. University of Cambridge 2012 www.cam.ac.uk/.../viking-mass-grave-linked-to-elite-killers-of-the-medieval world accessed 17 Jan 2014.

7. Naumann, Elise 2005.
8. Zuyderwyk, Janneke & Jan Besteman, 2010.
9. Lorenzi, R. 2011.
10. Rabin A, 2008.
11. Kalmring, Sven 2010.
12. Emerton, Ehpriam 1940.

Chapter 5 (pages 86–107)
1. Knight, B. 2007.
2. Bryan, L. 2006.
3. Hinton, D A, Keene S & Qualmann, K E, 1981.
4. Alan Mackley, Blythburgh, June 1999.
5. Williamson, T. 2007.
6. Cohen, E., 1980.
7. Hanawalt, B. 1975.
8. Hale, B., 2013.
9. Pisa, N. 2011: Posted by TANN ArchaeoHeritage, Archaeology, Europe, Italy, Southern Europe Daily Mail/UK.
10. Hanawalt, B., 1976.
11. Dvorsky, G., 2013.

Chapter 6 (pages 108–129)
1. Caputo, J. 2009.
2. Harte, J 2013.
3. Howard, S. 2004.
4. Freeman, J. 2004.
5. Currie, E.P., 1968.
6. Massey, Dr. A., 2000.
7. *Daily Mail* 2012 http://www.dailymail.co.uk/news/article-2154279/Has-Pirate-Kings-ship-found.html.
8. Kennedy, M. 2003 *The Guardian/*Porter, V. & Morison, P. 1998.
9. Bird, C., 2002.

Chapter 7 (pages 130–154)
1. Defoe, Daniel 1725.
2. Wilkinson, G.T. 2012.
3. Banks, S. 2013.
4. Hurren, E., 2013.
5. Lisa Hudgins 1997.

6. Grace Karskens 2003.
7. Casella, E., 1998.
8. www.met.police.uk/history / accessed 17 Nov 2013.
9. Dell, S. 2004.
10. www.met.police.uk/history / accessed 17 Nov 2013.
11. Crime and Punishment' www.exploringsurreyspast.org.uk accessed 22 Jan 2014.
12. Matteoni, F. 2012.
13. Charles River Editors, 2013.
14. Queen Anne's Revenge 1718, North Carolina Department of Cultural Resources, www.quaronline.org accessed 22 Jan 2014.
15. Platt, R. 2012 /Wood, G.B. 1996.

Chapter 8 (pages 155–178)
1. Davies, A. 2008.
2. Ritchie , J. Ewing 1858.
3. HSBC.com 2013.
4. http://www.btp.police.uk/about_us/our_history/crime_history/the_first_railway_murder.aspx accessed 10 Dec 2013.
5. Storey, N.R., 2010.
6. Harrison, P. 1993.
7. Erzinclioglu, Dr Z., 2000.
8. Heslop, P., 2009.
9. Starr, J., 2010.
10. Russell, J. & Cohn, R. 2012.
11. *Daily Telegraph,* 2011 'Head found in David Attenborough's garden was murder victim'.
12. Archaeological Institute of America 2012 archive.archaeology.org/1209/features/ned_kelly_bones_australia_old_melbourne_gaol.html accessed 12 Dec 2013.
13. Dell, S., 2004.
14. Morris, N. & Rothman, D.J. (eds), 1997.
15. Russell, M., 2003.

BIBLIOGRAPHY

Bahn, P 2000 *Archaeology – A Very Short Introduction,* Oxford: OUP.

Banks, S. 2013 *The British Execution,* Stroud: Shire Publications.

Bird, C., 2002, ' *Batavia's* Graveyard' in Bahn P. (ed) *Written in Bones,* (2007 edn) Rochester, Kent: Grange Books, 114–18.

Brown, S 'The Roman Arena', *Archaeology Archive,* Archaeological Institute of America 2007 archive.archaeology.org/gladiators/arena.html accessed 19 Sep 2013.

Bryan, L. 2006 'Marriage and Morals in the Fourteenth Century: The Evidence of Bishop Hamo's Register' *English Historical* Review, cxxi. 491.

Buckberry J.L. & D.M. Hadley 2007 'An Anglo-Saxon Execution Cemetery at Walkington Wold, Yorkshire' *Oxford Journal of Archaeology* 26(3) 309–29.

Camp, John McK. 2013 *Excavations in the Athenian Agora*: http://www.agathe.gr.

Caputo, J. 2009 'Forensic anthropologists at the National Museum of Natural History find answers to a colonial cold case' *Smithsonian magazine,* March 2009, http://www.smithsonianmag.com/arts-culture/Bone-Cops.html.

Casella, E., 1998 *Overview Report: Ross Female Factory Project 1995,* Parks & Wildlife Service of Tasmania, Cultural Heritage Branch.

Charles River Editors, 2013 Real Pirates of the Caribbean, Internet: Create Space Independent Publishing.

Churchill, Steven E., Robert G. Franciscus, Hilary A. McKean-Peraza, Julie A. Daniel, Brittany R. Warren 2009 "Shanidar 3 Neandertal rib puncture wound and paleolithic weaponry" *Journal of Human Evolution* Volume 57, Issue 2, 99–194.

Cohen, E., 1980 'Patterns of Crime in Fourteenth-Century Paris' *French Historical Studies*, Vol. 11, No. 3 (Spring, 1980), pp. 307–27 http://www.jstor.org/stable/286391 Accessed: 31 Jul 2013.

Cohen J. 2010 *Girl Possibly Murdered During Roman Invasion Found in* England: The 1,800-year-old murder mystery: Archaeologists unearth body *of young girl buried with her hands tied.* Sims P., 2010: http://www.dailymail.co.uk/sciencetech/article-1312338/ Murder-mystery-

1-800-year-old-girl-buried-ancient-Roman-barracks.html accessed 18 Sep 2013.

Conn, Robert 2007 "Prevalence and Profitability: The Counterfeit Coins of Archaic and Classical Greece" *Electronic Theses, Treatises and Dissertations.* Paper 3470. Florida State University.

Conti, C., *Mutiny in Modena? Decapitated Slaves in Roman Modena* http://www.archeobo.arti.beniculturali.it/index.htm, accessed 19 Sep 2013.

Currie, E.P., 1968 'Crimes without Criminals: Witchcraft and Its Control in Renaissance Europe' *Law & Society Review*, Vol. 3, No. 1, 7–32.

Davies, A. 2008 *The Gangs of Manchester: The Story of the Scuttlers, Britain's First Youth Cult*, Wrea Green: Milo Books.

Defoe, Daniel 1725 *A True & Genuine Account of the Life and Actions of the late* Jonathan Wild, Not made up of Fictions and Fable, but taken from his Own *Mouth and collected from PAPERS of his Own Writing.*

Dell, S. 2004 *The Victorian Policeman*, Stroud:Shire Publications.

Denison S. 2000 'Saxon Criminal' *British Archaeology* Issue 55.

Dvorsky, G., 2013 'Welcome to the macabre world of "execution site archaeology"' http://io9.com/welcome-to-the-macabre-world-of-execution-site-archaeo-474865725 accessed 17 Apr 2013.

Edwards, R., 2007 'Margate police fear trail of bodies in 20 homes' *Daily Telegraph* 19 Nov 2007.

Emerton, Ehpriam 1940 *The Letters of Saint Boniface.* New York: Columbia University Press.

Erzinclioglu, Dr. Z., 2000 *Every Contact Leaves a Trace* London: Carlton Books Limited.

Freeman, J. 2004 'Sorcery at court and manor:Margery Jourdemayne, the witch of Eye next Westminster' *Journal of Medieval History* 30 343–57.

Garoupa, N & Gomez Ponar, F. 2005 *Paying the Price for Being Caught: the Economics of Manifest and non-Manifest Theft in Roman Criminal Law*, Barcelona.

Hale, B., 2013 *Daily Mail* http://www.dailymail.co.uk/news/article-1162480/700- years-proper-funeral-teenage-witch-head-chopped-off.html accessed 10 Jun 2013.

Hanawalt, B. 1975 'Fur-Collar Crime: The Pattern of Crime among the Fourteenth-Century English Nobility' *Journal of Social History*, Vol. 8, No. 4, 1–17 http://www.jstor.org/stable/3786634 accessed: 31 Jul 2013 .

Hanawalt, B., 1976 'Violent Death in Fourteenth and Early Fifteenth-Century England' *Comparative Studies in Society and History*, Vol. 18, No.3 http://www.jstor.org/stable/178340 accessed: 31 Jul 2013.

BIBLIOGRAPHY

Harrison, P. 1993 *Hertfordshire & Bedfordshire* Newbury: Countryside Books.

Harte, J, 2013 *Crime in Tudor and Stuart Epsom and Ewell* Epsom and Ewell History Explorer http://www.epsomandewellhistoryexplorer.org.uk/index.html accessed 20 Oct 2013.

Heslop, P., 2009 *Murderous Women* Stroud: The History Press.

Hinton, D A, Keene S & Qualmann, K E, 1981 The Winchester Reliquary *Medieval Archaeology* XXV, 45–77.

Holmes N M McQ & F Hunter, 2001 Roman counterfeiters' moulds from Scotland *Proc Soc Antiq Scot,* 131 (2001), 167–76.

Hoth, Karin F, Robert H Paul et al. 'Associations between the *COMT Val/Met* polymorphism, early life stress, and personality among healthy adults' *Neuropsychiatr Dis Treat.* 2006 June; 2(2): 219–25.

Howard, S. 2004 'Investigating responses to theft in early modern Wales: communities, thieves and the courts' *Continuity and Change* Vol. 19 (3), 409–30.

Hudgins, Lisa 1997 "Dieting" the Prisoners: Ceramic Evidence from Old Gaol Excavations *University of South Carolina – Columbia,* hudgins@mailbox.sc.edu.

Hurren, E., 2013 'The dangerous dead: dissecting the criminal corpse' *The Lancet* Vol. 382 No. 9889 302–3.

Kalmring, Sven 2010 'Of thieves, counterfeiters and homicides: crime in Hedeby and Birka' *Fornvännen* 105:4, 281–90.

Karskens, Grace 2003 'Revisiting the World View: The Archaeology of Convict Households in Sydney's Rocks Neighbourhood' *Historical Archaeology* Vol. 37 No.1, 34–55.

Kelly, Martin A. 2011 *Slaves as Criminal Informers in Ancient Rome* published on line

Keys, David 2000 'Stonehenge used as Saxon execution site' *The Independent* http://www.independent.co.uk/news/UK/This_Britain/2000-07/henge140700.html.

Kind S, & Overman, M 1972 *Science Against Crime.* New York City: Doubleday.

Knight, B. 2007 *Crowner: The Medieval Coroner's Duties* www.britannia.com/history/coroner1.html accessed 19 Jan 2014.

Kuhnen, H-P 2009 The Trier Amphitheatre; an ancient monument in the light of new research, in Wilmott, T (ed) *Roman Amphitheatres and Spectacula: a 21st-Century Perspective,* Oxford: BARIS 1946 95–105.

Lichocka, B., 2006 *Forgery on the Nile*, Research Center for Mediterranean Archeology, Warsaw.

Lorenzi, R. 2011 *Did Zombies Roam Medieval Ireland?* London: Discovery Communications.

Lowther, A, 1989 Notes *Surrey Archaeological Society Collections* 79, 67–97.

Maddock, S & Mahon, P 2006 'A Romano-British prone burial from Bratton, Wiltshire' *Wiltshire Archaeol Natural History Magazine*, 99, p. 190–203.

Maspero, G. 1898 *Etudes de mythologie et d'archéologie égyptiennes* vol. 3, Paris.

Massey, Dr. A., 2000 'The Reigate Witch-Bottle', *Current Archaeology*, no 169, 34–6.

Matteoni, F. 2012 'Tom Otter's Gibbet' by E. Mansel Sympson, ed., *Lincolnshire Notes and Queries*, Vol.2, W. K. Morton, 1891 182–4.

Miller, H 2000 *Secrets of the Dead*, London, Channel 4 Books/Macmillan.

Morris, Alan G. 2012 'Trauma and violence in the Later Stone Age of southern Africa'. *South African Medical Journal*, [S.l.], vol 102, no. 6, 568–70, http://www.samj.org.za/index.php/samj/article/view/5792/4194 accessed: 01 Sep 2013.

Morris, N. & Rothman, D.J. (eds), 1997 *The Oxford History of the Prison: the Practice of Punishment in Western Society*, Oxford, Oxford UP.

Naumann, Elise 2005 *Archaeological Journal*, vol. 162, 215–55.

Pace, E. 2000 Konrad Kujau ,62, '*"Hitler Diaries" Swindler'*, www.nytimes.com/2000/.../konrad-kujau-62-hitler-diaries-swindler.htm accessed 28 Jan 2014.

Payne, S. 2008 'A grave is not just a hole in the ground' *British Archaeology* Issue 100, May/June 2008.

Platt, R. 2012 Smuggling in the British Isles, Stroud: The History Press.

Polybius, *Histories Book 6* published in Vol. III Loeb Classical Library edition, 1922-1927 (penelope.uchicago.edu/Thayer/E/Roman/Texts/Polybius/6*.html (accessed 2.8.14).

Porter, V. & Morison, P. 1998 'The Salcombe Bay Treasure', *British Museum Magazine: 3*, 30, 16–18.

Rabin A, 2008 'Anglo-Saxon Women Before the Law' *Old English Newsletter* Vol. 41.3, 33–6 University of Tennessee.

Reynolds, A. 2009 *Anglo-Saxon Deviant Burial Customs* Published to Oxford Scholarship Online: May 2009.

Richardson, M.E.J., 2000 *Hammurabi's Laws: Text, Translation and Glossary* Sheffield: Sheffield Acad. Press.

Ritchie, J. Ewing 1858 *The Night Side of London*, London: William Tweedie.

Roberts, C & Manchester K 1995 *The Archaeology of Disease*. Stroud: Sutton Publishing.

BIBLIOGRAPHY

Russell, J. & Cohn, R. 2012 *The Murder of Julia Martha Thomas,* Saarbrucken: VSD.

Russell, M., 2003 *The Secret Life of Charles Dawson,* Stroud: The History Press.

Sample, I. 'Swarthy, blue-eyed caveman revealed using DNA for ancient tooth' *The Guardian,* 28 Jan 2014.

Starr, J., 2010 *The Killer of Little Shepherds,* New York: Knopf.

Stavrakakis, Yannis 2012 'Athens Murder Court', *AIA* Vol 65 No. 4, archive.archaeology.org/1207/trenches/acropolis_athens_murder_court.htm l accessed 13 Nov 2013.

Stander, H.F. 2009 'Theft and robbery in Chrysostom's time' *Acta Theol.* vol.29 no.2 Bloemfontein.

Storey, N.R., 2010 *The Victorian Criminal* Stroud:Shire Publications University of Leicester. 'Discovery of remains of England's King Richard III confirmed.' *Science Daily,* 4 February 2013. <www. Sciencedaily.com/ releases/2013.

Watts-Plumpkin, E, 2012 'Richard III: DNA Analysis' *Current Archaeology* CA272.

Waugh, Rob 2012 '*Iron Age murder mystery as CT scan shows British man from 100AD was beaten, strangled, then beheaded in 'pagan ritual '*http://www.dailymail.co.uk/sciencetech/article-2112499/Very-cold-case-2-000-year-old-murder-solved-CT-scan-reveals-Iron-Age-man-bludgeoned-strangled-beheaded-human-sacrifice.html#ixzz2ciMrp9OM.

Whitehouse, Ruth 1977 *The First Cities* Oxford: Phaidon.

Wileman, J. 2009 *War and Rumours of War* BARIS 1984, Oxford: Archaeopress.

Wilkinson C 2004 *Forensic Facial Reconstruction* Cambridge: CUP.

Wilkinson, G.T. 2012 *The Newgate Calendar, The Making of the Modern Law: Trials, 1600-1926,* London: Gale Publishing.

Williamson, T. 2007. *Rabbits, Warrens and Archaeology.* Stroud:Tempus Publishing Ltd.

Wood, G.B. 1996 Smugglers' Britain, London: Cassell.

Zuyderwyk, Janneke & Jan Besteman, 2010 'The Roermond hoard: a Carolingian mixed silver hoard from the ninth century' *Medieval and Modern Matters*, Vol.1.